DECODING A DECADE

The Politics of Policy Making

DECODING A DECADE

The Politics of Policy Making

MANISH TEWARI

Vitasta

Let Knowledge Spread

Published by
Renu Kaul Verma
Vitasta Publishing Pvt Ltd
2/15 Ansari Road, Daryaganj
New Delhi - 110 002
info@vitastapublishing.com

ISBN 978-93-82711-62-9

Cover and Layout: Vitasta Publishing Pvt Ltd
Printed at Vikas Computer and Printers, New Delhi

Dedicated

To my dad, late Dr VN Tewari who fell to an assassin's bullet when he still had a lot to give...! the 3rd of April 1984.

To my mom Dr Amrit Tewari whose resoluteness in the face of adversity I have always admired.

To my wife Naaznin Shafa, who has been there always, pulling me back from the brink!

To my daughter Ineka who has grown from a bubbly baby into a beautiful young lady in a flicker of an eyelid.

Acknowledgement

My acknowledgements are due to some prior publications which formed the basis for updated and enlarged versions herein published: The *Indian Express*, *The Asian Age*, *Mail Today*, *Seminar*, *Tehelka*, The *Hindu*, *The Hindustan Times* and The Observer Research Foundation.

My sincere thanks to the publisher Renu Kaul Verma who had to bear with both my indolence and idiosyncrasies.

My gratitude to the copy editor Ms Veena Batra who was able to disassemble and cogently reassemble a mass of ideas and some verbiage too.

Preface

...Why ?

This collection of articles written between 2006 and 2016 is a comment on issues, events and trends. These reflect my opinion on an issue at that particular moment in time. This compendium also reflects how views on a particular issue may have evolved over the decade. At times they may be even contrary to each other but I guess that is how the human mind functions as it absorbs various influences and thought patterns. It then tries to assimilate them into a thread of coherence, if not consistency and continuity.

This compilation has been put together because even in its randomness it tells a tale of an eventful decade in India's public affairs—an era when the United Progressive Alliance government was charged with steering the ship of the Indian state and as it made way for a BJP-led NDA government in New Delhi in the May of 2014.

Some of the pieces have been edited to make them concurrent, though I have endeavored to leave most of them in their original form.

The book would not have been possible but for the persuasion of Professor (Dr) Rekha Saxena who took a very ardent interest and brought her academic perspective to the text as the project evolved.

Hope you enjoy browsing through it.

Manish Tewari
September 2016

Contents

PART A
Reforming Institutions of Governance
Perspectives on India

PART: B
India and the World: Issues and Challenges

PART A

Reforming Institutions of Governance: Perspectives on India

I. Constitutional Foundations

Introduction: Contours and context of India

A FUNDAMENTAL pre-requisite for any representative Government is a homogenous, small and an educated population. Thus spoke JS Mill, a political thinker of British origin. Mill was quick to point out that since all societies did not have these attributes representative democracy could not be a universally valid form of government. It is, therefore, not surprising that he opposed the transfer of power from the British East India Company to the British Parliament and, in fact, suggested that a despotic form of government was best suited to Indian conditions.

Almost a century and a half later the Indian democratic experiment has demolished all these theoretical postulates. Almost six decades of Republican experience puts us in the index of successful democracies around the world Even the severest of the critics of operation of Democracy in India have to accept its success at least in terms of its procedurality. It's on the substantive accounts that they can perhaps critique it. The regularity of more or less free and fair elections from the first general elections in 1951-52 to the fifteenth elections to the Lok Sabha in 2014, numerous rounds of elections for Assemblies in states and institutions of local self-governance bear eloquent testimony to this fact. It is the Indian political system that has largely given contour and character to our democratic processes.A system or order led by its much-maligned political class.

The continuation of the same Constitution established in the post-war period till today is an achievement that can be claimed by only three other countries in the Afro-Asian world, namely Japan, Sri Lanka and Malaysia. However, it is not the mere Constitutional Continuum but its effective adaptation to the changing circumstances and challenges faced over the decades that is the real tribute to its efficaciousness.

The perpetuation and institutionalization of the secular fabric is also no mean feat as diverse religious groups live in India. The danger of majoritarian tyranny always looms large and has become even more aggravated due to increased competitiveness in Indian politics leading to mobilization on religious and even ethnic lines. In such situations it becomes very important to emphasize the pluralistic principle because it is a matter that is existentially germane to over 400 million people belonging to one or the other minority groups.

The political system has succeeded in assimilating fundamental dissenters like communist revolutionaries who had started a revolutionary upsurge in Telangana in 1948. They have gradually been constitutionalized whereby they formally joined the electoral, parliamentary and the federal processes of governance. In the case of the Kashmiri separatists and those in the North East, although problems have not been fully resolved as yet but they have been partly diffused by restoring the processes of electoral democracy.

The Indian administrative and governance dynamic has been able to devolve and decentralize political power right down to the grass roots. Guided and inspired by Gandhian idea of a 'village republic' the political class was not content with devolution of power upto the state level only.

The political leadership understood that myriad numbers of voices are excluded from the political system. Thus to bring the unheard voices into the system, the 73rdand74th Constitutional amendments and enabling legislations were enacted. These legislations created a third tier of governance at the Village Panchayat level in the rural areas and at the ward level in urban areas.These institutions are not just decorative pieces but vested with real powers, real finances and real authority.

India successfully transited from a statist regime of Indian Socialism to a new regime of economic Liberalism and globalization when the economic system demanded such a change due to the triumph of the neo-liberal order in the ideological combat of economic systems of the United States and the former USSR. After the economic reforms, the rate of economic growth increased considerably and India joined the ranks of the fastest growing economies of the world.

Confronted with the question of distributive justice, Jawahar Lal Nehru once remarked: 'Let the size of the cake grow as we have nothing to distribute except poverty'. The political class successfully pursued the policy of growth with justice or development with a human face. Realizing that 'trickle-down' is not adequate for addressing the problem of socio-economic inequalities adequately, the political class legislated a Rights based entitlement architecture that is perhaps a first in socio-economic empowerment.

Governments, since the very beginning have practiced the policy of mainstreaming of marginalized groups. A conscious policy of mainstreaming and not co-option i.e. bringing such groups into the center without erasing their identities has been pursued. Several enabling, protective and progressive legislations have been brought in this regard. Consequently, the polity succeeded in bringing several groups living in the margins/periphery into the mainstream.

Has the Political Class betrayed India?

An oft-repeated gripe has been that the political class has let India down. On balance it has led the project of national renewal fairly satisfactorily. If we take the baseline of India as 1947, it was marked by abject poverty, political uncertainty, social disharmony and mass hunger. Balkanization of India was a prophecy that the imperialists and their lackeys thought was just a matter of time.

The India of today is seen as an emerging economic entity and presents a picture where some of the highest democratic values and ideals like the right to life and liberty, rule of law and the freedom of speech, expression and conscience prevail. The right to freedom to offend for a billion plus population, tolerance of dissent and celebration of plurality not withstanding , the aberrations of the past two years is a reality.

It is due to the vision and constant effort of the Indian political class, to quote Devesh Kapuran, Indian social scientist, that the Indian state can organize elections for an astounding 700 million voters with less controversy than the United States. It can also conduct a census for a billion people reasonably well. It periodically erects a temporary city for millions of people during the Kumbh Mela without mishaps, runs an efficient space program & has managed to keep one of the world's largest armed forces far removed from politics.

There have been occasions when some organ/tier like the legislature, executive or judiciary may have underperformed or have been overshadowed by the other but it should not be construed as failure of the political system or political class—rather it should be seen in totality or holistically. The relationship between various organs of the political system or sub-systems is not a relationship of trade-offs.

By way of example, if the judiciary has increased it's reach or impact (often described as judicialization of politics) it does not logically imply a failure of the executive or parliament.

If the popular appeal of judiciary has increased so has that of the Legislature as reflected by increasing voter turn-outs notwithstanding that the trust quotient in elected representatives has eroded sharply.

India is witnessing a democratic upsurge that has put enormous demands on the polity. This creates an impression that the system is in crisis but the reality is that it is reflective of the fact that people are approving the governance paradigm underpinning it to a popular base. What really secures democracy and ensures its survival is nothing but people and people only.

Bridging the generational divide

ON 26 NOVEMBER 1949, the Constituent Assembly adopted the Indian Constitution and mandated that it would come into force from the 26th of January 1950. The Preamble of this document declared the solemn resolve of the Indian people to constitute their nation as a sovereign, democratic republic. The words 'socialist' and 'secular' are of recent vintage, inserted by the 42nd Amendment to the Indian Constitution on 18 December 1976.

The democratic system that India adopted was based upon what is colloquially referred to as the Westminster system of government where the Council of Ministers is collectively responsible to the Parliament which embodies the sovereign will of the Indian people.

The Westminster model rests on a construct where political parties and individuals compete for space in the Parliament and assemblies on the basis of their programmes and policies. However, of late, with the mushrooming of regional and community based parties, religion, caste, muscle and money seem to have displaced the broad ideological architecture that provides the scaffolding for the policy and programme framework.

Political parties in India evolved out of the Indian liberation struggle with the Indian National Congress, from the late 19th to the

---

Seminar, 01 April 2009

mid-twentieth century performing the function of a broad platform. It accommodated the complete spectrum of national opinion cutting across every divide and focused solely on one objective—independence. The only other coherent political organization that emerged during this period was the Communist Party of India, incidentally founded not in India but in Tashkent on 17 October 1920 after the Second Congress of the Communist International (Comintern). Interestingly, there was no political party on the right of the ideological divide at the time. The RSS inspired Jana Sangh, now metamorphosed into the BJP, emerged only in the early 1950s.

It was only after independence, when the Indian democratic experiment started unfolding with the first general elections in 1952, that the political party system started acquiring roots in India. The noted historian, Ramachandra Guha, in his writings describes the process as such: 'Just before that election, two former cabinet colleagues of Jawaharlal Nehru established political parties to challenge the Congress. One was Shyama Prasad Mukherjee, who set up the Jana Sangh, and the other, BR Ambedkar, who revived the Scheduled Castes Federation (later named the Republican Party). Neither of these two doctors were, of course, ever members of the Congress itself. However, two more political parties were founded at the same time by lifelong Congressmen who felt compelled to leave their parent organization. One was the Kisan Mazdoor Praja Parishad, whose prime mover was Acharya Kripalani; the other was the Socialist Party, whose leaders included such gifted men as Ram Manohar Lohia and Jayaprakash Narayan.

'Shortly before the 1952 elections, these four challengers were joined by a fifth: the Communist Party of India, which came overground at the behest of Moscow, seeking to exchange the "bullet for the ballot". Despite their ideological differences then, the Communists, the Jan Sanghis, the Socialists and the Republicans all believed that Indian democracy would, in course of time, evolve around two poles: one represented by the Congress, the other, hopefully, by themselves. In this, they were influenced by the history of western democracies such as the United States of America and the United Kingdom, both marked by a more-or-less stable two-party system.'

The evolution of the Indian state coincided with the advent of the Cold War on the global stage. As India, for various reasons, including but not limited to, its anti-imperial and anti-colonial struggles became increasingly socialist in its predisposition, its political parties too started increasingly organizing themselves structurally and hierarchically on the pattern of similar structures in the socialist world. Unlike political parties in nations that Winston Churchill aptly described in Fulton Falls as 'outside the ambit of the Iron Curtain', where essentially temporary electoral platforms put individuals and ideologies in office, parties in the socialist world tended to be permanent and staffed by voluntary or paid whole-timers. This soon became the favoured model across the political spectrum in India also. It is interesting and perhaps the subject matter of some in-depth research whether this model was instinctively or deliberately adopted by almost all serious political formations in the newly liberated nations of Asia and Africa. And if some nations did not do so, then why not?

As time and elections merged into a collage between 1952 and 2004, the Indian democratic experience was widely hailed as successful by even naysayers around the world who had initially devoted tomes predicting the imminent demise, dismemberment or balkanization of the Indian nation state. From the windswept chic of Davos to the recently enfranchised black majority of Durban, the 'Indian phenomena' inspired the profiteer and the rebel alike. Even we started patting our own backs in appreciation, despite the million mutinies raging from Kashmir to Kalimpong and encompassing the Naxal heartland of Central India.

One crucial aspect which became a casualty in this thunderous crescendo of applause was how the political party system which scaffolds this democratic continuum faring? Between 1952 and 2009, though political outfits continued to mushroom, many of them remained fly-by-night operations structured around an individual/family/caste group, emerging only around elections. At last count there were as many as 730 political parties registered with the Election Commission, excluding the national and state parties. Unfortunately, even in the national and state parties, internal democracy remains more an exception than the rule. In some instances it is wilful while in others the sheer logistics of conducting credible, transparent and fair elections seems to have overwhelmed the intent. In the mid-1990s, the Election Commission of India made a valiant attempt to persuade political parties to follow their respective constitutions in letter and spirit on the pain of de-recognition/ de-registration if they failed to do so. Even as some parties complied, others merely amended their constitutions to formally do away with even the fig leaf of internal democracy that their respective constitutions and memorandums of associations envisaged. It is thus a piquant situation that the superstructure of the great Indian democratic experience is in the main underpinned by inherently undemocratic, if not totalitarian, political parties.

The challenge, therefore, is how do we ensure that each and every political party registered with the Election Commission holds regular democratic internal elections? The answer perhaps lies in the process being statutory rather than self-driven, with a separate commission exclusively tasked to fund, conduct, supervise and monitor the internal organizational elections of national and state parties. If this indeed happens, the largest democracy may thus finally have open, vibrant, inclusive and robust structures supporting its superstructure.

Judicial overreach or executive paralysis?

"STEP BY step, brick by brick, the edifice of India's legislature is being destroyed," moaned finance minister Arun Jaitley. He was referring to alleged judicial encroachment into the domain of the executive and legislature. The statement was in the context of the demand for judicial adjudication of dispute resolution on the proposed Goods and Services Tax Bill.

However, the bawling betrays the NDA government's inability to grasp the nation's transformed governance paradigm, where the executive is just one of the myriad stakeholders in India's power dynamics. Beyond the Narendra Modi government's bitterness at the Supreme Court quashing the National Judicial Appointments Commission Act by an overwhelming majority and the recent mauling it got from the courts on the Uttarakhand issue, there are much deeper issues at play. These go to the very heart of the lack of legitimacy of the executive and legislature.

In the republic's nascent years, though the judiciary was conservative and cautious, it didn't seriously oppose the policy thrusts of the political executive. Though affected interests challenged most progressive initiatives, including zamindari abolition and other land reforms, the government was able to have its way on almost all its statutory and policy prescriptions.

The Asian Age, 14 May 2006

The crunch came in 1973, when the Supreme Court propounded the "basic structure" doctrine in the Kesavananda Bharti case and proscribed the amending powers of Parliament. In addition to the inherent tension that began to manifest itself between the executive-legislature combine on one hand and the judiciary on the other, the growing perception that the executive had ceased to be the first frontier of justice took centrestage.

In every democracy, there are spirited contests between various political formations that vie to form federal or state governments. However, once governments are formed, the incumbent endeavours to administer keeping in mind the principles of equity, justice and fair play. The Indian political class, however, cast these time-honoured values by the wayside. Not only were their actions arbitrary, vindictive and even downright malicious against political opponents, the favours extended to political fellow-travellers at the cost of the deserving and meritorious instilled a deep distrust among ordinary citizens.

While participation in the democratic processes grew and got more broad-based, the trust quotient plunged. The credibility deficit became all the more pronounced due to boorish behaviour by elected eminences when Parliament or the Assemblies were in session. Hurling mikes, shoes and brawling became the norm rather than exception. Slowly and gradually, legislative institutions became irrelevant to the lives of citizens. They have even made themselves redundant to the national discourse.

The judicial institutions, on the other hand, not only maintained their quiet dignity and rectitude, but even expanded their remit through public interest litigation. People realised that if they wanted relief, it was far more efficacious to approach the judiciary and get directions issued rather than bang their heads against ossified and venal government structures. From getting footpaths repaired, refuse lifted, streetlights made functional, maintenance of public parks and even access to drinking water—every basic need of the citizen in both urban and rural areas—started landing at the court's doors. As a consequence of well-meaning judicial interventions, public confidence and trust in the judiciary grew and people now started perceiving it as the only bastion of justice.

As a result of this enhanced role, the judiciary soon took upon itself the responsibility of appointing judges. There was no public outcry at this reinterpretation of constitutional provisions that many jurists believe was detrimental to the system of checks and balances, going to the very core of how a democracy should structure itself. When the executive tried to wrest this power back through the NJAC by an overwhelming display of legislative unity, in Parliament and the Assemblies, its striking down by the Supreme Court hardly created a ripple among people except among those who wanted a say in judicial appointments.

If the courts had indeed trampled upon the sovereign will, as represented through elected representatives, why was there no outcry? The simple answer is that while politicians wanted a say in judicial appointments, people didn't. Here the elected representatives weren't articulating the people's will, but their own desires and aspirations. It was constitutional politics at play, in which ordinary people had no interest.

That is why even in dispute resolution over taxation between the Centre and a state, or for that matter between states, judicial determination as sought in the case of the GST paradigm is but at a subliminal level both an admission and acceptance by the political class that it is singularly incapable of surmounting the deeply divisive and polarised political divide. The judiciary is, therefore, the only natural and neutral umpire which can be trusted. It is thus logical that if the political class doesn't want its superstructure and foundations to be dismantled brick by brick, it would have to reinvent itself.

First, it would have to demonstrate that the government, irrespective of which party is in power, acts for the entire country and not just for the groups then in power. Second, politicians would have to re-learn what it means to be a legislator, and restore the decorum and gravitas of legislative institutions. Third, they will have to convince people that politics is a public duty and not a means of personal enrichment. Fourth, they must understand that voter turnouts essentially don't reflect the people's faith in the individual they are electing, but in the larger democratic principle, for elections are a contest between the given human material and for most people it is a zero-sum game.

Fifth and not last, it must dawn that expediency and opportunism no longer work. It isn't kosher to pompously pontificate that disruption is a legitimate parliamentary tactic while in Opposition, and then carp that the judiciary is overreaching itself while in government. In essence, politicians would need to rescue politics and the governance processes from their own depredations, a task that they singularly don't understand or don't want to understand.

Liberate the legislator

THE CONSTITUTION (Fifty-second Amendment) Act, 1985, added the Tenth Schedule to the Indian Constitution to curb the growing tendency of political defections by parliamentarians and legislators from one party to another after elections. The opening lines of the statement of objects and reasons of the said Bill described this disconcerting phenomenon succinctly: "The evil of political defections has been a matter of political concern. If it is not combated it is likely to undermine the very foundations of our democracy and the principles that sustain it." Members of Parliament and State legislatures are liable for disqualification if they leave the political party on whose symbol they got elected and join another, or violate the party whip to vote a certain way in the House.

Raising the defection bar

The original Tenth Schedule, however, failed to take into account the ingenuity of immorality that bedevilled some of the eminences that adorned our legislatures. While penalising individual acts of defection, it recognised the principle of splits whereby if one-third of the members of a legislative party broke away and formed a separate group or joined another political party, they could continue as members of the legislature.

The Hindu, 30 April 2016

Setting the one-third bar was explained in paragraph 3 of the Tenth Schedule in terms of "honest dissent"—that is, a critical mass of numbers would be swayed not by monetary considerations or the perks of office but by deep ideological or policy differences. In reality, individual defections got converted into a mass-scale malady.

The National Democratic Alliance government of Atal Bihari Vajpayee sought to address this aberration through the Constitution (Ninety-first Amendment) Act, 2003. It omitted paragraph 3 from the Tenth Schedule that allowed one-third of the parliamentarians/legislators to split from their parent party. However, it left paragraph 4 in place, which allows two-thirds of the members of a parliamentary/legislative party to merge with an existing political party or form a new political party. Essentially what this constitutional amendment did was raise the wholesale defection bar from one-third to two-thirds.

However, thirty-one years after the 1985 law, perhaps the time has come to assess as to how this statute-imposed morality squares up against a legislator's right to vote according to his conscience, convictions, common sense and constituency concerns.

Has the Tenth Schedule not altered the fundamental character of the Westminster model of parliamentary democracy whereby legislators, rather than articulating the predilections and priorities of the territorial constituency that they represent, have become but virtual hostages of a whip-driven tyranny? It is the political platform that selects a person to run that now exercises hegemony over the contours of legislation and policy formulation rather than the little chap who stood in the queue on a hot scorching summer day to press that elect button on an electronic voting machine. Did the framers of the Indian Constitution, when they chose the universal adult suffrage paradigm, contemplate that the system would be upended, whereby choice would be with an individual elector but legislative power would reside in a political party? Viewed from this perspective, is the Tenth Schedule not in violation of the fundamental tenets of the Constitution if not the basic structure doctrine?

Tyranny of the party line

Law making in India, far from being a consultative and transparent process that takes all stakeholders on board, essentially remains a bureaucratic function. On top of it is the party whip, which directs its members which way to vote, practically on each and every bill. This enforced adherence to the party line means that a member invariably ends up voting for a bill if he/she is on the Treasury benches and against a bill if he/she is in the Opposition, with the odd spectacle of parliamentarians sometimes voting against a legislative instrument which they had supported previously, depending on whether their party occupies the Opposition or Treasury benches.

This has the effect of disincentivising lawmakers from seriously thinking, researching or even rifling for best practices to incorporate into legislation that is before the House for consideration and focus their energies on procedural matters. This, when legislation is the principal function of Parliament. The problem becomes heightened as Indian laws do not come with a sunset clause. If a bad law is enacted, it would remain on the statute books for at least a century if not more.

An unfortunate trend that has recently manifested itself is the use of House majorities to get even Private Members' Bills defeated at the introduction stage. It restricts whatever little space individual members have left for legislative activity. The argument of the establishment (the collective of political parties) that standing committees of Parliament serve that very function doesn't hold, because an MP only serves on one standing committee and the practical possibility of getting onto even one more committee is almost non-existent.

Empowering the legislator

All this needs to change so that the empowerment of the individual can coexist with the imperatives of political stability and public probity. Some years back, I had introduced a Private Member's Bill entitled the Constitution (Amendment) Bill, 2010 (Amendment to the 10th Schedule) that lapsed, without a discussion, on my joining the government in 2012. The core provisions of the Bill envisaged that whips be issued only for those legislative items that threaten the stability of government. It would perhaps be instructive to reproduce the salient aspects of the Statement of Objects and Reasons of that lapsed bill: "After quarter of a century of the enactment of the Tenth Schedule, it needs certain adaptations and further strengthening so as to be of greater relevance to our democratic process today. The disqualification of a member of a House should be only on the grounds that if he votes or abstains from voting in the House with regard to a Confidence Motion, No-confidence Motion, Adjournment Motion, Money Bill or financial matters contrary to the direction issued in this behalf by the party to which he belongs to and in no other case."

The operative portion of the Bill stated: "A person shall cease to be a member if he votes or abstains from voting in such House with regard to a Motion expressing confidence or want of confidence in the Council of Ministers, Motion for an adjournment of the business of the House, Motion in respect of financial matters as enumerated in Articles 113 to 116 (both inclusive) and Articles 203 to 206 (both inclusive), a Money Bill, contrary to any direction issued by the political party to which he belongs or by any person or authority authorized by it in this behalf."

This little tweak restricting the rigours of the whip would free up the legislative space and ensure that every government strives not only for cross-party consensus on legislation but reaches out to individual lawmakers rather than just their leaderships, deepening participatory lawmaking in the process.

The case of Indian liberty

"THE CONSTITUTION promises liberty to all within its reach, a liberty that includes certain specific rights that allow persons, within a lawful realm, to define and express their identity."

— **Justice Kennedy**

The 800th anniversary of the origin of human rights universally, the Magna Carta, was recently celebrated. It is also the bedrock of the chapter on fundamental rights enshrined in Part III of the Indian Constitution. The right to equality and equal protection of all laws provided in Article 14, read with the right to life and personal liberty enshrined in Article 21 and the fundamental freedoms contained in Article 19 collectively form the golden triangle of rights. They have also been qualified as a part of the basic structure of the Indian Constitution.

Article 21 of the Indian Constitution states that "no person shall be deprived of his life and liberty except according to procedure established by law." Since most other constitutions use the term "due process of law", this gave rise to the apprehension that if the law laid down a tyrannical procedure it would still be constitutional. "Due process" envisages the larger concept of natural justice and the right to be heard before being condemned, etc. Thus, 28 years after the Constitution

---

The Asian Age, 11July, 2015

came into force, "due process" was read into Article 21, as an obvious part of our fundamental rights, by the Supreme Court of India.

However, on the aspect of the human rights of the LGBT (lesbian, gays, bisexuals and transgenders) community, the comprehension of liberty and equality by the Supreme Court of the United States and our Supreme Court are in apparent contradistinction.

Last fortnight, in the landmark judgment, Obergefell v. Hodges, the American Supreme Court by a wafer-thin majority of 5:4 held that all the states were mandated by the 14th Amendment to licence same-sex marriages and to recognise such marriages as lawfully licensed even if performed outside their states. This decision supplements the dicta in United States v. Windsor, wherein the Supreme Court had invalidated the DOMA (Defence of Marriage Act) to the extent that it barred the federal government from treating same-sex marriages as valid even when they were lawful in the state where they were licensed.

Compare this to the judgment of the Indian Supreme Court in Suresh Kumar Koushal vs Naz Foundation, whereby the enlightened if not radical decision of the Delhi high court to strike down Section 377 of the Indian Penal Code to the extent of sex among consenting adults, was reversed. It would not be entirely incongruous to say that the Supreme Court's decision was a disappointment for the LGBT movement and the promise of liberty to all.

The liberal epistle of the majority opinion (quoted above) authored by Justice Kennedy sets the pitch for the protection of the basic human rights of the LGBT community. Justices Ginsburg, Breyer, Sotomayor and Kagan supported the opinion while Chief Justice Roberts, Justices Scalia, Alito and Thomas dissented in four separate judgments.

The fundamental civil liberties preserved in the 14th Amendment of the American Constitution protect the dignity of an individual, and also the personal choices that define his or her identity, thereby protecting him or her from unequal treatment. The majority of the judges recognised that "the identification and protection of fundamental rights" was the primary judicial duty of the court while interpreting the Constitution. While holding that there was no basis for states to not recognise lawful same-sex marriages simply because they were marriages between same sex couples, the US Supreme Court noted, "The dynamics of our constitutional system is that individuals need not await legislative action before asserting a fundamental right. The nation's courts are open to injured individuals who come to them to vindicate their own direct, personal stake in our basic charter."

The contrasting decision of the Indian Supreme Court in Suresh Kumar Koushal vs Naz Foundation is anchored in conservatism. The court should have perhaps reflected whether it is appropriate to even entertain an appeal ostensibly filed by a self-styled minder of Indian morals on a matter of such fundamental import, especially when the then government was in support of the progressive view taken by the Delhi high court.

The conformist outlook towards the "miniscule" LGBT community is apparent in the phrase "so-called" prefixed to "rights of the LGBT persons" in its decision. This raises the question: Can the human rights of any individual be illusory?

The most arresting rationale not to endorse the rights of the LGBT community is the shift of onus on to the legislature. Noting that the criminal law had been amended in the aftermath of the December 2012 gangrape, and that Section 377 had been left untouched, the Indian Supreme Court held that it could not strike down or interpret a statute in such a way that its meaning would be completely altered.

For a libertarian court that is entrusted with the duty of preserving the primary personal privileges and self-esteem of the individual, this reasoning may be diminutive of the standards that the Supreme Court has always and correctly set for itself. Its liberal interpretation of the fundamental rights (especially right to life and liberty), and their elevation to be within the ambit of the basic structure of the Constitution has enlarged the soul of fundamental rights by placing them well beyond the black and white typescript of Part III.

The dignity of the individual has been placed on a pedestal by our constitutional scheme. A traditionalist interpretation of what constitutes the sweep of morals and values in the Indian ethos ostensibly ignores the very permissive expanse of ancient Indian texts and arts. Should they, in any case, be a source for an analysis of the right to equality before law and the right to life and personal liberty? The Supreme Court, in a recent obiter, has wondered whether watching pornography in the four walls of one's home should really be proscribed.

The interpretation of the "due process" clause missing from the text of Article 21 further shows the sensitivity of the apex court that liberty is indivisible, though it can be circumscribed by reasonable restrictions, but any excessive transgression of that liberty by the state or its instrumentalities ought to be curbed resolutely. The reluctance of the Supreme Court to void a provision which infringes upon the right of choice and to exercise it with dignity requires a revisit. Fascinatingly the same very court in NALSA v. Union of India has acknowledged the concept of transgender rights.

A financial daily quoted the minister of law and justice as saying that Section 377 requires a fresh pair of eyes. This led to an immediate clarification from him that he had made no such statement. He is right, as the present political establishment is the epitome of revivalism. Even the idea that sexual minorities can also have rights is anathema to them.

The Indian Constitution unequivocally echoes the words of Justice Kennedy. It eschews bias against a person for his or her sexual identity and lifestyle choice. As the government of the day is the most sterling example of medievalism, the Supreme Court should consider stepping in again, to let freedom reign.

Regression for progression the reservation imbroglio

THE AGITATION of the Patels in Gujarat has once again brought attention to the infuriating business of reservations in education and jobs. It may be instructive to recap the last two decades of the reservation imbroglio. On November 16, 1992, the Supreme Court of India by a majority of 6:3 upheld 27 per cent reservation for the socially and educationally backward classes (read Other Backward Castes) provided by the VPSingh government while striking down the 10 per cent reservation for economically backward sections of society provided by the successor Narasimha Rao government. This decision came in the wake of violent protests across the country that claimed the lives of hundreds of innocent students and brought the phenomena of self-immolations to university campuses in the year 1990.

Though the judgment did not re-ignite the anti-reservation fires, the simmering discontent against caste being the basis for determining backwardness still stirs passions. Quixotically, it has provided a spur for economically affluent, socially influential and politically powerful caste groups to agitate for entering the OBC domain.

Why did 10 per cent reservation for the economically backward, cutting across communities not covered by the existing quota architecture, not find favour with the Supreme Court? For the simple

---

The Asian Age, 05 September, 2015

reason that the Narasimha Rao government was only paying lip service to the cause of economic reservation. The only reason why the economic formulation was inserted into the equation was because Prime Minister Rao was petrified of another wave of self-immolations sweeping academic institutions.

When his government informed a Constitution Bench of the Supreme Court on August 8, 1991, that they too intended to implement the decision of the VP Singh government, the agitation recommenced and he held out reservation on an economic basis as a sop for future agitators.

While the Rao government amended the Office Memorandum of VP Singh's government on September 25, 1991, to provide for 10 per cent of vacancies in the civil services for other economically backward sections, it did not, despite repeated exhortations by the Supreme Court, evolve the economic criterion critical to actioning the amendment. His minister for social justice, Sitaram Kesri, who later succeeded him as Congress president, was virulently opposed to this concession. He wore his execration for the upper castes on his sleeve.

Kesri, therefore, ensured that despite the amendment to the earlier Office Memorandum, no economic criterion was ever evolved and presented to the Supreme Court and no enabling constitutional amendment was carried out. In the absence of a defined criterion, the court had nothing to go on except interpret as to whether the existing constitutional provisions covered economic backwardness or not. Rao found it convenient to believe that the solution lay in expanding the size of the economic pie through liberalisation and globalisation of the economy rather than getting caught in the quota conundrum.

It has been 24 years since economic liberalisation commenced and the quota genie still remains out of the bottle. Despite the Shangri-La of a neo-liberal economic order and the utopia of caste-based reservations, the depravation index, as evidenced by the preliminary data of the socio-economic caste census survey of 2011, paints a grim picture of the Indian milieu, especially rural India. Obviously, neither the benefits of economic liberalisation nor caste-based reservation have percolated to those who required them the most.

The philosophy of affirmative action in India rests on the plank that economic fillip leads to social mobility and political impetus. It is also anchored in the theory of generational guilt. Since the ancestors of the present day upper castes had committed atrocities and had ostracised the lower castes, therefore their progeny must be subjected to negative discrimination to carry the proverbial cross eternally for the sins of their forefathers.

This is distinct and opposed to the theory of positive affirmative action for the underprivileged, deprived and persecuted in most parts of the world. Positive affirmative action means that if there is one seat in an university or one job in the civil services and two people are identically situated then the one who is the beneficiary of an affirmative action paradigm would get it as opposed to the one who is not. It does not contemplate different benchmarks and qualifying criterion for different people for the same educational and employment opportunity. What we have in India is the spectre of different strokes for different folks.

The Indian template of affirmative action also leaves out of its ambit religious minorities. There is empirical evidence to demonstrate that they are victims of the most extreme forms of socio-economic marginalisation.

Then there is the related issue of quotas being open-ended. Article 334 of the Constitution had envisaged reservation of seats in Parliament and legislative institutions for a period of 10 years from the date of commencement of the Constitution. However, the said reservation has been extended every 10 years since then, making it almost perennial.

Former Prime Minister Rajiv Gandhi made the most eloquent critique of caste-based reservation in a seminal two-and-a-half hour address to the Lok Sabha on September 6, 1990. He pointed out that the data that constituted the foundation of the Mandal Commission report, that in turn underpinned the VP Singh Office Memorandum, was extrapolated from censuses that were between 70 years to a century old then. He observed that the commission had surveyed only 810 villages out of 5.5 lakh across the country and one urban block in each district to reach its conclusions. Eminent sociologists like Roy Burman, Srinivas and Jogendra Singh who were thanked for their contribution had distanced themselves from the report. Finally, the commission itself, in paragraph 11.27 of its report, had stated, "In the end it may be emphasised that the survey has no pretensions of being a piece of academic research", thereby betraying both its intent and lack of intellectual integrity.

The former Prime Minister prophetically warned his successors: "We have problems if caste is defined to enshrine casteism in our country. We have problems if the weakest amongst the classes are not helped and if the weakest among the minority religions are not helped. The Congress cannot stand by and watch this nation being divided for the political convenience of one individual." Unfortunately, Rajiv Gandhi was assassinated eight months later. Had he lived he would have found a smarter way of doing things.

The time has come to start an open debate. Is reservation in jobs and education required in the 21st century? If the answer is yes, then has the time come to move affirmative action to an economic platform cutting across caste, creed, region, religion and all the vivisections that bedevil the Indian experiment?

Though Justice Kuldip Singh was in a minority on the Indira Sawhney bench and failed to persuade his brethren to his point of view, his dissent is still relevant.

He said, "Poverty has a direct nexus to social backwardness. It is an essential and dominant characteristic of poverty. A rich belonging to backward caste—depending upon his disposition—may be or may not be socially backward, but a poor Brahmin struggling for his livelihood invariably suffers from social backwardness. The reality of present-day life is that the economic standards confer social status on individuals. A poor person, however honest, has no social status around him whereas a rich smuggler moves in high society. No statistics can hide the fact that millions of people, who belong to the so-called elite castes, are as poor, often a great deal poorer than a very large proportion of the backward classes. It is a fallacy to think that a person, though earning thousands of rupees or holding higher posts is still backward simply because he happens to belong to a particular caste or community whereas millions of people living below the poverty line are forward because they were born in some other caste, or communities. Poverty never discriminates; it chooses its victims from all religions, castes and creeds. The pavement-dwellers and the slum-dwellers, belonging to different castes and religions, have a common thread of poverty around them. Are they not the backward classes envisaged under Article 16(4)?"

The paradox is that India is perhaps the only country where castes and communities want to be backward to move forward. Regression for progression has become the mantra of a new India.

Politics of mercy petitions

THE SUPREME Court on Tuesday rejected Yakub Abdul Razak Memon's curative review petition, setting off the countdown to July 30, the date of his hanging. A few hours later, Memon, accused of criminal conspiracy in the Mumbai serial blasts of 1993, filed another mercy petition with the Maharashtra governor. The outcome will be known soon.

On March 21, 2013, the Supreme Court delivered its verdict in the case. A year later, on March 14, 2014, the President's secretariat received the recommendation of the ministry of home affairs on his clemency petition. A month later, on April 11, 2014, the President rejected his mercy petition.

This proposed execution—"to be hanged by the neck until death"—has once again focused attention on the politics of the mercy petition. In the autumn of 2008, a harangue was raging across the media space about delays in the disposal of clemency petitions by the President of India. The underlying and menacing subtext of the jeremiad was, "Why aren't we hanging the worthies sentenced to death by the courts?" As it was my remit then to offer an explanation for everything from the sublime to the obscene, I was compelled to examine the issue.

The Asian Age, 22 July, 2015

The data revealed that as on December 3, 2008, one mercy petition was pending since November 11, 1997, 15 between January 4, 1999 and May 14, 2014, and 12 between 2004 and till the end of 2008. In all, 28 mercy petitions were pending with the President of India.

The petitions were pending during the tenure of three governments —the United Front government headed by Inder Kumar Gujral, two National Democratic Alliance governments headed by Atal Behari Vajpayee and the first United Progressive Alliance government headed by Dr Manmohan Singh. They were also pending during the tenure of three Presidents: KR Narayanan, APJ Abdul Kalam and Pratibha Patil. The first and the third were the first dalit and women Presidents of India, respectively ,while the second was the third Muslim President of India.

Interestingly, Article 72 of the Indian Constitution vests executive authority to grant pardons, reprieves, respites or remissions from penal sentences, especially the sentence of death, in the President of India. Similar powers are also available to a governor of a state under Article 161 of the Constitution.

On June 26, 2012, the office of President Patil, in a widely reported press release, claimed, "The President is not supposed to act on her own judgment but is mandated to act in accordance with the aid and advice of the government in terms of Article 74 of the Constitution." However, there is contra jurisprudence with regard to presidential discretion under Article 72 and the mandate of Article 74 is not being binding on the President in this instance.

A constitution bench of the Supreme Court of India, while explaining the scope of Article 72 in the matter of Kehar Singh vs Union of India (1989) held: "The President in exercise of power under Article 72 is entitled to go into the merits of the case notwithstanding it has been judicially concluded. He can come to a conclusion different from that recorded by the court." The President can come to an independent decision on a mercy petition irrespective of the recommendation of the government.

If the government or the President had a view to the contrary to the one expressed by the court, they could have arrived at a different conclusion. It was legally valid. Why then the pendency? Was it that the ministry of home affairs was, by and large, dittoing the judicial decisions and recommending that the clemency petition be rejected, and successive Presidents, though chary of those recommendations, did not have the conviction to unequivocally state that they were not bound by the diktat of Article 74 while exercising power under Article 72?

Anyway, the pendency mounted. As on May 21, 2010, four mercy petitions were pending with the MHA and 25 with the President of India, after the President had commuted the death sentence of RGovindaswamy on November 23, 2009.

One June 23, 2010, the President's secretariat, in response to a Right to Information request ,confirmed that they were in fact 25 mercy petitions pending and in three cases the death penalty had been commuted to life benefiting nine death row convicts. By the end of her tenure, President Patil had commuted the death sentence in 19 cases, rejected three cases and 10 were still pending.

It was obvious that a closet debate was raging in the highest echelons of the Indian state about the efficacy of capital punishment. Nobody was unfortunately prepared to make it public.

A blood red pamphlet, "The Centre for Death Penalty", authored by the National Law University of Delhi and circulated at a consultation on death penalty hosted by the Law Commission of India, stated: "A predominant observation during the death penalty research project was that the recipients of capital punishment usually belong to the economically and socially backward classes". That's short hand for dalits, OBCs and Muslims.

President Kalam was the only one who candidly expressed his discomfort with capital punishment, stating that deciding mercy petitions was the most difficult task for him as President. In response to a Law Commission consultation paper, he submitted that there was a social and economic bias in the award of capital punishment.

While President Patil has not articulated her views on this question, it was widely believed that for religious reasons, she too was diffident about capital punishment. It is widely believed so was late President Narayanan.

As Justice APShah had invited me to the consultation on death penalty, on July 11, 2015, to speak on arbitrariness and discrimination in the application of death penalty, I decided to revisit the issue and update myself because somewhere this entire play was buried in my subconscious.

Interestingly, while re-reading old papers my office pulled out, a table from the website of Rashtrapati Bhavan came up. It stated that as of May 11, 2015, 24 clemency petitions had been rejected by President Mukherjee, two had been commuted to life and none were pending. Bingo!

Thus you had two paradigms—one across the tenure of three Presidents from 1997 to 2012 for 15 years, where pendency and commuting of death sentences was the rule and not the exception; and the current incumbent where upholding death penalty is the rule, commuting it the exception and pendency non-existent.

It raised the obvious question: In the rarefied environs of the Indian state were there any institutional processes at work in deciding clemency appeals or did it only go by the personal and ideological predilections of the incumbent in office? Since the answer was negative on the presence of any institutional processes, the conclusion was that the process was arbitrary. The Supreme Court in Madhu Mehta vs Union of India (1989) had held that "Article 21 is relevant in all stages. Speedy trial in criminal cases though not a fundamental right, is implicit in the broad sweep and content of Article 21. Speedy trial is a part of one's fundamental right to life and liberty. The principal is no less important for disposal of mercy petitions."

Chief Justice Bhagwati, in his famous dissent in the Bachan Singh case on capital punishment, observed there is no objective manner of awarding the death penalty and therefore it falls foul of Article 14. All of this left me wondering. The Bombay blasts took place in 1993, the wheels of justice cranked at a glacial pace with Supreme Court finally pronouncing its view two decades later. What if Memon's clemency appeal had come up before the earlier Presidents and not Pranab Mukherjee? Does the issue of capital punishment not require a dispassionate debate in the public space?

The politics and poetics of death

YAKUB MEMON, a convict in the Bombay serial blasts case of 1993, was hung by the neck until death on July 30, 2015. He had turned 53 on that day. A ghoulish birthday gift by the Indian state, to say the least. An article written by a former Research and Analysis Wing (R&AW) officer, the late B Raman, in August 2007, tells the tale of Memon's cooperation with the intelligence and investigation agencies. In it, he alludes to a "commitment" made by the Indian state to Memon in return for his assistance. If indeed that were true, and there is no reason to believe otherwise because by all accounts Raman was an honourable man, there would certainly be a paper trail in some government file classified as "secret". No officer would have made a commitment in a matter of such import without authorisation from the political masters. If for nothing else then to cover his own posterior.

It merits an inquiry because jurisprudentially, courts in other parts of the civilised world have been candid enough to admit that they erred in handing down the sentence of capital punishment even after the execution. Muslim leaders and even distinguished columnists correctly ask why three Muslims held guilty by the courts, and their mercy petitions rejected by the President of India, have swung from the gallows, while others who have been held equally guilty by the

---

The Asian Age, 08 August, 2015

courts long before them and had their clemency petitions rejected by the President or the respective governors, continue to live.

What are going to be the physiological implications of this conduct on a community that is combating both a siege mentality and ghettoisation ever since the Partition of India may be hard to predict at this point in time, but they would surely be menacing. What Yakub Memon's hanging has done is that it has brought the focus back on the entire issue of death as a penalty for criminality. At a recent Law Commission consultation on death penalty, enough empirical evidence was presented to demonstrate both socio-economic and class bias, as well as an asinine arbitrariness from investigation to even the disposal of clemency petitions in death penalty cases. Has a communal mutant also been advertently injected into this prejudice? Notwithstanding the fact that judges have repeatedly articulated that capital punishment should be given only in the "rarest of the rare cases", there is no modus to determine this dicta.

The legality of the death penalty was validated by a bench of five justices of the Supreme Court of India in Bachan Singh vs State of Punjab in 1980, by four in favour and one against. The lone non-conformist, Justice PN Bhagwati, declared that death penalty was repugnant to the provisions of the founding document of the Indian Republic: "It is obvious on a plain reading of Section 302 of the Indian Penal Code which provides for death penalty as alternative punishment for murder that it leaves it entirely to the discretion of the court whether to impose death sentence or to award only life imprisonment to an accused convicted of the offence of murder. This section does not lay down any standards or principles to guide the discretion of the court in the matter of imposition of death penalty." Over time, in almost identical cases of abhorrent crimes, courts have arrived at wholly contrasting decisions. Dhananjoy Chatterjee is the last convict to be executed for acts that cannot be designated as an archetype terrorist transgression. He was held culpable for the rape and murder of a teenager residing in the apartment block where he was assigned as a guard. Even the Supreme Court upheld his conviction and classified it in the "rarest of the rare" category in 1994.

Subsequently, even the late President APJ Abdul Kalam, who had publicly expressed his discomfort with the concept of capital punishment per se, rejected Dhananjoy's mercy petition and he dangled at the end of a hangman's rope on August 14, 2004. In contradistinction is the case of Amit vs State of Maharashtra, where Amit had been convicted for the rape and killing of a 12-year-old girl. In 2003, the Supreme Court held that he was young, with no previous record of odious offences and would not be a threat to humanity. Death penalty was commuted to life, holding that the case was not "rarest of the rare". Is it really possible for even the most evolved judges to really make a cogent distinction between the cases of Dhananjoy and Amit? Would it not be a brief that is impossible? Another instance is the case of Vasanta Dupare, a 47-year-old man who raped a four-year-old girl and then murdered her by crushing her with stones. Dupare, a repeat offender, was given the death penalty by the trial court. It was upheld by the high court. In 2015, a three-judge bench of the Supreme Court concurred that it was unlikely that Dupare would be reformed, was likely to remain a menace to society and hence deserved to be given the death penalty. Now discern the contradiction with the case of Neel Kumar who raped his own four-year-old daughter and then killed her. The apex court said the case did not fall within the "rarest of the rare" category since there was no reason to believe that Neel Kurnar could not be reformed. Intriguingly, in Shankar Khade's case, the apex court in 2013 observed that there was no fair process of "conferring" death penalty or thereby commuting it to life. And, that the application of the "rarest of the rare" principle was exceptionally friable. These doubts are identical to those raised by Justice Bhagwati in his celebrated dissent.

Why was it so that Dhananjoy and Dupare were given the death penalty for crimes that were similar to the ones Amit and Neel Kumar committed, while the latter were spared the noose? Such incongruence bolsters the argument that this is primarily based on the "eminence" who presides over the matter—much like the disposal of mercy petitions that are circumscribed by the personal predilections of the person occupying the highest office in the country - and not on any merit at all. There are many cases pertaining to terrorist related offences, including the assassination of a former Prime Minister, where ironically the Supreme Court upheld its own decision to commute the death penalty to life imprisonment on the same day it decided Yakub Memon's fate. Then there is the matter of a former chief minister's assassin where all legal processes, including the clemency petition option, have run their course. If someone pounds the pulpit and asks why different strokes for different folks, and he happens to be a Muslim member of the Indian Parliament, can anyone provide him with a cogent explanation that is convincing rather than attempting to hang the guy for asking?

The Indian state is on a slippery slope when a perceived sense of injustice coalesces into a mass conviction. It leads to alienation that breeds radicalisation. All that's required then is for someone to put a match to the ready gunpowder. There are two parallel narratives at play—one in the mainstream media and the other in the Urdu press. The day these tectonic plates grind against each other, the Partition will be like a boot camp joust. In the 35 years since the "rarest of the rare" doctrine was evolved, several methods of discerning what this norm is may have been outlined, but the final use eventually boils down to the discretion of the judge administering it. It is this vagueness that Justice Bhagwati said made the provision of death penalty fall foul of the hallowed principles of right to equal protection of the laws and the right to life. There is no ambiguity to the fact that the discretion in applying the principle of the "rarest of the rare" differs from judge to judge. The question that needs to be answered is whether a convict must leave the decision about his life to fluke. Given the demonstrable unfairness in its application, it is time for the Supreme Court to pay heed to the sagacious librettos of Justice Bhagwati and re-visit the constitutional validity of the death penalty, as the legislature would not be able to rise above its inanities to debate the matter with any measure of seriousness or sagacity.

II. Institutional Framework

When Centre cannot hold

OUR CONSTITUTION mandates a clear division of responsibility between the executive, legislature and the judiciary, with the sole responsibility of governance and day-to-day administration vested in the executive. However, the nature of parliamentary democracy creates a de facto fusion of roles, with the executive drawing legitimacy and sustenance from parliamentary majorities notwithstanding the de jure separation. Not only do parliamentary majorities ensure passage of legislation but also provide the executive with moral legitimacy to become the key driver of policy choices in terms of content and implementation.

Some of these institutional certainties driven by majoritarianism that were a given in the first four decades of the Republic have come under strain in the past two decades, resulting often in policy paralysis. While the undermining of parliamentary and legislative institutions, unfortunately by elected members, has got a good deal of attention in the national discourse, the erosion of executive authority has not been commented upon, presumably because the executive once was so powerful that it has created a residue of permanent antipathy.

The foremost reason for the weakening of the executive is the emergence of coalition governments at the Centre and variegated power

The Indian Express, 21 December, 2011

configurations in state party systems. The excessive regionalisation of the party system has created regional centres of power that have come to exert federal pressures on the parliamentary executive that go beyond the normal scheme enshrined in the Constitution.

Since the 1990s, centrifugal tendencies coupled with political fragmentation have resulted in a systematic erosion of both the mystique and omnipotence of a strong Centre. Coalitional strains on cabinet collegiality and cohesion, along with the stretching of the collective responsibility of the council of ministers beyond Parliament, have resulted in a situation whereby the capacity of the Centre as the driving dynamic of programmes and initiatives, even in the conduct of international relations, is hobbled. While the advent of coalition governments may have rejuvenated certain federal principles, it has weakened the unitary paradigm, thus presenting a profound challenge to the twin imperatives of governance and administration.

The second reason is the institutionalisation of an innovation known as "judicial activism". The power vacuum created by unstable coalition arrangements has impelled the judicial establishment to try and fill this vacant national space. The diffidence of the executive and the legitimate impatience of the people have resulted in judicial intervention in areas which the Constitution had intended as an exclusive executive preserve. Judicial activism, initially forged as a benign instrument to rein in a belligerent executive from disregarding checks and balances, has now appropriated for itself the role of being the driver of executive processes.

The third reason for the weakness of the executive has been the resistance to any worthwhile reform of the colonial administrative structure that is antiquated and straining at the seams. The excuse trotted out by the bureaucracy that any tinkering with the steel frame of governance may lead to a complete collapse, obviates the reality that the system is unfit to respond to contemporary expectations. The permanent establishment has stymied attempts at a holistic overhaul. While legislation like the Right to Information has empowered people, it has exposed the inability of the system in dealing with the expectations unleashed. More often than not, government finds itself incapacitated if not overwhelmed by the deluge. The answer lies in looking afresh at the structure of the administrative system, from recruitment to retirement.

The fourth reason undermining the institutional autonomy of the executive is the tendency of certain non-governmental organisations to insist upon making laws on the streets rather than in Parliament. Their utterances cannot mask their contempt for democracy even if they cloak their actions under an obtuse ideological construct called direct democracy, which is only a sure-shot recipe for anarchy.

Notwithstanding institutional infirmities that have weakened the executive, the reality is that under our constitutional scheme the sole responsibility for protecting national sovereignty, ensuring political stability, maintaining internal security, preserving communal amity, deciding economic policy and conducting international relations is the executive's, and it is accountable principally, if not only, to Parliament.

The next two decades are critical for India's growth trajectory. The imperatives of internal consolidation and increasing international responsibilities can only be surmounted by a strong and relatively autonomous executive. Given that decentralisation of power would keep throwing up coalition governments, thereby rendering the Centre susceptible to institutional weakness, and that this political reality may be here to stay, any attempts to hobble the executive further by creating statutory structures and oversight mechanisms that compel it to look over its shoulder before taking any decision would have ominous implications.

As the government prepares to move the Lokpal bill, and Parliament to debate it, it must be borne in mind that what India needs are laws that resuscitate and reform—that strengthen the executive, not weaken it.

Cure far worse than disease

IN JULY 2011, India will enter the third decade of its economic liberalisation programme, with the last seven years having being spent in trying to humanise the fruits of that labour. As paradigm shifts continue on the economic and social landscape, what India urgently requires is a comprehensive overhaul of its antiquated governance processes and delivery mechanisms to keep pace with these changes. They must be efficient, transparent and free from the taint of corruption.

In this context, the move to establish a Lokpal is welcome. However, it is at best a quarter-measure. With 78 per cent of India's GDP in private hands and power being distributed across the spectrum—and not concentrated, as previously, in the executive—what is required is a new regulatory architecture that can police not only reformed administrative structures but also all those institutions that have a direct bearing on national life.

This overarching framework must stand on the sturdy foundations of a judicial accountability and standards bill; administrative reform commencing with the repeal of Article 311 of the Constitution; a robust anti-trust legislation that provides the instruments to regulate the pernicious use of "influence" that accompanies the concentration

---

The Indian Express, 07 June, 2011

of wealth; laws to regulate cross-holdings, private treaties, and paid news in the media; and of course the Lokpal.

Why are these measures being advocated now? Is it to try to deflect attention from the Lokpal, currently on the front burner? Is it that the political establishment and the permanent executive are quivering at the thought of the mechanism being drafted? The answer is a big no. They already stand substantially covered by the provisions of the Indian Penal Code and the Prevention of Corruption Act among a host of others. A part of this edifice is in the design stage; it would thus be appropriate to look at the issue holistically, so that an all-encompassing superstructure is created.

However, what must be seriously considered is whether we ought to allow manifestations of street power and contrived rage to drive the discourse on these complex issues. Is McCarthyism, driven by evangelist hysteria, going to become the order of the day? Are all legitimate representatives collectively going to be convicted and hanged just because they chose to be a part of the greatest of all human experiences—politics?

Even the United States found it difficult to surmount the trauma of Senator McCarthy's excesses. If guilt by association becomes the rule rather than the exception, then the scar tissue it creates would be a permanent abrasion on our national life.

India has dealt with a million mutinies, from the well-orchestrated violent separatist impulses in the north-west and the north-east to the more emotional identity-based upsurges of religion, caste and language. They have been handled with a dexterous combination of flexibility and firmness.

However, even the most vibrant of democracies, with the safety valves of a representative legislature, free speech and a functional judicial system, are still not completely immune to street coercion.

History provides many examples of the utilisation of street power to subvert functional states. In 1935-38 Adolf Hitler used the street power of the Austrian Nazi party under the leadership of Dr Arthur SeyssInquart to prepare the ground for the absorption of Austria. The same pattern was repeated in Czechoslovakia, when the Sudeten Germans led by Heinlein were encouraged to revolt, which paved the way for the annexation and dismemberment of that nation. After the Second World War ended and the iron curtain descended upon Europe, the Communists used a combination of street and state power to subvert democratic processes throughout East Europe, thereby subjugating vibrant societies to totalitarian one-party rule. Closer home we find that such is the terror of Islamic fundamentalists who rule the streets of Pakistan that the governing establishment did not even muster up the gumption to attend the funeral of Punjab Governor Salman Taseer, and no maulvi was prepared to even perform his last rites—all while his assassin is extolled as a defender of the faith.

Thus the mobilisation of street power and the manner in which it is used can have very dangerous implications, even if the intent is noble and inspiration fired by idealism. While across-the-board reforms are the need of the hour they must be subjected to the calm and deliberative wisdom of the high temple of democracy—Parliament—rather than be allowed to fall victim to venting.

While it is the measure of confident governments to be sensitive to the concerns of their citizenry, there is a very thin line that divides accommodation from capitulation—and eternal vigilance is the price of freedom. The Constitution provides the space for a spectrum of ideological predilections but the developments of the past ten months make me wonder if the campaign is only about purging the toxins from the body politic or it is the unfinished battle for the idea of India in yet another avatar. There is a need for all those who believe in the core values of the Indian state to be vigilant because there may be some malaise intrinsic to the cure we're being offered.

Why the CAG is wrong ?

WHAT IS the constitutional and legal remit of the Comptroller and Auditor General of India—the ubiquitous and omniscient CAG? In other words, what does the Constitution and the law enjoin upon it to do?

Article 149 of the Constitution is the fountainhead from where the CAG draws its legal sustenance. It would be worth its while to reproduce it in full: "The Comptroller and Auditor General shall perform such duties and exercise such powers in relation to the accounts of the Union and of the states and of any other authority or body as may be prescribed by or under any law made by Parliament and, until provision in that behalf is so made, shall perform such duties and exercise such powers in relation to the accounts of the Union and of the states as were conferred on or exercisable by the Auditor General of India immediately before the commencement of this Constitution in relation to the accounts of the Dominion of India and the provinces respectively".

A bare perusal of this provision makes it amply clear that the founding fathers circumscribed the extent of the CAG's powers only to such duties and powers in relation to the accounts of the Union and states and had further qualified the mandate by explicitly stating

---

The Indian Express, 28 August, 2012

that, pending the enactment of a law by Parliament in this regard, the CAG would perform only such duties as were performed by the Auditor General in relation to the accounts of the Dominion of India and the provinces respectively before the commencement of the Constitution. Mark the emphasis on accounts and the clear absence of a remit to audit policy.

This constitutional directive held the field till 1971 when Parliament enacted the Comptroller and Auditor General's (Duties, Powers and Conditions of Service) Act 1971. The Act was last amended in 1994. Chapter III, Sections 10 to 17, list the statutory mandate of the institution. It can be summarised as: a) to audit all money paid into and expanded from the consolidated fund of the Union and that of the states/ Union Territories; b) to audit all transactions of the Union and of the states relating to contingency funds and Public Accounts; c) to audit all trading, profit and loss accounts and balance sheets and other subsidiary accounts kept in any department of the Union or the state; d) to audit the accounts of bodies or authorities substantially financed by government; e) to audit accounts of government companies, statutory corporations which have provision for audit by him and other bodies and authorities, even though not substantially financed by government at the request of the President/ Governor or at his initiative after obtaining President/ Governor's approval; f) to ensure that the Appropriation accounts and Finance Accounts of the Union/ states are prepared correctly; g) to prepare accounts of the states and Union Territories; h) to audit and report the account of the stores and stock kept in any office or Department of the Union/ states or Union Territories. Once again, note the emphasis on accounts and the clear absence of even a whisper of policy.

The CAG justifies its current audit practices by relying on an Office Memorandum (OM) dated June 13, 2006, whereby the finance ministry had ostensibly clarified whether a performance audit fell within the scope of the CAG (DPC) Act. Paragraph 3 of the OM makes it evident that only a performance audit "which is concerned with the audit of economy, efficiency and effectiveness in the receipt and application of pubic funds is deemed within the scope of audit by the Comptroller and Auditor General of India". Once again, mark the absence of even a convoluted reference to policy.

This notification is itself bad in law and needs to be withdrawn or quashed because the principles of jurisprudence state what cannot be done directly should not be done indirectly. An OM cannot override the explicit mandate of a constitutional provision and the enabling act which nowhere provides for such creative latitude. However, assuming for the sake of argument that the OM is correct, let us turn to the Regulations on Audit and Accounts 2007 made by the CAG itself to give effect to the said act, to understand as to how it interprets a performance audit.

Chapter 7 states that performance audit is an independent assessment or examination of the extent to which an organisation, programme or scheme operates economically, efficiently and effectively. It then goes on to define these three Es. Mark the emphasis on organisation, programme or scheme, not policy.

Anybody with even a nodding acquaintance with the English language can discern that the constitutional provisions, parliamentary enactment, rules, regulations and even the OM, read together, do not permit the CAG the kind of role and approach it has arrogated to itself of juxtaposing its personal policy prescriptions against the policy choices made by a democratically elected government and arriving at quixotic estimates of presumptive loss or windfall gain numbers which by themselves are incorrect and open to both dispute and demolition.

The Supreme Court, while quashing the 2G licences on February 2, 2012, had correctly refrained from making any observation on the presumptive loss figure of Rs 1.76 lakh crore and left it to the wisdom of the PAC and JPC to quantify the loss, if any.

Similarly, the Rs 1.86 lakh crore figure that the CAG has computed as gain to private players in the allocation of coal blocks is seriously flawed as it disregards the fundamental reality that these coal blocks were not given to mine coal and sell at elastic prices in the open market but were predicated upon certain tangible national development goals inter alia the generation of 18,300 MW of power, augmenting sponge iron capacity by 35 MPTA and steel capacity by

1,325 MPTA (million tones per annum) respectively, cement capacity by 7 MPTA and the production of 1,70,000 barrels of oil per day by a proprietary technology that converts coal to liquid. Power tariffs are fixed by statutory regulators in the states after ascertaining input costs; cement and steel prices are subject to market dynamics that enable the consumer to get the most competitive price; and fuel prices, except petrol, are regulated by the government.

It is unfortunate that 56 out of the 57 coal blocks audited by the CAG are non-functional, pending a plethora of clearances mostly by state governments.

The CAG also conveniently decided to overlook the fact that coal is to be extracted over a 30-year period when it decides to hypothetically mine all the coal on a given date in 2012 and sell it all at the Coal India market price on that given date without bothering for the niceties of discounting practices to rationalise the figure at net present value (NPV), which incidentally it chooses to do in its other two reports submitted concurrently.

Incidentally, out of the 57 coal blocks audited, 54 are in non-Congress-ruled states where the state government has the sole responsibility of selecting the developer, recommending his case for a coal block, participating in the proceedings of the screening committee, which should not be confused with an allotment committee, executing the mining leases and giving a bulk of the clearances.

In conclusion, the CAG does not have the constitutional or legal mandate to make its own policy prescriptions and then utilise them to compute notional or even mythical loss or gain. Even when it chooses to do so, it ends up getting it grievously wrong. Headline-hunting is a volatile vocation—perhaps it is time to stop this parody.

Are CBI, IB, R&AW Illegal Organisations?

THE LAWYER in me has always been intrigued by the legal architecture that empowers both our central law enforcement and intelligence services. In response to a series of questions during the recently concluded budget session of Parliament, the government provided answers that only underscore the ambivalence, procrastination and perhaps even the dilemma of successive governments to break out of the status quo mold and address this critical governance issue. The objective of this piece is to explore and navigate the legal underpinnings of the Central Bureau of Investigation, Serious Fraud Investigation office (SFIO), Intelligence Bureau and the Research and Analysis Wing. (R&AW).

The Central Bureau of Investigation was created by an executive order on the April 1, 1963. However, it was really born 22 years earlier as a Special Police Establishment in the Department of War in 1941. In 1943 it was constituted by an ordinance into an independent entity, namely the Special Police Establishment (War Department), in exercise of the Emergency powers conferred upon the then Viceroy and Governor General of India Lord Linlithgow by the India and Burma (Emergency Provisions Act) 1940 passed on June 27, 1940 by the British Parliament.

The Emergency Provisions Act interminably extended the validity of ordinances promulgated by the Governor General invoking the

---

ORF Issue Brief (20), August, 2009

powers available to him under Section 72 of the Ninth Schedule of the Government of India Act 1935 which otherwise mandated that the maximum validity of an ordinance could be six months.

With the Second World War coming to a close in 1945, the said act stood repealed by His Majesty's Order in Council, namely The India and Burma (Termination of Emergency) Order 1946, which declared the end of emergency with effect from April 1, 1946. The emergency had occasioned the passage of the Emergency Provisions Act in the first instance.

Fearing that all acts done under the Emergency Powers Act would either lapse with effect from October 1, 1946 or get extinguished as the validity period of an ordinance stood revived to six months as envisaged in Section 72 of the Ninth Schedule of the Government of India Act 1935 with effect from April 1 1946, the government of the day promulgated another ordinance on September 25, 1946 called the Delhi Special Police Establishment (War) Department ordinance. On October 1, 1946, in exercise of powers conferred by the said ordinance dated September 25, 1946, the then Federal government mutated the Special Police Establishment (War Department) into the Delhi Special Police Establishment.

However this apprehension was later proved to be unfounded as the Supreme Court of India in an another matter challenging the legality and life of ordinances promulgated under the Emergency powers Act 1940 held that while the Act itself may have been repealed by the termination order of 1946, the ordinances promulgated under it are valid into perpetuity unless an ordinance itself had a self limiting time frame (Hans Raj Moolji vs State of Bombay AIR 1957 SC 497).

The ordinance of September 25, 1946 was also subsequently repealed by the Delhi Special Police Establishment Act that came into force in November 1946, even though the 1946 ordinance was to remain valid till March 1947.

In the discharge of its legal duties the CBI still functions as the Delhi Special Police Establishment ostensibly constituted before independence, on October 1, 1946. It is not quite clear as to whether a subsequent notification re-constituting the Delhi Special Police Establishment under the said act was ever issued as the 1946 ordinance only midwived and morphed the Special Police Establishment (War Department) into the Delhi Special Police Establishment. Jurists, however, may propound that the earlier transition is saved by the Provisions of the General Clauses Act 1897, which is also open to dispute as to whether constitution of a force is a substantive right saved by the provisions of the said Act.

Before you get lost in a legal jungle let me demystify the legalese. The CBI has no independent standing in law. Simply put, it is a piece of legal fiction whose underpinnings in law are tenuous to say the least. It still draws all its powers of investigation and arrest from the antiquated 1946 act which essentially being a local act provides that each state through an executive order under Section 6 of the said Act has to give the Special Police Establishment, what is colloquially called the CBI, permission to investigate particular offences in that state. In other words, the CBI can investigate a case only if requested by the concerned state government or directed by the High Court or Supreme Court, except if it is a matter that pertains to the Central government.

At various points of time in the past, several states had revoked orders giving consent, that too with retrospective effect to the Special Police Establishment (read CBI) to investigate matters. The beneficiaries, alas, were card carrying members of the much maligned political class. The Supreme Court finally put paid to this practice in Kazi Lhendup Dorji v CBI 1994 Supp (2) SCC 116 by holding that state governments can not revoke consent given to the Special Police Establishment to investigate and prosecute any matter with retrospective effect. It is also questionable whether the constitutional scheme provides for a Central police force. Entry I and 2 of the state list seventh schedule makes police a state subject.

The moot point is that when legislative powers are available to the Central government in terms of Entry 8 of list 1 of the seventh schedule, that speaks of a Central Bureau of intelligence and investigation, why does the government not enact a straight and simple law empowering the CBI rather than let it function on the basis of a dubious piece of legislation whose basic legality is open to question. Incidentally, the government has recently constituted the

National Investigation Agency drawing upon these very legislative powers mentioned herein above.

Similar is the case of the Serious Fraud Investigation office (SFIO) that has investigated 36 cases and has filed 574 complaints for violation of various provisions of the Companies Act and the Indian Penal Code from May 2004 to July 2009. The SFIO again draws its powers from the investigative provisions of the Companies Act but has no independent locus or standing under the Companies Act. That is the reason why it had to approach the courts to gain accesses to the Satyam scam accused, something that should have been its inherent right given the nature of the Satyam scam. The irony is that the SFIO, despite existing and operating, does not even find mention in the Companies Bill 2009 introduced in Parliament on the August 3, 2009, what to speak of embedding it in a proper legal framework.

The case of our intelligence agencies is even more interesting. In response to a question pertaining to the legislative act or legal architecture from which the Intelligence Bureau draws its legal/statutory authority or right to function, the government came up with a very quixotic response. "The Intelligence Bureau figures in Schedule 7 of the Constitution under the Union list". When pressed that possibly this may not be an appropriate answer the government emphatically reiterated, "The intelligence Bureau finds mention at S.No.8 in the Union list under the 7 Schedule of the Constitution of India".

Even an aspiring student of law knows that Article 246 (1) gives Parliament the exclusive right to make laws on matters enumerated in the Union list in the seventh schedule of the Constitution. In other words, Entry 8 in the Union list enunciated in the government's response merely gives it the legislative power to enact a statute to bring a Central Bureau of Intelligence to be called by whatever name (IB or BI) into existence. A mere mention of a subject in the laundry list of legislative powers neither gives an organization life or legitimacy. Unfortunately, no such law has ever been enacted by successive governments since the commencement of the Constitution.

Similar is the case of India's external intelligence service, the Research and Analysis Wing (R&AW). In response to a question about the law/statute which gives R&AW the powers/authority to discharge its functions/mandate efficaciously and efficiently, the government did not try and hide behind any obfuscation but candidly admitted, "There is no separate/ specific statute governing the functions/mandate of the R&AW". However, in 2000 following the report of the task force on Intelligence Apparatus which examined the entire intelligence system in the country, a formal charter listing the scope and mandate of the R&AW was formally approved by the government of India".

Contrast this with the position in various other countries of the world. The Federal Bureau of Investigation of the US government draws its powers from Title 28 of the United States code. Title 28 (Judiciary and Judicial Procedure) is that portion of the United States Code (federal statutory law) that governs the federal judicial system.

The Serious Fraud office of the United Kingdom draws its legal authority and powers from the Criminal Justice Act 1987 (as amended). The impetus for introducing the Criminal Justice Act 1987 and creating the SFO was the Fraud Trials Committee Report, popularly known as 'the Roskill Report' published in 1986. Its main recommendation was the setting up of a new unified organization responsible for the detection, investigation and prosecution of serious fraud cases.

Similarly the Central Intelligence Agency (CIA) of the United States, created by the National Security Act of 1947, was specifically empowered by the Central Intelligence Agency Act of 1949 (CIA Act) to carry out the duties assigned to it by the 1947 Act. MI5, the domestic intelligence service of the United Kingdom, draws it's legal authority from The Security Services Act 1989 and its sister organization, the James Bond Fame, MI6 or the SIS, from the 1994 Intelligence Services Act, thereby subjecting it's activities to the scrutiny of the British Parliament's Intelligence and Security Committee.

The Foreign Intelligence Service of Russia draws its legal basis from the Law on Foreign Intelligence Organs 1996. The German Federal Intelligence Service, Bundesnachrichtendienst (BND), draws its legal sustenance from the Federal Intelligence Service Law 1990. Its activities are supervised by the Parliamentary Control Commission (PKK) for intelligence services which in turn is empowered by the Law over the Parliamentary Control of Intelligence Activities 1978. Even in Japan the Public Security Intelligence Agency, that post its reorganization in 1996 started focusing upon foreign intelligence collection, is empowered by the Subversive Activities Prevention Law that came into force on July 21, 1952. PSIA is credited with collecting information on Russia, China and North Korea through their HUMINT networks.

Both from the national security and the civil liberties point of view, it is inappropriate to allow law enforcement and intelligence services to function without a sound and well defined legal basis. There can be no case that an equivocal or indeterminate legal mandate gives greater operational flexibility. In fact, in an information and litigious age it has both, an inhibiting and, even worse, a debilitating impact.

It makes one shudder to think that when the spectre of multiple security challenges ranging from Jehadi terrorism, economic espionage to Naxalism threaten the sovereignty of India, the sentinels of the nation, i.e. its principal law enforcement and investigative agencies, are bereft of the armor of legal sanction and protection. It is equally horrifying to even imagine that organizations that wield enormous powers of depriving people of both life and liberty do it in accordance with legality whose underpinnings are at best tentative if not completely non existent, thereby undermining Article 21 which lies at the heart of the Indian Constitution.

It is imperative in a democracy that every organization of the government must draw its powers, privileges and authority from clearly defined legal statutes. The legal basis must not be fuzzy but sharply defined to obviate any obfuscation about both the intent of the legislature and the mandate it seeks to bestow. This ispo-facto addresses the issue of oversight and provides the structure of checks and balances that is critical for the healthy functioning of any constitutional system.

Maybe, competing priorities edged out this critical issue from the 100-day radar of UPA II, but to put our democratic ethos on an even sounder footing, it is imperative to provide our central law enforcement and intelligence structures with proper legal shields.

Postscript: This piece was written a full 4 years and 3 months before a Division Bench of the Guwahati High Court quashed the constitution of CBI on 6th November, 2013.

An idea whose time has come

ON THE 12th of August 2009, in these very columns, I had underscored the need to provide India's law enforcement and intelligence structures with a comprehensive legal architecture that balances the twin imperatives of national security and civil liberties. With Parliament in recess and in the wake of the debate around alleged phone tapping it may perhaps be an opportune moment to calmly re-visit the issue of both the legal foundations and oversight mechanisms of our intelligence organizations.

The evolution of the debate on the twin issues of surveillance of electronic communication and reform of intelligence paradigms, both in Britan and India, has uncanny parallels. In part, it may be due to shared legal and constitutional traditions. In both instances the process in it's embryonic stage, was kick started externally and driven judicially rather than springing from internal imperatives eminently desirable with reform renaissances .While in Britain the process has fructified into legislation, in India it remains mired by institutional resistance. However ,there are useful lessons that can be learnt from the British experience that may help shorten the learning curve. The decision of the European Courts of Human Rights in Re James Malone's case, that the tapping of his phone had contravened

---

The Hindustan Times, 19 May, 2010

his right to privacy guaranteed under Article 8 of the Human Rights Convention ,directly led to the 1985 Interception of Communication Act in the United Kingdom. Though Malone could not succeed in a UK high court, the Judge, Sir Robert Meggary, while delivering the verdict, observed in open court that "telephone tapping is a subject that cries out for legislation."

Compare this with the pronouncement of our Supreme Court in PUCL vs UOI 1997(1) SCC 301, Justice Kuldip Singh speaking for the bench observed, "In the absence of a just and fair procedure for regulating the exercise under Section 5(2), it is not possible to safeguard the rights of the citizens guaranteed under Article 19 (1) (a) and 21 of the Constitution of India." Section 5 (2) is that provision of the Indian Telegraph Act that under certain circumstances empowers the state to eavesdrop on citizens. The bench laid down the guidelines to be followed for phone tapping which hold the field even today.

By the mid 80's British juries repeatedly expressed their reluctance to convict people under the discredited Official secrets legislation. The inability of the British government to prevent the telecasting of a documentary in which a former Security Service officer Cathy Massiter claimed that prominent members of the peace movement and trade unions were under MI5 surveillance, coupled with the public ridicule it invited while attempting to obtain an injunction in the Australian Courts against the publication of a former Security Service official Peter Wrights memoirs entitled *Spy Catcher,* and the decision yet again of the European Court of Human Rights in the matter of a Swedish Marxist-Torsten Leander ,convinced the M1 5 leadership that it required sound legal footing.

Exhaustive intra-agency deliberations led it's annual report for 1987-88 to conclude,"There is complete acceptance among the staff of the desirability of legislation for the security service". This paved the way for the enactment of the Security Services Act in 1989 and the Intelligence Services Act in 1994. Again, compare this with the contours of the Indian debate. There have been repeated calls by opinion leaders to repeal the Official Secrets Act 1923. The continuing prosecution of the Tehelka co-founders Tarun Tejpal and Annirudha Behal on the strength of a specious FIR filed against them in 2001 to harass them for a Defense expose—Operation West End exemplifies the absurdity of the situation . These demands have become even more urgent after the enactment of the Right to information Act in 2005 as the inconsistency between both these legislations stands out in sharp contrast. The handling of our own La-Spy Catcher affair, Gen VK Singh's book on the RAW, makes the Indo-British parallels more compelling. The implications of this handling are reflected in the demand of furtive NTRO whistleblowers flagging the VK Singh episode to demand full immunity in return for full disclosure.

The parallels do not end here. In the wake of opposition charges that the British government had ignored intelligence warnings of an impending Argentinean invasion of the Falklands, the government appointed a commission of six Privy Counsellors headed by Lord Franks to undertake the Falklands Islands Review. By establishing the Franks committee ,Prime Minister Thatcher conceded in practice the principal of an oversight committee for the intelligence community. This paved the way for the establishment of a Parliamentary Standing committee on Intelligence and Security a decade later.

Similarly, in India too, the furor over intelligence lapses that resulted in the Kargil intrusions in 1999 impelled the Vajpayee government to establish the Kargil Review committee chaired by the distinguishedK Subhramanyam. The recommendations of the KRC led to the constitution of a Group of Ministers to implement its recommendations. While it may not have amounted to a parliamentary review the Vajpayee government did, in a convoluted manner, ensconce the canon of oversight on intelligence structures.

The time has arrived to abandon the two puritanical constitutional doctrines that have perpetuated opacity around intelligence structures. First—the dogma that since intelligence operations require secrecy therefore the word intelligence itself is taboo. Second ,the precept that Parliament must entirely abdicate its powers in this field to the executive. Victorian naiveté that enemy agents are found under Gooseberry bushes and intelligence is brought by storks must cede to the next logical step i.e. providing the intelligence services with an appropriate legal framework including a Surveillance of Electronic Communications Act complimented with robust parliamentary oversight.

NJAC Bill needs some introspection

THE STAGE is set to refer the 121st Constitutional Amendment Bill that deals with the appointments and transfers of Judges of the Supreme Court and the High Courts to the State Legislatures for ratification. This follows Article 368 of our Constitution, which requires one half of the State Legislatures to ratify by resolution an amendment to the Constitution in relation to the Union Judiciary, State Judiciary or those provisions which relate to Centre-State relations.

The time has come for the State Legislatures to take this exercise with profundity rather than "a party whip"driven, unthinking process. How judges are appointed has relevance for all Indians, because judicial independence is the cornerstone of democracy. In fact, there is a very strong case for diluting the rigors of the Anti Defection Law as proposed by the writer in a Private Members Bill in the previous Lok Sabha.

Constitution

The consideration of the Constitution (121st Amendment) Bill, 2014 along with the National Judicial Appointments Commission Bill, 2014, can only be termed as a Constitutional and a legislative aberration. Until and unless the amendment process was complete, after ratification by one half of the Legislatures of the States, the provisions of the NJAC Bill ought not to have been introduced, much

---

The Mail Today, 28 August, 2014

less considered and passed by the Parliament. The same can only be termed as a constitutional impropriety.

The reason why the State Legislatures must apply themselves to the provisions of the Constitutional Amendment Bill is because the framers of the Constitution were very clear in their conception that judicial independence is the cornerstone of democracy. It is the final frontier of justice for the last person in the last row when the executive fails him or tramples upon his legal and Fundamental Rights.

It, therefore, provided in the amending article that any constitutional amendment that deals with the judiciary must be scrutinized by legislators in addition to parliamentarians as they have an equal, if not a greater stake in the issue, being closer to the grass roots dynamics. India lives not in New Delhi, but its states.

The flaws in the Constitutional Amendment and the bill are myriad. However, what is of concern is that the Commission to select and transfer judges has a quixotic provision whereby its eminent members are not required to be jurists. Though the process mandates that a High Powered Committee will decide whom these eminent persons are, it may have been wiser to have the President and the Chief Justice appoint such persons (as suggested by the Venkatachaliah Commission), thereby precluding any executive influence. The provision with regard to reservation of one of the eminent members can only be described as regressive. Our higher judiciary does not contemplate any reservation for appointment, and such a reservation in the membership of the Commission would only spur demands for a system of reservations in the appointments, as also transfers of the higher judiciary itself.

Governance

What is also pertinent is that if the Government of the day has a vote in the appointment of Judges, it would be incumbent that the political opposition also has a direct and an equal say to maintain the balance of a democratic polity. After all, the appointment of Judges is too serious a business to be left to the tender mercies of the executive, which incidentally is the biggest litigant across the country.

The procedure contemplated by the NJAC Bill also leaves many questions raised against the Collegium System unanswered. What is interesting to note is that while the consultation system is completely done away with for the appointment of Judges of the Supreme Court, it is partially maintained for the appointment to the High Courts. The requirement of a 5/6th majority for the appointment of Judges of the Supreme Court can only be termed extremely arduous.

If two members of the NJAC are given a veto to stall the appointment of Judges, one can reasonably apprehend a gridlock in judicial appointments. Intriguingly, the appointments of the Judges of both the High Court and Supreme Court are contemplated by the Commission in terms of the regulations to be prescribed. The NJAC Bill excessively delegates power to prescribe the procedure to be followed by the proposed Commission.

Even prior to the introduction of the two Bills for consideration in Parliament, there was no effective consultation with Bar Associations. The least that needed to be done was to have broad-based stakeholder consultations across the country involving people across the spectrum, as everyone has a stake in the functioning of the judicial system.

Justice

The primary grievance of the secrecy of the Collegium has not been cured, and the proposed system is as opaque as the existing one. Our Constitution is a living document, whereby the Supreme Court has been given an important role with regard to judicial review. There is no doubt that the proposed changes will see another round of litigation. What would be interesting to see is how the Government will bring the amendment to the Constitution within the framework of the basic structure doctrine laid down in Kesavananda Bharati, which has successfully surmounted legislative and constitutional and legal challenges. It, therefore, is important that members of the state legislatures must apply themselves to the provisions of the Constitutional amendment bill.

Political parties, in the larger national interest, must ensure that no whips are issued and legislators are permitted to exercise their conscience on a matter germane to the rights of the sovereign and the very existence of the republic. Given the experience of the post colonial world, the reason why India was able to maintain its democratic continuity is because of the doctrine of separation of powers.

If the Constitutional Amendment fails to pass legislative muster the interests of posterity would be protected in perpetuity.

Beware of the tyranny of the elected

IT HAS BEEN a fortnight since the Supreme Court struck down the Constitution (99th Amendment) Act and also declared the National Judicial Appointments Commission Act, 2014, as unconstitutional and void. The fine print of the decision has been analysed to death. However, the unspoken 600-pound gorilla in the room is the power dynamic between the executive and the judiciary and how it evolved since the commencement of the Constitution.

From the dawn of the Constitution in 1950, till 1967, the Supreme Court adopted a rather conservative approach towards the interpretation of the Constitution. It had, by majority, held that parliamentary sovereignty was supreme and Parliament had unlimited powers to amend the Constitution.

In context of property rights, juxtaposed against the socialist narrative of the then government, the Supreme Court, for the first time in 1967, in Golak Nath's case barred Parliament from taking away or abridging basic human rights by amending the Constitution. These entitlements are enshrined in the Constitution and ubiquitous in the chapter on fundamental rights.

Then came the landmark Kesvananda Bharati judgment in 1973. The Supreme Court propounded the basic structure doctrine,

---

The Asian Age, 31 October, 2015

whittling down the power of Parliament to amend the Constitution by holding that there were certain basic features of the Constitution that even Parliament could not alter. Although there was nothing in the text of the Constitution limiting the power of amendment, the judges discerned some implied limitations, thereby designing the basic structure construct.

At that point in time, the basis of the judgment, or the lack of it thereof, came under dense denunciation from the Bar and the political executive. On the very next day, three senior judges of the Supreme Court, who had voted in favour of limiting the power of amendments, were superseded. The fourth senior-most judge, Justice AN Ray, was appointed as Chief Justice of India.

Whatever may have been the rationale, this was perceived as an insalubrious departure from the tradition established since 1950 of nominating the senior-most judge as the Chief Justice of India. The three judges resigned in protest. Lok Sabha member Mohan Kumaramangalam speciously validated the perception of bloodletting by hyperventilating in Parliament that the country needed judges who were committed to the political ideology of the government of the day.

The new Chief Justice reinforced this perception further by constituting a bench of 13 judges to reconsider the basic structure doctrine. Fortunately, the attempt had to be aborted due to the embarrassment caused during the hearings.

A struggle for supremacy between the executive and the judiciary became the order of the day. The sardonic pejorative "court packing" was freely bandied about. Since the executive exercised primacy in the process of appointment of judges, a canard gained credibility that only such persons would be considered for appointment as judges who were in tune with the ideology of the government.

This was then followed by the supersession of Justice HR Khanna. He had rightly held in the ADM Jabalpur case towards the end of 1976 that the right to life enshrined in Article 21 of the Constitution could not be suspended even during the Emergency. He was not appointed as the Chief Justice of India.

Although in the First Judges case in 1981, the Supreme Court upheld the supremacy of the political executive in the appointment process, the judiciary was not only queasy but also extremely uneasy with this arrangement. This found reflection in the lead judgment of Justice PN Bhagwati in which kernels of the collegium system were seeded.

It took another 12 years for the seeds to flower into the present day collegium system that was institutionalised by the Supreme Court in the Second Judges case in 1993. The Supreme Court, by a majority, held that the term "consultation with the Chief Justice of India" in the constitutional scheme for appointment of judges to the Supreme Court and the high courts must be read as concurrence. This changed the balance of power. What, till yesterday, was an executive privilege became a judicial prerogative. The equation of primacy was now in favour of the judiciary. The judiciary, in a 1998 presidential reference, or the Third Judge's case, unequivocally reinforced this primacy.

The key reason, therefore, for the Supreme Court to appropriate to itself the power of appointments to ostensibly preserve the independence of the judiciary was the rancorous legacy of the earlier decades as much as the merits of a matter that it was considering at that point in time.

Turning to the present, the events leading up to the passage of the 99th Constitutional Amendment and the NJAC Act did not exactly create the right ambience. In fact, the malevolent conduct of the government muddied the waters. Right after the National Democratic Alliance government was sworn in, it took umbrage to the proposed elevation of the former solicitor-general of India, Gopal Subramaniam to the Supreme Court on completely frivolous grounds.

Mr Subramaniam, in a display of statespersonship, withdrew his candidature rather than allow the government to belittle the process through an inspired campaign of calumny and insinuation.

Even though the proposal to have a Judicial Appointments Commission was made by the previous UPA government, much like the Judicial Accountability Bill, the government did not attempt to push it through. It allowed it to linger deliberately so that the process could find its own equilibrium. When it did not, it was allowed to lapse. On the contrary, the haste with which the present government carried it through was astounding. In a Parliament of more than 750 members, the debate centered primarily on the demerits of the collegium system. With only one member voting against the amendment, the bill sailed through smoothly. The rare political consensus also ensured that one half of the states ratified it.

When the hearing of the challenge to the amendments began, the Constitution Amendment Act and the NJAC Act were not yet notified by the government. Only two days prior to the final hearing did the government think it appropriate to notify the acts, thereby sending a clear signal that it had started having second thoughts about its "Don Quixote" initiative.

The lead judgment by Justice Jagdish Singh Khehar expresses apprehension about the ability of the political executive to be a participant in the appointments process of judges to the constitutional court for a myriad and one reasons.

However, the primary reason for the rejection of the NJAC was delineated as the perceived threat to the integrity of the appointment process from the political executive and threat to the primacy of the judiciary in the entire paradigm. The lone dissenting voice based his judgment on the lack of transparency in the appointment process under the collegium. In a display of both fairness and candour, even the judges who ruled against the constitutional amendment have underscored the flaws in the collegium arrangement and have posted the matter for a "consequence hearing" in November.

Perhaps, one of the esoteric triggers for the almost unanimous striking down of the constitutional amendment and the NJAC could be the return of a majority government after almost a quarter century of coalition governments. Maybe, that is why the court, even for deciding a constitutional question, has rightly found the attendant political circumstances relevant. They find prominent mention in the body of the judgment. One can only wonder whether the Supreme Court may have come to a different conclusion if a coalition government had been in office. Only four times before has a constitutional amendment been struck down by the Supreme Court, and three of those four occasions have been because it barred the fundamental power of judicial review. This time around, and notably so, the principle of separation of powers and independence of the judiciary have been invoked to strike down the 99th Constitutional Amendment.

The argument made by the government in the Supreme Court, and outside, that the NJAC represents the "will of the people" and, therefore, must be held as valid by the courts, is legally subversive and morally insidious. If accepted, parliamentary majorities can then resort to unconstitutional actions, like abrogation of the Constitution, replacing democracy with dictatorship, and tell the courts that they cannot hear a challenge to these actions, much less strike them down as it reflects the will of the people as expressed by the legislature. This would ring the death knell of the court system. The most hilarious of course was the "tyranny of the unelected" hyperbole coming as it did from a gentleman whose electoral credentials are nothing much to write home about.

With the spectre of fascism hanging low, a great evil stalks our land. It is better, for now, that judges continue to appoint judges, howsoever imperfect the system may be, rather than leaving it to the tender mercies of Narendra Modi and his not very merry men. It is undoubtedly the lesser of the two evils. For judges will retire, governments will change, but the Constitution would remain to be revisited at a more fortuitous time. As war is too serious a business to be left to generals, judicial appointments are too critical to be allowed any monkeying around with.

No case for Uniform Civil Code

AN INVITE to a conversation on "Constitutional politics and judicial will relative to the Uniform Civil Code" made me examine the matter beyond the bluster. The idea of a Uniform Civil Code flows out of Article 44 of the Indian Constitution that is a directive principle of state policy. It declares, "The state shall endeavour to secure for the citizens a uniform civil code throughout the territory of India."

The preamble to the Indian Constitution enshrines secularism as a fundamental value of the Indian state. The first question that would arise then is this: Is there an inherent conflict between a preamble ideal and the remit of Article 44? The second query that would arise is whether there is an intrinsic inconsistency with Article 25 that allows for freedom of conscience and free profession, practice and propagation of religion. The third enquiry that needs to be flagged is whether, on a wider plane, there is a basic incompatibility between retrofitting religious continuums dating back millennia into the conception of modern Westphalian nation states?

Eminent jurist HM Seervai, in his treatise *Constitutional Law of India*, delineating on fundamental rights qua directive principles posed the following interrogatories: "What would have happened if directive principles had not been enacted in our Constitution or are struck out?

The Asian Age, 15 November, 2014

And what would have happened if fundamental rights would not have been enacted or were struck out." He then proceeded to answer the conundrums. "I came to the conclusion that if directive principles had not been enacted or struck out nothing would have happened. But if fundamental rights had not been enacted or were struck out, the result would have been a disaster." The issue of a Uniform Civil Code needs to be scrutinised within the framework of the preceding inquiries and this postulation.

Secularism is the separation of the church and the state. It essentially means that the state shall not interfere in the religious activity of any denomination and no religion shall be permitted to exercise any influence on the affairs of the state. What it also implies is that while the state should look at the materialistic aspects of life, religion is really the spiritual salve that operates in the individual domain. The underlying assumption being that the state must be atheist or at the very least agnostic in its conception.

This is how the construct was perhaps originally conceived as the forerunners of India endeavoured to shape a modern state out of an ancient nation. However, here lay the quintessential contradiction between intent and reality. That the subliminal Indian ethos was deeply religious is an actuality that just could not be overlooked. Over a period of time, secularism was modulated and Indianised by succeeding generations of statespersons to mean Sarv Dharam Sambhav—that the state would have equal respect for all faiths. What was implicit in this formulation was that the state had now given itself the license to patronise faith. This was a definitional leap of faith that allowed the politics of religious revivalism to get a second wind.

However, in the perspective of the Uniform Civil Code, irrespective of whatever definition of secularism is assumed, it can by no stretch provide a lever for the state to transgress into the religious beliefs of an individual.

Coming to Article 25 of the Constitution—doesn't the right to practice a faith encompass all the conventions and practices that go with it? Since the Westphalian conception of sovereignty post-dates the religious continuum, can that by any stretch provide a warrant to interfere with the fundamental beliefs of an individual?

There is an obvious caveat to this proposition. If there are faith based or associated practices that are retrogressive and repugnant to the very ideal of a progressive ethos, for example, diktats of caste oligarchies (read khap panchayats) or unequal inheritance laws that discriminate against women, should the state not decisively intervene to put an end to such abhorrent practices. The answer is certainly a yes, but is the way to do so reform of that particular aspect of personal law or the adoption of a common civil code?

There is also no clarity on what a common or uniform civil code means? Would it mean that all personal laws relating to marriage, divorce, inheritance, succession and guardianship would cease to exist and there would only be one law governing the personal and private affairs of all the 1.2 billion people of India or would it just be another law open to those who seek to utilise it?

If it were the former, would it not militate against the sheer diversity that is the essence of the whole idea of India? In 2012, Parliament legislated an amendment to the Anand Marriage Act because the Sikh community, and rightly so, wanted certain ambiguity pertaining to the phraseology of their marriage ceremony be clarified. This is not withstanding the fact that Hindus, Sikhs, Jains and Buddhists fall within the overarching ambit of the Hindu Marriage Act. In fact, the movement among non-Hindu communities is to break free from this omnibus legislation. Similarly, in many communities succession is matriarchal. Another issue that is provocative is—would it provide rights to transgenders, gays and lesbians? Would it legitimise same sex marriages?

If it is going to be the latter, then don't we already have the Special Marriage Act, 1954, and the Indian Succession Act, 1925, that are non-denominational in character. Does that not constitute a voluntary Uniform Civil Code?

Experience establishes that reform of personal laws should really come from within the communities. It ensures that there is the broadest possible consensus on change rather than change being imposed from outside. The example of the Bharatiya Muslim Mahila Andolan is a case in point. They have ostensibly drafted a New Muslim Marriage and Divorce Act and are now canvassing support for it within the community.

To conclude, the commandment of a Uniform Civil Code is not a polemical political issue to be used for partisan purposes. It has a very grave import. Thankfully, it is non-enforceable. Given the sheer multitude of different intra-faith social conventions and traditions, without even embarking on an exercise to map out inter-faith divergence, any hasty action on this score would be catastrophic. Certain dead letters must be allowed to fade.

Talabira-II upheld Federal principles

ON MAY 7, 2005, an industrialist called Kumar Mangalam Birla wrote a letter to the then Prime Minister requesting allocation of Talabira-II coal block in Orissa to Hindalco for a 650-megawatt captive power plant at its integrated aluminum project in the Sambalpur district and a 100-megawatt captive power plant for the expansion of its Hirakud aluminum plant, both situated in Orissa. Dr Singh acknowledged the letter and noted, "Please get a report from the coal ministry". Is it unknown for businesspersons to write to the Prime Minister to plead their case? Is it inappropriate for a Prime Minister to acknowledge a letter and ask for a report? The answer to both the questions would be an emphatic no. It would be relevant to point out that Dr Singh was holding the additional charge of the coal ministry due to the continuing trials and tribulations of the then coal minister Shibu Soren.

On May 25, 2005, the Prime Minister's Office forwarded the said letter to the coal ministry, requesting them to examine the letter and send a report. Forty days later, Mr Birla wrote another letter to Dr Singh on June 17, 2005, reiterating his request. This letter was linked to the earlier reference. Again, it was sent to the coal ministry requesting for a report on the matter. In August 2005, the coal

---

The Asian Age, 15 March, 2015

ministry sent its file to Dr Singh. In the said file, it was mentioned that the screening committee had considered three major contenders for allocation of Talabira-II and decided to allocate the block to Neyveli Lignite Corporation (NLC), as adequate coal linkages had been provided to Hindalco from Mahanadi Coalfields Limited (MCL) and they had not ostensibly used the coal. Talabira-II & III needed to be developed together to extract an additional 30 million tonnes (Mt) of coal that would have gone waste otherwise at the boundaries of each block. Talabira-III had been separately allotted to MCL and both these public sector companies could develop these two blocks as one large mine through a joint venture. On the other hand, Mr Birla contended that Hindalco was the first applicant for the said coal block way back in 1996. The coal linkage allocated to it could not be used since a bauxite mine lease relating to the aluminum plant had not materialised. MCL would not be able to supply the coal as per earlier linkage and the Government of Orissa favoured allocation of Talabira-II to Hindalco over NLC.

While the file was being processed in the PMO, a letter arrived on August 17, 2005, written by none other than the chief minister of Orissa strongly advocating the claim of Hindalco for the allotment of the Talabira-II coal block, as it would be more beneficial for the state. The letter gave myriad reasons why it would be so. In the light of the said letter, the file was sent back to the coal ministry for re-examination on August 29, 2005.

On September 16, 2005, the coal ministry recommended a joint venture between MCL, NLC and Hindalco for the joint mining of both Talabira-II & III with a shareholding pattern of 70:15:15 respectively. The rationale for this proposal was that under the sharing arrangements, 70 per cent of the total annual production would go to MCL and the remaining 30 per cent would be shared equally between NLC and Hindalco. Out of the estimated reserves of 553 Mt, 100 Mt would go to Hindalco, while the remaining 453 Mt would go to both the Central public sector units, thus, fully protecting their fuel requirements for a proposed power plant.

It needs to be explained that under the Mines and Minerals Development and Regulation Act, the mining lease is actually granted by the state government. The prior approval of the Central government is, of course, taken but an important caveat is that under the Federal framework of sharing mining rights, as provided by the statute, both the Central government and state government need to concur before an allottee gets a mining lease. It is not the sole prerogative of the Central government. In the present case, the government of Orissa, keeping the best interests of the state in mind, had not only strongly supported the case of Hindalco in the screening committee but also pointedly underscored that aluminum plants should get higher priority as they generate more employment, create more wealth and add to the growth of the manufacturing sector directly. The state government, underlining the federal principle, opined that it is equitable to accord higher priority to units adding value to manufacturing within the state where the mine is located. Now, for any decision-maker, the quintessential dilemma is how to balance competing interests. On the one hand, the interests of the public sector undertakings need to be protected, while on the other one cannot overlook the fact that 75 per cent of India's $2 trillion GDP comes from the private sector. That is where growth and development trajectories are steeper.

Moreover, should the federal imperative be totally ignored? If a state government is being so emphatic, is it wise for any Prime Minister to disregard its point of view? It was in the light of these competing interests, that every policymaker has to balance, that the former Prime Minister, on October 1, 2005, approved the allocation of Talabira-II & III to a three-way joint venture between MCL, NLC and Hindalco with 85 per cent of the equity in the hands of the two Central public sector undertakings. Does this even smack of malfeasance much less corruption?

III. Political Economy of India

Moving past the financial crisis

CREATING PRACTICAL Answers: Overcoming Political and Economic Obstacles.

The subprime crisis that emerged in the US housing mortgage market in 2007 snowballed into a global financial crisis, leading to a global economic recession. The financial landscape has changed significantly after the collapse of Lehman Brothers in September 2008. An important lesson learnt, post-September 2008, is that irrespective of the degree of globalization of a country and the soundness of its domestic policies, a financial crisis could spread to any economy.

India too was affected by the crisis as several sectors reeled under stagnation. The major IT companies such as Infosys, Wipro and Tata Consulting Services were hit hard by the financial crisis, due to the fact that many of the loss making US financial institutions were their key clients. Foreign institutional investors withdrew $12 billion from the stock markets and foreign credit suddenly vanished. India's merchandise exports were badly hit by the Great Recession. They declined by around 30% during 2008.

Having said that, let me underline the fact that India largely remained immune to the larger and more venomous consequences of the Global Financial crisis, primarily because of its unique financial

---

Speech in Doha, 02 June, 2010

and economic architecture. Also, let me emphasise the fact that the stability of the Gulf region is very much in the interest of India. The region collectively hosts the largest expatriate Indian community. The total size of the Indian community in all the six countries of the GC, taken together, is over 5.5 million, constituting 36.5% of the total expatriate population. The remittances from the Indian Diaspora were US$50 billion of which a significant portion comes from the gulf region. Nearly 75% of the crude oil requirement is met from this region which plays a crucial role in our energy security.

Table-India during the recession

Indicator	2007-08	2008-09	2009-10	2010-11	2011-12	2012-13	2013-14
Real GDP Growth (2004-05 Price)	9.32	6.72	8.59	8.91	6.69	4.47	4.74
Industrial GDP Growth	9.67	4.44	9.16	7.55	7.81	0.96	0.35
Services	10,27	9.98	10.50	9.67	6.57	6.96	6.78
Exports Growth	28.94	13.72	-3.49	37.34	23.67	-1.03	3.9
Imports Growth	35.08	19.76	-2.56	26.78	31.07	0.54	-7.2

Source : Reserve Bank of India, Central Statistical Organisation, Finance Ministry, CSO 30/05/2014, 29/11/2014 and Economic Survey 2013-14 etc.

I would like to place before this forum some lessons, we in India, have learnt from one of the dreariest financial crisis of this century. Timely interventions by the government helped to avoid systemic collapse and stabilise the finance system.

Indian initiatives and policy framework

The financial sector is the life blood of any economy. Our Government's approach to the banking and financial sector has been to ensure robust oversight and regulation while expanding financial access and deepening markets. The merit of this balanced approach has been borne out in the recent experience, as the turbulence in the world financial markets has left the Indian banking and financial sector relatively unaffected. Never before has Indira Gandhi's bold decision to nationalise our banking system, exactly 40 years ago—on

14th of July, 1969—appeared as wise and visionary as it has over the past few months. Her approach continues to be our inspiration even as we introduce competition and new technology in this sector.

The setting up of the Financial Stability and Development Council (FSDC) was announced by the Finance Minister Pranab Mukherjee in his Budget Speech 2010-11. This body will be responsible for financial stability and also deal with issues and disputes between financial regulators. FSDC will be multilayered. The council's members will include the heads of financial regulatory organizations such as RBI, SEBI, IRDA, and PFRDA. FMC (Forward Market Commission) is the latest member included in December 2013.On 28 September 2015, it got merged with SEBI. The idea to create such a regulatory body was mooted first by Raghu Ram Rajan Committee in 1998.In addition, the Financial Secretary and chief economic adviser of the Ministry of Finance will also be members of this council. It has the freedom to invite experts in its meetings if it feels the necessity of such expert advice.

The council performs its task without endangering the autonomy of the regulators. The council has conducted 11 meetings and the last such meeting was held on 7th June, 2014.

The FSDC sub-committee has been set up under the chairmanship of Governor, RBI. All the members of the FSDC including 4 Deputy Governors of the RBI and Additional Secretary DEA in charge of FSDC, are members of the sub-committee. It is a forum that meets more frequently than FSDC. It has met 13 times so far and its last meeting was held on 9th August, 2014.

An inter- regulatory technical group has been set up in September, 2011 for better inter-regulatory coordination among the financial sector regulators. The group holds its meeting every two to three months and discusses issues related to risks to systematic financial stability and inter-regulatory coordination to provide input to the sub-committee. The group has met 16 times so far.

Early Warning Group and Macro Financial and Monitoring Group were also set up in 2012. Another group named Working Group on Resolution Regime for Financial Institutions was set up in January 2013. The initiative has led to better regulation of the economic assets and provided better conditions to prevent and face strongly the conditions of economic meltdown in future.

The financial crisis has put a question mark on the role of the central banks worldwide. The autonomy and the independence of central banks are being reviewed. In India, I can say for sure that the prudential norms enforced by our central bank saved the day for us. The Reserve Bank of India operated in an atmosphere where it had the complete backing of the government in suggesting and adjusting the monetary policies such that the Indian financial system remained largely immune to the spreading tentacles of the crisis. So much so, that the role which the RBI played was applauded by many foreign nations.

In India, current account has been opened fully, though gradually. Over the 1990s, a more calibrated approach has been followed to the opening of the capital account and to the opening up of the financial sector. This approach is consistent with the weight of the available empirical evidence with regard to the benefits that may be gained from capital account liberalisation for accelertion of economic growth, particularly in emerging market economies. The evidence suggests that the greatest gains are obtained from opening to foreign direct investment, followed by portfolio equality investment. The benefits emanating from external debt flows have been found to be more questionable until greater domestic financial market development has taken place.

Accordingly, in India, while encouraging foreign investment flows, especially direct investment inflows, a more cautions, nuanced approach has been adopted in regard to debt flows. Debt flows, in the form of external commercial borrowings, are subject to ceilings and some end-use restrictions, which are modulated from time to time, taking into account evolving macroeconomic and monetary conditions. Similarly, portfolio investment in government securities and corporate bonds are also subject to macro ceilings, which are also modulated from time to time. Thus, prudential policies have attempted to prevent excessive recourse to foreign borrowings and dollarisation of the economy. In addition to the exercise of normal prudential requirements on banks, the Reserve Bank has also successively imposed additional prudential measures in respect of exposures to particular sectors, akin to a policy of dynamic provisioning. For example, in view of the accelerated exposure observed to the real estate sector, banks were advised to put in place a proper risk management system to contain the risks involved. They were advised to formulate specific policies covering exposure limits, collaterals to be considered, margins to be kept, sanctioning authority, level and sector to be financed.

An additional feature of recent prudential actions by the Reserve Bank relate to the tightening of regulation and supervision of Non-banking Financial Companies (NBFCs), so that regulatory arbitrage between these companies and the banking system is minimized. The overarching principle is that banks should not use an NBFC as a delivery vehicle for seeking regulatory arbitrage opportunities or to circumvent bank regulation(s), and that the activities of NBFCs do not undermine banking regulations. Thus, capital adequacy ratios and prudential limits to single / group exposures in the case of NBFCs have been progressively brought nearer to those applicable to banks. The regulatory interventions are graded—higher in deposit-taking NBFCs and lower in non-deposit-taking NBFCs. Thus, excessive leverage in this sector has been contained.

In brief, the Indian approach has focused on gradual, phased and calibrated opening of the domestic financial and external sectors, taking into cognizance reforms in the other sectors of the economy. Financial markets are contributing to efficient channeling of domestic savings into productive uses and, by financing the overwhelming part of domestic investment, are supporting domestic growth. These characteristics of India's external and financial sector management, coupled with ample forex reserve coverage and the growing underlying strength of the Indian economy, reduce the susceptibility of the Indian economy to global turbulence.

Impact of the crisis on GCC

As global shocks tightened financing conditions, and oil production and prices declined, the global financial crisis took its toll, particularly on the UAE, Kuwait, and Bahrain, given their linkages with global equity and credit markets. Across the region, economic activity contracted in the second half of 2008 and the first half of 2009, and was accompanied by a decline in credit, broad money growth, and inflation. Decisive policy actions by the authorities have helped moderate the effect of the crisis, although its full impact, particularly on the financial sector, may not have materialized yet.

The GCC countries have been hit by the decline in oil prices and production, as well as by liquidity shortages in global financial markets. The direct impact from US subprime assets, however, was limited, given a relatively low direct exposure of GCC commercial banks to these assets. Oil market developments affected government finances and external positions directly, but they also had an indirect impact on banking and corporate liquidity and funding costs as speculative capital inflows reversed and investor confidence in the GCC declined. Due to lower oil revenues, the fiscal and external balances of GCC counties have weakened in 2009 and are expected to have a partial recovery in 2010, in line with the expected oil price increase. Suggested reforms to overcome the economic and political obstacles

1. Banking Sector—The crisis revealed some vulnerabilities related to banks' exposures to asset markets, their increasing dependence on foreign financing, and a general weakness in their liquidity management framework. It also exposed instances of weak supervisory enforcement. For example, the severe liquidity shortages that banks faced in 2008 were due, to a large extent, to the use of short-term speculative capital inflows to finance rapid credit growth.

Formal state ownership of banks is low, though informal channels of influence can be significant. Bahrain, Kuwait, and Qatar had limited public sector ownership of banks prior to the intensification of the crisis in 2008, although Qatar banks have recently received extensive support, and one bank in Kuwait was recapitalized, partly with public sector funds. Oman and Saudi Arabia have a relatively higher public sector component. UAE domestic banks stand out in the GCC, either in the form of direct government ownership or via royal families' ownership. More recently, key Abu Dhabi and Dubai banks received significant public support in the form of equity injections to mitigate the impact of the current crisis. Regardless of formal ownership arrangements, de facto state influence over domestic banks remains pervasive wherever hydrocarbon wealth is important. In these countries, state control over hydrocarbon resources fundamentally determines activity in the non-hydrocarbon sector of the region, through strong connections between state and core industrial and financial groups.

2. The non-banking financial sector—The crisis also revealed weaknesses in the regulatory and supervisory framework of non banks. The systemic importance of non-banking financial institutions in many GCC countries has increased in recent years with the rise in their number, activities, and market share. However, similar to the international experience, the development of regulatory and supervisory framework for nonbanks has lagged behind, resulting in a build-up of vulnerabilities in some cases.

In this regard, authorities should facilitate the restructuring of non-banking institutions, including by recapitalizing systemic and viable ones while ensuring a smooth exit of nonviable ones. Furthermore, to address weaknesses in the regulatory and supervisory framework of non banks, the authorities should:

- strengthen oversight of the risk management practices of those institutions;
- adopt tighter conditions for granting licenses;
- introduce an appropriate minimum set of fit and proper criteria for the appointment of managers and board members;
- enhance disclosure.

These measures, if strictly enforced, would enhance soundness, encourage consolidation, and provide a quality hurdle to entry, leading to fewer and well-managed institutions.

3. Corporate governance and transparency—Improving corporate sector transparency has become a priority. The corporate sector in the GCC is largely owned by family business groups or GCC governments. This has tended to decrease overall disclosure, internal controls, and corporate governance, particularly in view of the limited disclosure requirements for unlisted companies. While these groups had comfortable access to credit prior to the crisis, both domestically and externally, lenders are now putting pressure on them to enhance disclosure, particularly in view of the default of the two Saudi conglomerates and DW developments. The immediate challenge—for maintaining public confidence in the banking sector and supporting credit growth—is to ensure that the process of cleaning up of the

banks balance sheets is completed smoothly, based on continued upfront recognition of losses and immediate bank recapitalisation. The should be accompanied by enhancements to regulatory, supervisory and resolution frameworks, where needed.

4. Communication—Communication during the crisis showed some weaknesses. Clear communication on policy actions, objectives, and rules and procedures of governing authorities' actions would help ensure their success and speed up recovery. Improved communication would also help ease investor uncertainly and reduce speculation and market volatility.

5. Fiscal policies and diversification—The crisis has re-emphasized the risk of high dependence on oil revenues and the importance of revenue diversification and rationalization of fiscal spending. Notwithstanding progress made by the GCC in diversifying economic activity in the past two decades, the oil sector continues to contribute heavily to total GDP and is the main source of fiscal revenue. The volatility of oil revenue and production also underscores the importance of accumulating fiscal savings during economic upturns to allow for counter-cyclical fiscal policies during downturns.

6. Strengthening cross-border cooperation—The need to exchange information among cross-border supervisors has not been critical so far given the still limited number of GCC banks with cross-border operations. However, cross-border cooperation should be strengthened in light of the changing regional financial landscape and increased integration. Harmonization of regulation and supervision within the GCC will also be essential.

Conclusion

With this degree of openness, in the economy today, developments in international markets are bound to affect any economy and policy makers have to be vigilant in order to minimize the impact of adverse international developments on the domestic economy. It is, therefore, essential that nations work in tandem with each other and develop a framework to prevent the financial crisis from turning into a humanitarian crisis.

Green Revolution now in the red

TO MAKE agriculture profitable, relax or remove land-ceiling limits and corporatise farm inputs to keep the costs down. Travelling through the Punjab hinterland is always a learning experience for me. Recently, on a hot May afternoon, I had a long and detailed conversation with a group of farmers on the rustic realities of farming today.

To understand the essence of the conversation, we need to look at some data first. The average size of a land holding in India is 1.16 hectares. This is roughly 2.8 acres. Conventional wisdom holds that 84% of the farmers in Punjab have a landholding of less than five acres. Though official data puts the average size of a landholding at 3.77 hectares in the state, this is more a statistical sophistry than an accurate analysis of the situation. Most farmers grow only two crops: Wheat that is sown in November and harvested in April and rice that is planted in June and reaped in early October. The farmers I spoke to described the agrarian crisis using a rough-and-ready tutorial on the economics of farming in layman terms. One acre of land in a good year yields about 20 quintals of wheat. A quintal is equal to 100kg. In a bad year, like the current one, the yield can go down by half or three-fourths i.e. 7-10 quintals. At a minimum support price (MSP) of Rs 1,450 per quintal, a farmer can get about Rs 29,000 per acre.

The Hindustan Times, 12 May, 2015

But we need to take into account the cost of inputs. Each acre requires about one quintal of fertiliser that costs about Rs 2,000. It requires about one-and-a-half quintal of urea (Rs 1,000), a dose of zinc (Rs 200), three sprays of pesticide (Rs 1,500), seed (Rs 800), four rounds of watering (Rs 800), and manual harvesting (Rs 3,000) . There are sundry expenses like tractor and diesel of around Rs 2,000.

So a farmer spends about Rs 11,300 per acre considering that electricity is free. He thus earns about Rs 17,700 per acre for six months of hard work that translates into Rs 2,950 per month and if he has a plot of three acres, it comes up to Rs 8,850 per month. This does not take into account the wages of an entire family of four or five persons who would be toiling ceaselessly to make these numbers a reality.

Then the agriculturists explained the economics of the second crop. The yield of rice per acre is about 25 quintals in a good year. At an MSP of Rs 1,400 per quintal, it translates into a figure of Rs 35,000 per acre. With an input cost of Rs 13,800, which is slightly higher than wheat, the farmer earns about Rs 21,200 per acre for six months of hard work that translates into Rs 3,500 a month. Now if he has a three-acre plot, it means Rs 10,500 per month for the whole family.

Thus in a good year, a family can earn about Rs 19,350 a month but if there is any unnatural occurrence it can all go down the drain. However, if you are a contract farmer, who has taken the land on lease and are paying to the owner Rs 40,000 per acre annually, then your monthly income is down to Rs 9,500 per month for a three-acre agricultural holding. These figures do not take into account the all-pervasive spectre of rural indebtedness where a farmer is on an average paying an 18% annual rate of interest to the moneylender from cradle to cremation.

How does a farmer then sustain himself? He grows his own vegetables, has an odd buffalo for milk, and leads a very rudimentary existence. If there is an illness in the family or when a marriage is supposed to take place, the farmer is caught between a rock and a hard place. Children's education on such meagre earnings is a non-priority.

What then keeps the farmer going? "Two things," explained one of the older men. The "notional satisfaction" that the value of land is multiplying—if you are near a city, it could be Rs 2-3 crore an acre and if you are in the hinterland it could be Rs 25-30 lakh an acre. The value is the only social security net. Coupled with that is the insecurity over what to do if they sell the land.

But the younger generation is not prepared to wait. They want to monetise the land not because they want to buy flashy cars or pay for their drug habits. The sensible ones see that as the only head start that can give them a better quality of life than what their parents have had.

With immigration barriers at their zenith, recruitment in the armed forces dwindling and even terrorism having been experimented with, alienating land holdings is no longer about choice but a compulsion. If the price is right, acquisition is not a taboo.

What is the solution? Surprisingly, the old gentleman gave an answer that one would have expected from a kulak. Address the structural issues beginning with relaxing or removing land-ceiling limits altogether so that agriculture becomes remunerative and collectivise, or corporatise farm inputs so that input costs can come down. Some farmers would lose out in this shake-out but farming would survive.

This is a dormant volcano in the crucible of the green revolution—with fertile soil, means of irrigation and an open-ended MSP supported public procurement programme to boot. The situation is fast evolving—from the death of farmers to the death of farming.

The dialogue left me wondering whether the concerns of India for the vast unknown called Bharat were still as far removed as the physical miles between Delhi and a smouldering settlement called Dedka, tucked away in the what was a 'no go' area during the height of militancy in Punjab.

The colour of money

AT THE HEART of the debate on electoral reforms lies the vexed issue of campaign finance reform. The four fundamental questions that need to be answered to understand this conundrum are: How are electoral processes currently funded? How much should a candidate and a political party be allowed to spend on an assembly or a parliamentary campaign? How to ensure that the source of electoral funding is legal and accounted for to tax authorities? Finally, how to police the whole process?

Candidates for public office are invariably funded in myriad ways and at multiple levels. The principal funding comes from the political parties they represent, corporate houses and even private individuals. The Indian diaspora is also a top-dollar contributor to electoral campaigns. A significant part of the funding to candidates also comes from government officials, from the patwari to the highest echelons of the bureaucracy, for current or future patronage. Politicians funding their personal campaigns in entirety are also a growing phenomenon.

The second issue is: What rationale should be used to determine an electoral expense ceiling? It is possible to fight a Lok Sabha election with Rs 25 lakh (which is the permissible limit now), and also possible to burn through Rs 25 crore (which certain candidates are rumoured

---

The Indian Express, 11 March, 2011

to have spent). Given this level of variation, there is a real dilemma in finding a reasonable limit for expenditure.

The government has already accepted the Election Commission's recommendation to increase the limit to 40 lakh. One can ask how Rs 40 lakh is any better than Rs 25 lakh when crores are in play? Then, why shouldn't money spent by a political party in a constituency be counted towards the expenditure incurred by its candidate? After all, it is being spent for and on behalf of the candidate.

Instead of prescribing an arbitrary limit, the Election Commission should float a consultation paper specifically on, and limited to, the issue of campaign finance reform, hold open discussions with people across the social and economic spectrum including civil society and election watchdogs, meet representatives of political parties under Chatham House rules to get the real picture, and then arrive at the ceiling on election expenditure—which must be reviewed after every Lok Sabha election.

The third issue is how to ensure that legitimate funding drives electoral campaigns. As a first step, the entire regime of corporate funding needs to be revisited by relaxing the irrational limit prescribed by Section 293-A of the Companies Act that places a 5 per cent cap on net profits that can be contributed to a political party. Why should it be 5 and not 50 per cent of net profits? There should be no ceiling in law. It should be between the management and the shareholders to decide the level of contribution that a corporate wants to make. The government should only ensure that companies contributing are legitimate business entities and not mere money-laundering fronts.

Even if you liberalise the regime, corporate groups would still prefer to pay in cash because of the coercion and the element of vendetta that accompanies these transactions. To surmount this reality, the government must, by law, establish an independent campaign finance trust to be chaired by a former president of India, consisting of a former vice president and former chief justice of India as its trustees. This trust would receive funding from corporate entities, NGOs, individuals and others, as well as confidential advice as to which political party the funds should be transmitted.

The recipient must be a political party registered with the Election Commission. No court of law or any right to information request should go into the advice given, unless the trustees themselves find that a receipt is suspect and order an investigation into its origin. All the funds from diverse sources which are advised for a particular political party can then all be bundled up and one cheque every quarter or half-year could go to that registered political party. This would ensure both the anonymity of the contribution and insurance against coercion. Thus, by protecting the confidentiality of the transactions, corporate houses and others could be encouraged to contribute by cheque.

The final question is: how to police and regulate a reformed architecture of electoral finance? A possible solution could be the setting up of a three-member exclusive election tribunal in each state, headed by a retired Supreme Court judge and including two retired judges of the high court.

These tribunals would be empowered to hear election petitions, with only a statutory appeal straight to the Supreme Court, so that the entire legal journey could culminate in a final decision in 18 to 24 months. If the panel of observers appointed by the Election Commission makes a consensus reference to the tribunal that a candidate is violating or the winner has violated the expenditure ceiling, and the tribunal makes a prima facie assessment that there is merit in the report, it can disqualify a candidate during the campaign process or the winner even after the results are declared—thereby shifting the onus on him to dispute the findings of the observers and establish his innocence.

A related but standalone issue is that of state funding of elections. The moot question remains: how to ensure that other forms of funding can be stopped if state funding is brought into play? Yogendra Yadav's proposal of reimbursing candidates per vote secured, is an interesting idea that needs to be explored and developed further—with the caveat that it should only qualify a candidate polling at least 20 to 25 per cent of the valid votes cast, and private funding is effectively policed, if not eliminated.

Black money, white lies

WHAT IS "black money"? Black money is wealth held by an individual or a company in violation of the laws that are applicable to them. It can broadly be classified as capital that has been subject to tax evasion or are the proceeds of crime. Where is this money then parked? Among other places it is kept in autonomous jurisdictions that are colloquially referred to as tax havens or offshore financial centers (OFCs).

What are tax havens or OFCs? They are countries that utilise their sovereignty to create Preferential Tax Regimes (PTRs) that are backed by a legal architecture that guarantees confidentiality to those who utilise these arrangements.

The Bank of International Settlements (BIS) estimates that around half of all international banking transactions are channelled through such tax havens. About one-third of all foreign direct investment of international conglomerates goes through these OFCs. While corporate tax avoidance is difficult to ascertain, it is estimated that individual tax evasion is close to $1 trillion yearly.

In India, the size of the black or non-formal economy is assessed at about $2 trillion. This is equivalent to the GDP of India. Paradoxically, the formal Indian economy floats on top of a capacious black economy. Most of this money is either invested in the stock markets or the real

---

The Asian Age, 29 October, 2014

estate sector. Just compare the difference between the market value and the registered value of land, houses or commercial complexes in any part of the country. The cash component varies between 50 to 80 per cent even today.

How did tax havens originate? Like all things modern, it has an American touch to it. In the late 1880s, the state of New Jersey was in dire need of revenues. Legend has it that a New York attorney persuaded the then governor of New Jersey, Leon Abbot, to enact such legislation that would attract businesses to set up their headquarters in that state. The law had two constructs, easy incorporation and low rate of commercial taxation.

The state of Delaware soon followed suit with a new General Incorporation Act in 1898. While both these states were not tax havens in the strict sense of the word, they were the designers of the archetypes of easy incorporation and amenable regulatory ecosystems for non-resident companies and individuals. This is the basis of all contemporary tax havens even today. From 1920 onwards this practice started getting plagiarised by some Swiss cantons led by the canton of Zug. It soon got replicated on the European mainland also.

In the 20th century, most of the noteworthy tax havens around the world developed around two principal geo-political poles: Some evolved with close links to the City of London that, even today, remains an important financial center. It consisted of the British crown dependencies and overseas territories. It included the Channel islands, Jersey, Isle of Man, Cayman Islands, Bermuda, British Virgin Islands, Turks, Caicos and Gibraltar to name a few. The other developed in Europe and consisted of the Benelux countries, namely Belgium, the Netherlands and Luxembourg—Ireland, Switzerland and Liechtenstein. They were supplemented by Hong Kong, Singapore, Dubai, the Bahamas and the islands in the Pacific Ocean over a period of time. The only other important tax havens that were not a part of this axis were Panama and, to some extent, Uruguay.

Tax havens now span the entire world serving all the major financial and commercial centers. They have thrived with the patronage of influential global powers. In fact, judicial decisions in various countries have facilitated their growth. A landmark judgment being the 1929 ruling by a British court in the matter of the Egyptian Delta Land and Investment Co Ltd vs Todd, that laid down the principle for the entire British Empire, that if a company is registered in a particular domain but does not have activities there it would not be subject to taxation. The maxim "onshore but offshore" became a reality.

How does a nation then get intelligence or information from this web of offshore financial centers that circumscribe the globe? They are, after all, sovereign entities that have enacted edicts as a part of their developmental strategy to attract a certain type of global investment. Research establishes that those states that have a population of less than one million are more prone to become a Preferential Tax Regime. The European Commission during its investigation into tax abuse among the member states of the European Union discerned 206 such tax refuges. The number is only increasing. Since their entire economy is based upon this activity, their appetite to cooperate with countries that are looking for information on their nationals or companies for tax evasion or criminal acts is non-existent. It is only after the global economic meltdown of 2008, when the developed economies were under pressure and were looking for revenues, that they started focusing on these tax sanctuaries.

The 2009 London communiqué of the G-20 devoted a whole section to re-regulating tax shelters. Between 2009 and 2014, India also signed and updated 92 Double Taxation Avoidance Agreements (DTAAs) and 16 Tax Information Exchange Agreements (TIEAs) with various countries. It became a part of various multilateral arrangements to share information with regard to financial crimes and delinquencies. Thus, the UPA government laid the foundation for accessing information on Indian nationals and companies from such nations and tax havens.

Conventional wisdom has it that all these pacts presumably come with a confidentiality clause that broadly states that the information provided can only be used for the purposes of legal prosecution and associated processes and should not be made public. What can be the consequence of the information being made generically public? The implication may be that other countries could refuse to sign agreements with India and those who have signed them already may either repudiate them or refuse to provide information. Reneging on such commitments could also create trust issues qua a broad spectrum of other multilateral accords India is a party to.

The BJP and its proxies were cognizant of the provisions of these compacts. That did not, however, inhibit them from riotously demanding that the names be made public immediately. They promised to do so once in government. It was then politically expedient to crow that the UPA had something to hide.

Correctly cornered by the Supreme Court recently, which is monitoring the black money matter, the current government did a U-turn and was compelled to concede that it cannot divulge the names that it has got from other countries till the departmental and judicial processes against those entities reach fruition. The names divulged till now are ostensibly post the culmination of these processes. With the Supreme Court rightly deciding to hold the government to its rhetoric and directing that all names be provided to the court the chickens have come home to roost rather early for the NDA government. The BJP has been caught in the trap of its own loquaciousness.

Honey, I shrunk the economy!

EVER WONDERED why the Budget is such an important event in India? Why on the last day of February everyone goes into a tizzy? Why after the usual platitudes from corporate India, even if the finance minister has messed up the economy, the Budget is forgotten till the next year? Why is the public discourse not prepared to go beyond that "one-day shenanigan" and spend the next two months between the presentation of the Budget and its passage in a piercing and detailed scrutiny of every aspect of the budgetary proposals as if it is the panacea for all our ills? Finally, why is the Budget a non-event in all other democracies?

The reason is not difficult to discern. Unlike the rest of the world where there is stability in fiscal and monetary policies over the medium term and no gerrymandering with the taxation structure, budgets are but an accounting exercise to serve the ends of financial housekeeping.

Earlier, the Planning Commission used to be a fair arbiter between the Centre and the states. With the abolition of the Planning Commission and its replacement by the Niti Aayog that, at the last count, was a one-and-a-half-man band, not only has enormous power, propensity to arbitrariness and unfettered latitude been concentrated in the finance ministry, but, more importantly, even the institutional

---

The Asian Age, 05 March, 2016

mechanism of taking a long-term view of India's economic trajectory has been dismantled.

Be that as it may, let us turn our attention to the Union Budget for 2016-17. Finance minister Arun Jaitley opened his Budget speech with a pat on the back. He rather triumphantly declared, "The International Monetary Fund has hailed India as a 'bright spot' amidst a slowing global economy. The World Economic Forum has said that India's growth is 'extraordinarily high'."

How does this square up against the government's own numbers? The Ministry of Finance, Department of Economic Affairs, Economics Division, puts out monthly economic reports. In its report for the month of January 2016, the last available, it outlines the macro-economic indicators as follows. The index of industrial production (IIP) is in the red now for many months. It was (-)1.3 per cent in December 2015 as compared to 3.6 per cent in December 2014. It was (-)3.2 per cent in November 2015 as compared to 5.2 per cent in November 2014. Do not forget that in its first six months the National Democratic Alliance government was riding the positive economic momentum created by the previous United Progressive Alliance government even in the closing years of its decade-long tenure.

In December 2015, eight core infrastructure sectors—coal, crude oil, natural gas, refinery products, fertilisers, steel, cement and electricity— grew by a measly 0.9 per cent as compared to 3.2 per cent in December 2014. In November 2014, growth in these sectors had contracted by 1.3 per cent—it was in the negative as compared to positive growth of 8.5 per cent in November 2014. The manufacturing sector also recorded negative growth of 4.4 per cent in November 2015 and again negative growth of 2.4 per cent in December 2015.

During April 2015-January 2016, merchandise exports and imports declined by 17.6 per cent and 15.5 per cent, respectively. The rupee that stood at 59.26 against the dollar on an average in the May of 2014 had depreciated to 68.29 by February 2016 and continues to slide. The bad news does not end here. The moot point is the data put out by the finance ministry does not square up with the delusional world that Mr Jaitley wants to live in. He, before patting himself on the back, opened his innings by referring to the global economy being in serious crisis. However, is the crisis as serious as the global economic meltdown of 2008 and the eurozone catastrophe of 2010-11? Despite such grave challenges, the UPA delivered 7.8 per cent growth on an average year on year for 10 years.

What prescriptions to surmount this precarious situation did Mr Jaitley provide in concrete terms in the Budget? The answer, disappointingly, is none. May be for the first time ever a finance minister refrained from putting a headline number for gross domestic product growth in 2016-17. The apologists for the government stated on TV show after TV show that they had adopted the number given in the Economic Survey, conveniently forgetting that it is an academic sweep of the economic landscape while the budgetary exercise, for whatever it may be worth, is a governance remit. The Economic Survey assumes a rate of about 7 per cent for 2016-17. The Budget papers have given the GDP figures for 2015-16 and 16-17. It calculates the nominal growth at 11 per cent. If these are government's numbers and the Reserve Bank of India's target for inflation in the current fiscal is 4-6 per cent, then it can be safely inferred that GDP growth in the next financial year would be a meagre 6 per cent. Remember this number is also premised upon 2011-12 as the base year. It is a number that even the RBI and many economists are deeply sceptical about. At the previous base year of 2004-05, the 6 per cent growth rate would translate into 4 per cent, which is what the economy really feels like.

Even the revenues of the government have not been augmented by increased collections of corporate income-tax or widening the tax base. They have been bolstered by multiple increases on excise duty on petrol and diesel myriad times since the Budget was presented last year. This brought Rs 54,334 crore to the government's kitty, an amount that should have been legitimately passed on to the consumers because of the sharpest drop ever in global crude oil prices in recent times.

On the three major challenges of agrarian distress, private investments and exports the government has done precious little. While the Budget talks about doubling farm incomes in five years by 2021, it does not offer a clue as to how it is possible with the agriculture sector growing at 3.4 per cent. The government has not even given a meagre increase in the minimum support price (MSP) over the past two years. In fact, MSP increases have been virtually nil and the government has reneged on its electoral promise of giving cost plus 50 per cent more to farmers as remuneration for their produce.

Similarly, the government has shortchanged all the oligarchs who had bankrolled the 2014 elections of the BJP. They are bitter about being used, abused, and then finally dumped. The Budget has some paragraphs devoted to public investment which, in any case, cannot kick-start the economy if the path of fiscal consolidation has to be followed. There is nothing to spur private investment that they can create the much-needed employment and trigger domestic demand to get the wheels of the economy turning.

On exports, the government seems to have just thrown in the towel. After 14 successive months of negative growth, there is no roadmap or incentive structure to revive exports which have played a critical role in India's growth trajectory over the past three or more decades. The government has spent less than budgeted on education, medical and public health, housing, social security and development in the current fiscal. Even the outlays of gender-based ministries went south in the revised Budget estimates.

Finally, there is nothing for the middle class or the small and medium entrepreneur. Neither is their any substantive relief to the taxpayer. The government has delivered a double whammy by deciding to tax withdrawals from the Employees' Provident Fund (EPF), the object of the tax being to encourage people to stop investing in the EPF scheme and to invest in market-based annuities that can then be leveraged by the pirates and carpetbaggers of the financial sector. This has the potential of virtually wiping out the life savings of millions of ordinary people, as it happened with pension funds of many countries during the arbitrage, derivatives and leverages-driven economic meltdown of 2008. Mr Jaitley's Budget would have the singular distinction of shrinking if not sinking the Indian economy.

IV. Modi's Empty Promises

Thirty days of u-turns

THE NATIONAL Democratic Alliance-Bharatiya Janata Party government has completed a month in office. Given that foreign policy initiatives were the flavour of the first 30 days, their examination is in order. An analysis of the government's inertia on rescuing Indians trapped in Iraq would require a separate piece altogether. A host of leaders from the region were witness to the birth of the new dispensation. The invitation to the neighbourhood lends itself to the assessment that India's near abroad is a focus area of this government. However, the choice of invitees laid bare the rather limited worldview of the new government because over the years India's role has not been limited to the Saarc (South Asian Association for Regional Cooperation) but extends deep into the new construct called Indo-Pacific. Even with regard to the region, what was missing was the articulation of a Monroe Doctrine that could possibly distinguish the approach of the new government from the previous one.

Beyond the atmospherics ,what did the invites really yield? Afghan President Hamid Karzai is winding down his presidency and triple transitions are at play in Afghanistan. With allegations of electoral fraud vitiating the presidential election process, the new order may take a while to emerge. If the recent events in Iraq are any indicator,

---

The Asian Age, 28 June, 2014

Afghanistan may descend into a cesspool of violence. Has New Delhi even contemplated establishing relationships with the emerging players in Afghanistan beyond the embassy level interactions during their manifesto/campaign deliberations? Would they contemplate a boots on the ground response if requested for by Afghanistan or an international organisation/coalition at some stage? Are they inclined to, if required, an expansion of the terms of the India-Afghanistan strategic partnership signed in October 2011. There seems to be no indication of a gameplan on Afghanistan as yet.

Moving onto Pakistan, the BJP's approach towards India's most contentious relationship has been marked by the most muscular rhetoric ever since its inception. However, the Vajpayee years saw an abandonment of the rhetoric. The invitation to Pakistan's Prime Minister Nawaz Sharif is perhaps indicative of this turnaround once again. The attack on the Indian consulate in Heart, hours after the invite, was a shot across the bows allegedly by the permanent establishment in Pakistan underscoring that they continue to call the shots on Pakistan's India policy. However, the most disturbing signal this invitation has sent to the people who matter in the Pakistani power calculus and their non-state instrumentalities is that whatever may have been the bombast before assuming office, the new order is now more than willing to play ball on their terms. In other words, terror and talks can go hand in hand. This about turn by the government would have serious implications for India in the coming days. Contrast this with the United Progressive Alliance's approach. Prime Minister Manmohan Singh did not visit Pakistan even once in 10 years as no substantive breakthrough on prickly issues with Pakistan happened. Ironically, the UPA was blamed for being pusillanimous on Pakistan.

Turning attention East, the Prime Minister of Bangladesh Sheikh Hasina chose to send the Speaker of the Jatiyo Sangshad. There are allegedly serious questions about the legitimacy of Sheikh Hasina's government, and if history is any guide, Bangladesh looks set for a rocky time ahead. Again, with regard to Bangladesh, has there been any re-thinking within the BJP on the land boundary question or the Teesta waters issue which are extremely germane from Bangladesh's point of view? There is no indication of any rethink on these questions. Paradoxically, there seems to be backtracking on the BJP's pet electoral issue—illegal infiltration from Bangladesh despite ostensible attempts to tinker with the visa regime.

Moving South, the government of Sri Lankan President Mahinda Rajapakse has been under fire from a number of international organisations for alleged war crimes during the final days of the conflict with the Liberation Tigers of Tamil Eelam (LTTE). This evokes very strong sentiments in Tamil Nadu. The invitation to Mr Rajapakse—without any assertion as to where the new government stands on the question of the rights of the Tamil minority—brought into question and raised legitimate apprehensions about India's continuing commitment to the very concept of human rights, especially given the fact that the BJP's approach towards the minorities in India is not the most glorious chapter in its history.

Turning to Nepal, Bhutan and the Maldives, our relationship with all these three countries is extremely critical given the growing Chinese influence in the region. Again, there seems to be no clue as to whether the government is even cognisant of this concern, what to talk about giving any positive indications to these countries which would give them the confidence that India would continue to be a countervailing influence to the pervasive embrace of the Chinese dragon. Even during the Prime Minister's maiden foreign visit to Bhutan the stress seemed to be more on communicating in Hindi rather than discerning the great balancing act that Bhutan has successfully been doing between China and India. Coming to China, the visit of foreign minister Wang Yi was again heavy on friendly rhetoric and short on substance. The new regime seemed to suffer from a bout of selective amnesia insofar as its ostensible aggressiveness on border intrusions and the question of Arunachal Pradesh being an inalienable part of India were concerned. Except for an ambiguous one-liner—that we expect China to respect a one-India policy—there was no firm message to the Chinese leadership.

It can thus be inferred that the foreign policy outings of the new government during its first month were more in the nature of a meet and greet exercise rather than a calibrated attempt at defining a fresh policy outlook, if at all any does exist or is under contemplation. If it cogitates that continuity in foreign policy is in national interest, then it must acknowledge the correctness of the UPA's approach upfront.

Unfortunately for India, there was no shortage of U-turns in the first 30 days, coupled with the complete absence of "the big idea" that would underpin India's interaction with the world. As Sylvia Plath reminisced in the Ennui, "Tea leaves thwart those who court catastrophe, designing futures where nothing will occur."

Century worth a duck

HOW DO you benchmark the first hundred days of the Bharatiya Janata Party-led National Democratic Alliance government? There are five objective criteria on which the performance of any government must be evaluated.

They are: political stability, social cohesion, internal security, economic development and international relations. How does the government then square up on these parameters?

After 1984, this is the first government where a single party has a majority in the Lower House and, therefore, political stability should be a given, but here lies the rub. The agenda of the Rashtriya Swayamsevak Sangh (RSS) and the paradigm of governance in a democracy are defiantly at cross-purposes. While the RSS, as the fountainhead of Hindutva, wants its ideological agenda to be implemented, the reality is that the nation has moved beyond the fundamentalist dogmatism that is the sine qua non of the ideological mentor of this government. RSS chief Mohan Bhagwat's public disapproval of attempts to assign credit of the election victory to "one individual" is only an overt manifestation of an intense internecine struggle.

Coupled with that is the marginalisation of the old guard in the BJP, who may be getting on in years but are present in Parliament

---

The Asian Age, 04 September, 2014

and have deep roots in the party organisation. They have not taken too kindly to the attempts to ostracise them.

The perception of centralisation of power in the Prime Minister is indicated by enigmatic source-based reports that keep surfacing regularly as to how the Prime Minister or his office have upbraided his ministerial colleagues for lunching with industrialists and instructed them on the kind of clothes they should wear on foreign trips. The public overruling of Home Minister Rajnath Singh on the choice of interlocutor for the Naga peace talks and his implicit exclusion from the Appointments Committee of the Cabinet point to the discord inside. The contradictions with the RSS and the instability intrinsic in the BJP will manifest itself over the short term and the facade of stability will give way to instability sooner than later .

Social cohesion and communal harmony have been the biggest casualties of the past 100 days. The government kicked off its innings with a statement that Article 370 would be repealed. It followed that up with a reiteration in Parliament that a uniform civil code would be implemented. Its affiliates use phraseology that amounts to telling the minorities that they should consider themselves second-class citizens of India. MPs belonging to its ally, the Shiv Sena, misbehaved with a Muslim employee on a Ramzan fast.

Mr Bhagwat declared that India was a "Hindu rashtra". The oxymoron of "love jihad" was invoked by the BJP to communally polarise Uttar Pradesh, where 600-odd communal incidents have taken place in the past 100 days. To top it all, a BJP MP invoked community demographics to propagate a bizarre theory of communal violence. In the midst of all this, the silence of Prime Minister Narendra Modi is deafening.

The country's internal security situation has also become unstable with estrangement both with Jammu and Kashmir, as shown by the unprecedented resolution on the Indo-Pak talks passed by the state Assembly, as well as with the troubled parts of the Northeast, especially after a particular state was singled out for transferring, humiliating and then removing governors. The lull in anti-Maoist operations has also given the Maoists time to recoup and consolidate. What is also a matter of concern and has not happened over all these years of the proliferation of revivalist Islam in West Asia is the radicalisation of Indian youth as a consequence thereof.

It may be a mere coincidence or perhaps not that young Indians are involved with the most barbaric Islamist group, the Islamic State of Iraq and Syria (ISIS), and are fighting alongside them in Syria and Iraq. This could be a direct result of the insecurity that is becoming increasingly internalised among younger people of minority communities as a consequence of the Sangh Parivar's politics of majoritarianism. The BJP's coming to power and its obvious "Hindutva" agenda in its 100 days in office may have given a fillip to this feeling. It has the potential of becoming India's biggest security nightmare in the years to come.

The disappointment on the economic front has perhaps been the most palpable. While the government can take comfort in the fact that the GDP grew by 5.7 per cent in the first quarter of the current fiscal, it should not be forgotten that for 57 days of that quarter there was a UPA government at the wheel of the economy and the NDA government was there only for 33 out of the 90 days that make up the quarter. The first Budget of the new government has been exceptional for being so mundane that it was forgotten even before the finance minister's speech got over. Financial pundits who wrote reams of criticism about the UPA's economic policies, hoping that their critiques would serve as handy resumes for a job in the new dispensation, were scrambling around red faced to unearth virtues in the Budget. For the common man there was a triple whammy of high food prices, increase in rail fares and an increase in fuel prices. It, therefore, has become increasingly evident that the government has no gameplan for the economy.

The most disquieting issue has been the summersaults that the government has performed on foreign policy. No vision has been articulated that could possibly delineate the contours of a long view from New Delhi. The Pakistan policy has swung between extremes of feting Nawaz Sharif to calling off the foreign secretary-level talks. The silence on China's cartographic invasion is eloquent. There is no clarity on outstanding issues with Bangladesh and a complete failure in maintaining the balance between China and Japan in East Asian politics.

In conclusion, it can be safely said that if the first 100 days are any indication of the road ahead, this country could find itself in extreme strife, often sponsored, if not patronised, by the government as the challenges mount and the pressure grows. For a government that has gone into hibernation mode already with regard to its media interface, the default option of increased polarisation would appear extremely attractive and that eventually would be its nemesis.

Koi lauta de mere beete hue din

ON MAY 16, 2014, a Friday morning, as results started trickling in, it became clear pretty soon that Narendra Modi was headed towards an absolute majority—the first in 30 years after 1984. India's Rockefeller moment had arrived. Corporate India's first overt intervention in the sweepstakes of electoral democracy had paid off. Bombay Club version 2.0 popped the champagne. Their war chests and historic print media domination coupled with the muscle of 400-odd news channels created the blitzkrieg that resulted in this windfall. Their decision to back "a man" as opposed to hedging their bets across the political firmament, as they had always done, heralded the most significant power shift in Indian politics. Euphoria was in the air as the Shangri-La of "achche din" was at India's doorstep. One year later, on a balmy Saturday morning as you open this newspaper, the ecstasy has all but disappeared. It's been replaced by a weary sense of resignation—a sense of being conned, though the sullenness that crystallises into cold anger is yet to coalesce.

On September 4, 2014, in this very paper, in a piece titled *Century worth a Duck*, the first 100 days of the Modi government were benchmarked on five criterion that help provide a macro overview of any government. Let us deploy the same yardstick after 365 days.

The Asian Age, 16 May, 2015

The first is political stability. It is imperative to make a distinction between legislative stability and political coherence. While the numbers in Lok Sabha do provide a degree of comfort to the government, there is, however, a reality that even Arun Shourie alluded to—that the sum total of this government is only three men in a boat, namely the Prime Minister, his finance minister and the president of the Bharatiya Janata Party. The centralisation that excludes even the home minister from the all-important Cabinet Committee on Appointments—he sees files on their way down rather than on their way up—is an alarming tale about how this government is structured.

Delhi is replete with stories about how the higher bureaucracy is omnipotent and the political executive—read ministers—are mere pygmies. Instructions on important issues are directly conveyed to the secretaries from the Prime Minister's Office (PMO), who then process the papers accordingly and the ministers just sign on the dotted line. Yet, nothing moves in the government. The emasculation of the political executive has dire portents for the Westminster Model that is premised on the supremacy of the Cabinet system in governance.

Coupled with that is the complete marginalisation of the veterans in the BJP, Messers Advani, Murli Manohar Joshi, Yashwant Sinha and the rest who are trotted out only for photo-ops but otherwise have to suffer the ignominy of being made redundant. There is a storm brewing. It is only a matter of time before it makes a landfall.

The wipeout of the BJP in the Delhi Assembly elections is a clear manifestation that people have moved away from the "three men in a boat". The "canny" one in the boat possibly sensed a defeat in Delhi and made Kiran Bedi the unwitting fall lady.

The next benchmark is social cohesion. This perhaps has been the biggest casualty in the previous one year. The Rashtriya Swayamsewak Sangh and its ideological fellow travellers have left no stone unturned to medieval India. Every abomination, from "love jihad" to "ghar wapsi", from calling minorities second-class citizens to asking Hindu women to procreate more to increase their demographic numbers, and attacks on places of worship, especially churches, is meant to create a fear psychosis among the minorities.

Equally ominous are the systematic appointments of ideologically inhibited individuals to autonomous bodies with the remit of documenting India's hoary past and saffronisation of education by tampering curricula. This is the most overt assault to change the very narrative of India. However, the most glaring failure of this government has been on the third benchmark—economic development. The raison d'etre of Narendra Modi of Gujarat fame during the most expensive election campaign in India was that a policy paralysis had gripped this nation and a strong leadership was required to rescue the economy from its state of morass. The most telling accomplishment of the "strong leadership" of Mr Modi in one year has been the free fall of the Indian currency.

In August 2013, the current foreign minister and the then Leader of the Opposition in the Lok Sabha had notoriously tweeted: "The Rupee has lost its value, PM his grace". On May 16, 2014, $1 was (equivalent)to Rs 58.86. Three hundred and fifty-seven days later, on May 8, 2015, one American dollar is equivalent to Rs 64.04. Against six currencies, the trade weighted real effective exchange rate (REER) has ascended from 109.58 in February 2014 to 124.34 in February 2015.

The monthly economic report of the department of economic affairs (DEA) of the finance ministry pegs the growth of gross value added (GVA) for agriculture and allied services at 1.1 per cent in 2014-15 as compared to 3.7 per cent in 2013-14. No wonder there is agrarian distress all around and farmers are committing suicide during public protests.

Eight core infrastructure sectors of the economy registered a measly 1.4 per cent growth in February 2015 as compared to 6.1 per cent in the February of 2014—when the UPA was in office. Five sectors of the economy—crude oil, natural gas, refinery products, fertilisers and the steal sector—have recorded negative growth. Growth in broad money (M3) decelerated to 11.3 per cent in March 2015 from 13.4 per cent during the corresponding period of the previous year. Growth in bank credit also decelerated to 9.2 per cent in March 2015 from 11.7 per cent during the March of the previous year. Even deposits with scheduled commercial banks went south to 10.9 per cent in March

2015 as compared to 14.6 per cent in March 2014. Non-food credit too went down to 9.4 per cent in March 2015 compared to 11.7 per cent during the same period last year. Business confidence is at an all time low. The economy is emanating gigantic red warning signs. No wonder the chummy capitalists now appear morose. The champagne corks appear ready to go back into the bottles.

On the fourth benchmark, that is the internal security situation, the scenario is depressing if not distressing. Even during the worst days of militancy in Jammu and Kashmir, never, ever were Pakistani flags so openly waved, as they were in the past one-month. The Central and the BJP-People's Democratic Party government in the state was, at best, a helpless bystander if not collusive in this brash and brazen challenge to the Indian state. The release of Massarat Aalam—the mastermind of the stone-pelting incidents in the summer of 2010—brings into question the resolve of the National Democratic Alliance government to tackle terrorism.

Given that the release was orchestrated while the state was under President's Rule belies the BJP's rhetoric about being tough on terror. Left-wing extremism has again reared its snakehead with back-to-back attacks in Chhattisgarh. What perhaps was most telling of the weakness of the Indian state was the abduction of 300 villagers from near a bridge building site on the Baru river in Sukma district, the day the Prime Minister was in Dantewada, pleading with the Maoists to see their sins in the eyes of militancy-affected children barely 60 km away. The battalions tasked with fighting the Maoists in an inhospitable terrain are complaining of being equipped with inferior weaponry and are literally sitting ducks for the better-armed reds.

The situation is no better in the Northeast. There has been no breakthrough on the Armed Forces Special Powers Act issue and no headway in resolving the million mutinies that plague the picturesque Northeast. It recaps the famous couplet, "Shahenshah Bahadur Shah Alam, Delhi se Palam". The writ of the BJP-led NDA government is circumscribed by its inefficaciousness.

On to the final benchmark—international affairs—there is complete absence of a vision or even a coherently articulated strategy. There is no clear sense about where the NDA government would want to see India in 2019 when its term ends. Though the Prime Minister has been a fleeting visitor to India in the past one year, his trips across the world have been more of the meet and greet variety than having any substantive policy content in them. Collecting non-resident Indians in stadia and "king konging" does more harm to India's interests than helping it.

Imagine if the Prime Minister of Nepal would fill the Indira Gandhi stadium with the Nepalese living in India and hold forth on all and sundry matters—how would that go down with the Indian foreign policy establishment? Or what if the Prime Minister of Bangladesh collected a million Bangladeshi's at the Boat Club, presuming she got permission to do so, to declare victory over the Land Boundary agreement with India? The endemic screaming of our television anchorites and hosts would rise to vein-bursting proportions. Mr Modi's interlocutors in the US, Australia and Canada have been more than polite, but as to how long would this restraint last is an open-ended question.

On substantive issues this government has lost the plot. Calling off the foreign secretary-level talks with Pakistan over the Pakistani high commissioner's meeting with Hurriyat leaders in August last year and then burying its head in the sand when the same exercise was repeated this year on Pakistan Day sent out a very clear signal to the hawks across the western border—that they are dealing with a bunch of novices in Delhi. The government unfortunately, much like the previous one, has reached its "Sharm el-Sheikh" moment rather early in its term. The relationship will continue in the state of frozen turbulence as it has been for the past six decades.

The most devastating evaluation of this government came from a rather mellow group of investors whom I came across at a legendary watering hole in Mumbai on a Saturday evening. One of them turned to the crooner after a couple of doubles and asked if she could sing *Koi lauta de mere beete hue din* — an evergreen Bollywood song that loosely translated means, "Could someone please return me to the old times!"

Koi lauta de mere beete hue din Season II

ON THE FIRST anniversary of the NDA government, I had written a piece underscoring the budding scepticism of the people with the BJP-led government. At the end of 24 months, cynicism and disillusionment are the two overriding emotions that summarise mass opinion about the functioning of this government, notwithstanding the odd electoral success in Assam. It would perhaps be appropriate to measure the performance of this government on the same five benchmarks that were used last year—social cohesion, political stability, economic development, internal security and foreign relations.

Social cohesion has further deteriorated in the past one year. There are abysses and crevices in the hearts and minds of people. Yet, invisible but solid walls have come up between communities as a result of polarising and noxious rhetoric orated by the government functionaries.

Never before has it ever happened that writers, poets, artistes and filmmakers have risen as one against the spectre of intolerance created by this government. The silence of Prime Minister Narendra Modi on the lynching of an innocent Muslim on the false charge of storing beef has been deafening. The crude attempts by Union ministers and chief

---

Deccan Chronicle, 26 May, 2016

ministers to demonise culinary choices by proclaiming that those who eat beef can go to Pakistan, and criminalising mere possession of beef are but overt manifestations of the revivalist and medieval mindsets in the ruling dispensation.

The spurious debate on nationalism of the "Bharat Mata ki Jai" variety that found protuberant mention even in the resolutions of the BJP and attempts to brand Jawaharlal Nehru University as anti-national on the strength of allegedly fake and spurious videos, amply demonstrated that this was no loony fringe at work but very much a mainstream ideological enterprise of the BJP-RSS to try and change the fundamental narrative of India and anchor it on the extreme Right. All this has upset the intricate social balance of India, with the worst yet to come in the years ahead.

Political stability is yet another area where the country has taken a huge hit. The relentless attack on institutions, beginning with the judiciary, demonstrates the inability of Mr Modi to reconcile to the changed power dynamic of India where the political executive is just one of the stakeholders in a multi-stakeholder rubric. The demolition of the Planning Commission and its replacement with a one-and-a-half man-act called the Niti Aayog has removed a fair financial arbiter between the Centre and the states.

The unprecedented assault on the Reserve Bank of India and its governor Raghuram Rajan for its refusal to toe the government line and persevere with the protection of the interests of millions of small depositors is, perhaps, the worst form of fascist intimidation through vilification and calumny. The message this government is sending out to upright professionals is—if you do not play ball with us we will hound you, harass you and finally run you into the ground.

However ,what is even more ominous is the sledgehammer blow dealt by this government to Indian federalism. The toppling of elected Congress governments by misusing the instrumentalities of the state, including the office of governor, shows the scant regard the Centre has for democratic traditions and conventions. It took the combined heft of the high court of Uttarakhand and the Supreme Court to prevent the blatant subversion of democratic principles. The verdict of the Supreme Court in the Arunachal Pradesh matter is still awaited.

Even the role of the President in not preventing the misuse of Article 356 of the Constitution of India by the BJP-NDA does not really warm the cockles of the heart.

On the economic front, this government has been able to achieve the impossible. They have actually sunk and shrunk the Indian economy. The Indian economy is growing at a derisory 4.5-5 per cent annually. The government's own economic numbers put out by the department of economic affairs tell a sordid story. Amid unparalleled agricultural distress across a third of the country, agriculture grew by a measly 1.1 per cent in 2015-16. From April 2015 to February 2016, the Index of Industrial Production (IIP) grew by a measly 2.6 per cent only.

During the same period eight core infrastructure sectors namely coal, crude oil, natural gas production, refining, steel, cement and fertilisers grew by only 2.3 per cent. Out of the 24 months that this government has been in office exports and imports have been in a free fall for 18 months in a row.

The internal security situation in the past one year has taken a turn for the worse. Punjab, a frontline border state that had been peaceful since 1995 saw two back-to-back terrorists attacks in Gurdaspur and Pathankot respectively. In Jammu and Kashmir, the situation is on a razor's edge with stone pelting crowds back on the streets to welcome the second stint of the BJP-PDP alliance. In the Northeast, and the Naxalite menaced areas of Central India security forces are being repeateuly ambushed and killed by terrorists.

However, the worst cock-up has been in the area of international relations. After two years of chest thumping spectacles, especially curated for pliant people of Indian origin (PIOs), the Modi government has nothing substantive to account for in terms of a foreign policy. South Block has allowed the Pakistani deep state to run circles around it putting the country's national security in grave peril. Despite Pakistan rubbishing the Ufa joint statement even before the ink had dried on it, in spite of repeated terror attacks emanating from that country, Mr Modi chose to drop by at Lahore to meet Prime Minister Nawaz Sharif for no ostensible reason.

The bilateral relationship with China is also in the chiller with China openly blocking India's candidature for the Nuclear Suppliers Group (NSG) and the designation of Masood Azhar and the Jaish-e-Mohammad as terrorist entities respectively.

There has been no big idea or initiative qua the United States. The Free Trade Agreement with the European Union remains frozen. India's foreign policy is adrift and rudderless at a point in time when events in the South China Sea, the throat of the Indo-Pacific region, are reaching a flashpoint. Even India's most trusted ally, Russia, of yesteryears has now started striking a linear equation between India and Pakistan.

The best one-liner on the performance of this government came from a little boy working at a ramshackle teashop on the GT Road. When queried about the Prime Minister's performance, he replied: "Gaccha de gaya Modi". Loosely translated in English, it means the honourable Prime Minister has made a chump of us.

V. Make or Break: The Role of Media

The golden mean

A FIVE-JUDGE bench of the Supreme Court is currently hearing a batch of matters pertaining to, inter-alia, the formulation of norms and guidelines for reporting sub-judice matters, coverage of news by the electronic media, minimising presentation of sexual abuse and violence on TV channels, contempt proceedings against journalists for publishing confessional statements of an accused made to the police, and to making the police liable for tarnishing the reputation of an accused by releasing details of a matter under investigation.

Concurrently, a division bench of the Lucknow bench of the Allahabad High Court has passed an order restricting reportage on the movement of troops. The Standing Committee on Law and Justice and the Lok Sabha recently saw an animated debate on the issues of oral observations made by the judiciary during court proceedings and obiter dicta. It culminated in the incorporation of an axiomatic clause in the Judicial Accountability Bill that bars judges from making "unwarranted" comments against constitutional and statutory functionaries. It further ordains that judgments should speak for themselves.

Reports have appeared that a state government is planning to launch a TV channel and a newspaper to disseminate "correct"

The Indian Express, 28 April, 2012

information to people. The social media has empowered almost everyone who chooses to become a part of it to instantly turn broadcaster, throwing both restraint and responsibility to the winds. The government is attempting to balance competing interests in trying to find an acceptable middle ground. To top it all is the ever increasing anxiety, if not unease, among a large swathe of the population about the sensational, if not hysterical, nature of media discourse. An intense and undulating debate is unfolding across institutions and societal paradigms to define both the core and the frontiers of the freedom of speech and expression. The jury is still out on where the golden median lies in apparently conflicting narratives.

Article 19(1)(a) of the Constitution of India guarantees to all citizens the right to freedom of speech and expression. However 19(2) caveats the right by giving the state powers to make laws to impose reasonable restrictions on these liberties. Notwithstanding these constitutional caveats in Indian legislatures, judicial authorities and people's movements across democracies have consistently struggled to not allow any substantive erosion of the freedom of speech and expression that forms the core of any liberal, plural and democratic ethos.

The Supreme Court in Re: Kushboo's matter (2010) 5 SCC 600 held, "The framers of our Constitution recognised the importance of safeguarding this right since the free flow of opinions and ideas is essential to sustain the collective right of the citizenry. While an informed citizenry is a precondition for meaningful governance in the political sense we must also promote a culture of open dialogue when it comes to societal attitudes".

Though this observation was made in an entirely different context, the import is indeed prophetic. It should become the trigger to reflect on the attitude that we have as a society towards the institutions of national security, be it the armed forces or intelligence structures. For over six decades now these organisations have been treated as sacrosanct and insulated from public scrutiny. An ethos has been perpetuated that seeks to view with scepticism any attempt to transparently examine issues and problems that make the rounds in Chinese whispers in the rarefied echelons of power.

While it should not be argued that confidentiality and discretion are not intrinsic to the defence of the realm, the furore over the leak of a recent letter purportedly written by the army chief to the prime minister was, with due respect, a bit of a stretch. Similarly, there was a front page story by *The Indian Express* with regard to troop movements. While everyone has the right to disagree with the contents of a story, what we need to determine is whether, in a democratic nation, a newspaper does not have the right to make an editorial judgement as to what should and should not be disseminated in the public domain. Anybody who is aggrieved by the content has recourse to legal remedies, which brings to the fore the need to tighten libel laws in the country.

The rash of recent controversies with regard to alleged shortages of equipment, material and personnel in the armed forces are partly due to the fact that substantive issues of defence preparedness have never ever been seriously discussed by Parliament during times of peace. Even after five decades, the Henderson Brooks report on the Sino-Indian border war has not been put in the public domain. Even after a decade, there is a lack of clarity about the implementation of the recommendations of the Kargil Review Committee. One can only hope that the Naresh Chandra Committee report would be placed on the table of the House, so that the issues that it flags can at least be discussed in a transparent manner.

India has a professional defence force that is paid for by the taxpayers. If there are problems or portents that could manifest even in future because of a perceived strain in civil-military relations, they are better out in the open rather than being consigned to the closet.

Institutionally, Parliament must rethink its reluctance to engage with doctrinal strategic and military issues. The constitutional courts also need to assess and weigh the pros and cons as to whether sustained and comprehensive journalistic engagement with issues of national security would perhaps be a more enlightened method to discern areas of concern and address them holistically.

Policing the Internet

THE INTERNET is the boldest attempt at anarchism and it has succeeded. It epitomises the vastest ungoverned sphere on the globe. Never earlier in the human saga has so much influence concurrently resided in so many fingertips around the world. There is more data that is churned out every two days than since the dawn of civilisation and till the advent of the current century. The new or the social media rides on the back of this incredible marvel.

What has emerged is a tale of two civilisations—a physical realm that took millennia to evolve and a virtual domain that is still emergent. At the junction of both these empires lies the future of humankind, especially when all eight billion people are online, perhaps in less than a decade from now. That is precisely why there has been a lot of deliberation about the basic personality of the Internet. Is it a global commons like the seas, space and the environment, or an enterprise owned and operated by a diverse array of private entities and governments? Unlike the former that are bounties of nature, the virtual world is an innovation that represents both, the cutting-edge creativity of the human race and a crystallisation of human wisdom.

Why is this colloquy imperative? Because associated to it is the issue of the governance of the Internet.

The Asian Age, 13 December, 2014

This vast expanse provokes the spirit of liberty to prevail in its most majestic manifestation. Here freedom of speech and expression is largely untrammelled. Here the right to offend is an integral part of the right to articulation. Here the discourse is egalitarian, bottom-up and horizontal rather than top-down and vertical. Here the agenda of the media owner or the tyranny of editorialites or anchorites do not skew the conversation. Here new friends are made, old sweethearts found, emotions transmitted and business is done. Should this virtual civilisation be left to itself and be allowed to find its own natural equilibrium?

The deployment of this medium for catalysing political change during the Arab Spring has been hailed as one of the finer moments of people's power harnessed to technology. It is another matter that the libertine ideal could not strike root in the harsh maelstrom of West Asian politics.

Why would anybody like to impose rules, restrictions or limits on this utopia? The fact that it is even being seriously contemplated, should it not qualify the proponents for an automatic admission to a psychiatrist's facility?

However, there is the other side of midnight also. The Internet has become a veritable playground for cyber criminals of every shade and hue. Identity theft, financial scams, political and economic espionage, cyber attacks and child pornography, to name but a few. The spectre of the Deep Web and the hidden people who misuse the privacy that the Net provides to perpetrate their nefarious activity is also a hard reality. The freedom of one person easily translates into the fear of another.

Terrorist organisations and non-state actors exploit the open architecture of the Net not only to push their perverse agendas but also to recruit and radicalise impressionable minds. It has become a key platform to plan, coordinate and execute strategy for such groups.

However, there is a far graver dilemma that confronts policymakers and administrators. At what point does a cyber attack qualify as an act of war? Cyber warfare is conventionally defined as actions by a nation state to penetrate another nation's computers or networks for the purpose of causing damage or destruction. If the attack is perpetrated on physical infrastructure, like disrupting power grids, crashing stock markets or attempting to assert remote dominance over nuclear command and control systems causing humongous casualties, how should then the victim state respond, especially given the fact that the aggressor can more often than not cover his tracks. What if the attack is the handiwork of non-state actors operating from ungoverned spaces in a sovereign entity?

Should the response be in the cyber or physical domain? Would raw public opinion allow the retaliation to be limited to the virtual domain?

These are precisely the reasons why the governance question becomes germane. How and who should administer the Net? What should be the shape of the governance architecture and what areas should it cover? These posers require urgent answers.

A bewildering array of global institutions with exotic acronyms, from the International Telecommunications Union to consultations such as the Netmundial convened by Brazil in April 2014, are grappling with the issue but without apparent success. The summitry and torque that nations have brought to bear onto the climate change negotiations or for that matter the World Trade Organisation confabulations on various access, subsidy and tariff barrier related issues is conspicuously absent in the case of the Internet governance dialogue.

The profound peril is that if globally acceptable and uniformly enforceable rules of engagement do not emerge, we may, during our lifetime, see the demise of the Internet as we know it just as we saw its rise. The first step would be the Balkanization of the Net along shared cultural alignments, value systems and even hegemonistic spheres of influence. Just as the great firewall of China has virtually turned the Web into a Chinese intranet, similarly you may find that there is an Anglo Saxon Net or an Islamic Net or for that matter a virtual space that corresponds to the power projection capacity of a Westphalian state. This would necessarily also mandate that some form of visa requirement would emerge for users wanting to transit from one intranet to the other.

With the underlying hardware the transmission towers, routers and switches that anchor the flora and fauna of the Net, namely the websites and the applications, being still under the control of states, there is no guarantee that they would not abuse their position as the "gatekeeper" to erect barriers under the ubiquitous guise of national interest. It is millions of newly empowered people around the world who have the greatest stake in preserving the Internet in its current form. They must wrest the chance they have to aggressively campaign for participatory process in designing the governance architecture of the Net. This task cannot be left to governments, conglomerates or corporate fronts masquerading as think tanks.

Let freedom reign

WHAT THEN would the remedy be for those offended by free expression? Decriminalise defamation but make it a civil wrong with punitive and exemplary damages accompanying the offence. Should Freedom of Expression be an absolute right was the provocative punt that set the Hooghly ablaze one cool evening in Kolkata? Coming at a time when the government is tying itself into knots to ban the Nirbhaya documentary and the Censors are proscribing *Fifty Shades of Grey*—how would this maxim square up in a progressively xenophobic cosmos?

To answer this ante it is imperative to step back in time. Way back in 1644, John Milton in his *Areopagitica* affirmed ,"Give me the Liberty to know, to utter and to argue freely according to conscience, above all liberties". Milton placed the freedom of expression at the acme of all freedoms.

One hundred and forty five years later, as the United States took baby steps towards proliferating its tenets, it did so by adopting the first amendment to its Constitution in 1789. It declared "Congress shall make no law respecting an establishment of religion, or prohibiting the free exercise thereof: or abridging the freedom of speech or of the press, or the right of the people peaceably to assemble, and to petition the Government for a redress of grievances". It was an explicit,

---

The Asian Age, 07 March, 2015

unambiguous articulation, without any caveats. Not that the US of those times was the most evolved and tolerant ethos bereft of hotheads and bigots. That is not the case even today as it has its own bunch of loonies. The framers of the US Constitution, who had forsaken the hierarchical straitjacket of the feudal oligarchies of Europe, realised the pitfalls of allowing the state to gerrymander with the freedom of speech, press, religion and protest in any manner.

Ironically, one hundred and sixty one years later, when the Indian Constitution was adopted, freedom of speech and expression as enshrined in Article 19 was caveated with as many as eight omnibus restraints, each more restrictive than the other. They include sovereignty and integrity of the state, security of the state, friendly relations with foreign states, public order, decency or morality, contempt of court, defamation or incitement of an offence.

India had a vibrant tradition of fearless and adversarial journalism during the struggle for liberation. It included, but was not limited to, papers like the *Bengal Gazette* founded in 1780, *Amrita Bazar Patrika, Kesri, Mahratta, Satyagrahi* and the *Bombay Chronicle* edited by the distinguished BG Horniman.

However, this illustrious lineage notwithstanding, the freedom of the press was, inexplicably, not included as an explicit right in the Constitution. It had to be deduced or extrapolated from the rights settled for a citizen.

Even more paradoxically, Article 10 of the European Convention of Human Rights, adopted in 1953, has nine caveats stretching from national security to health and morality. The short point being that over time countries and societies have become more regressive rather than progressive on the issue of freedom of speech and expression.

The freedom of speech includes the right to offend. You have every right to have a quarrel with Charlie Hebdo, dislike the cartoons, even abhor them for what they caricature, but the manner of settling the spat can not be to mow down the cartoonists in cold blood. Similarly, the brutal hacking of Avijit Roy in Dhaka because he had the temerity to question religion raises a central inquiry. Something said or written in Vancouver can be culturally, or even in civilisational terms, offensive to a person living in Vanuatu. Given that information travels in real time, does that mean each sensitivity needs to be accounted for before someone opens his mouth or pecks at a keyboard?

The Pope, in the wake of the Charlie Hebdo massacre pontificated, "Disparage another's faith and you can expect to be punched." His Holiness is in error. Few subjects demand more urgent scrutiny and critical examination than religion. It would be blasphemy to do otherwise. The abuse of religion for revivalist purposes and to subterfuge violence has been the most destructive impulse down the ages. Now juxtapose this conservatism with the information order that we live in. In India alone, there are 99,660 print publications reaching out to about 168 million people. There are 160 million TV houses reaching out to about 800 million people. 800 odd TV channels out of which 400 are news channels service this spectrum. There are 243 private FM stations and 389 community radio stations and 245 million netizens out of which 110 million, or even more, are active media users. These are the numbers in one country alone.

As of June 30, 2014, there were 3,035,749,340 Internet users globally accounting for 43.2 per cent of the world's population. Within the next decade it is estimated that 90 per cent of the world's population would be hot wired or connected to the Internet. How would the increased means of information dissemination measure up against growing intolerance for someone else's point of view? The quintessential paradox of the short fuse. Would it be possible to confine speech or expression even if there is a global compact to do so?

The new media that rides on the back of the great mobocracy called the Internet has democratised public discourse by making it horizontal rather than vertical. It allows anyone and everyone to articulate a point of view without restraint and even any responsibility that is good, bad and ugly. Good because every dark secret eventually bubbles up, bad because it allows anonymity to masquerade as privacy, thereby opening the doors to malice and malevolence. Ugly because there is child pornography, and spectres of hidden people—the ubiquitous "dark" net. The way to tackle these aberrations is not to contain, control and circumscribe free speech but to ensure that consensual rules of engagement emerge in the information paradigm. Even the Chinese, who have firewalled the Internet by turning it into an intranet, are hard pressed to contain the million mutinies that take place everyday on the Chinese hybrid of Twitter and Facebook —SinaWeibo.

What then would the remedy be for those offended by free expression? In the Indian context, decriminalise defamation but make it a civil wrong with punitive and exemplary damages accompanying the offence. Thus the unbridled freedom of speech is matched by unlimited liability to be paid by the delinquent. In the final analysis, freedom is indivisible and therefore the right to free speech cannot be less than absolute.

Make way for the new media

WITH THIS piece, I complete one year of writing for *The Asian Age* and *Deccan Chronicle*. It has indeed been a gratifying experience to transcend the entire paradigm of the media cycle from 160 characters on Twitter to 60-second sound bytes on television and 1,600 words in print. In the case of the latter, much to the consternation of the editors who had to contend with pieces way over the word limit. An oft-repeated transgression that they have overlooked with generosity and magnanimity.

Over this period of time, I have deliberately refrained from writing about the media to put some time, space and distance between my thoughts on this matter and my former remit. In the first of the occasional and staggered pieces on the media to follow, let us commence by looking at the structure of the Indian media and the contradistinction between the traditional qua the new media. India has 99,660 print publications, 832 permitted private TV channels out of which 406 are news and 426 non-news. Twenty-one odd TV channels are run by the public broadcaster, some in the terrestrial mode. There are 245 private FM radio stations and 179 operational community radio stations. Supplementing this is a network of 229 broadcasting centres, 148 medium frequency, 54 high frequency and 168 FM transmitters of the All India Radio.

The Asian Age, 13 June, 2015

The print media has a combined penetration of 14 per cent of the population that translates into 173 million households. One sixty eight million homes have access to cable and satellite TV. All India Radio alone covers 99.19 per cent of the population. There are 952.34 million mobile phone subscribers in India out of which 116 million have Internet-enabled smartphones. The number of Internet connections are estimated at 302 million and the number of social media users at 145.2 million and rising. In all, it is a bewildering but vibrant paradigm.

What, therefore, are the projections for the traditional media and how would it square up to the challenge of the new media? The golden lining for the print sector is that it is projected to grow at a combined aggregate growth rate (CAGR) of 8 per cent in the medium term when many global print institutions have shut shop and switched over to the digital space. India is bucking the trend, though most of the growth is expected in the regional space.

The proliferation of television still remains the poster child of the liberal information order that came to hold the field post—the opening up of the skies to private players. New players are still entering the TV genre everyday. Radio has got a new lease of life due to the hand-held phone explosion. The upcoming FM phase-3 auctions that have been in the works since 2011, could add another 839 stations across 294 cities. If the Supreme Court rules that news should be permitted on private radio stations it would make the state of play all the more stimulatingly chaotic.

The cheeky dare to the traditional media is the new media that rides on the back of the Internet—the most impudent tryout with ochlocracy and the largest ungoverned space on planet earth. The sardonicism of the Internet is that it is one thing built by humans of which they understand less and less as it evolves.

In the next few years, the world's virtual population would outnumber the physical population on planet earth. A virtual civilisation exists in the ether that is increasingly becoming immune to the rules of engagement of the corporeal world, and governance gurus have no clue how to deal with this apparition.

As the new or social media becomes the first port-of-call for all information, the virtual world would be awash with massive amounts of low-grade and unverified content a-la-citizen journalist marvel. It would make the contest to put the feed out first among the traditional media almost rapacious. In the process, credibility, which, in any case, is at an all time nadir, would be a casualty.

Rather than compete in an unwinnable race, the traditional media can evolve into a credibility filter, certifying as to which virtual source is credible. A kind of ISO 9002 or a standards organisation, while continuing with it's originally envisioned role of a more profound and informed voice in the public discourse. It would liberate both print and television from the breaking news syndrome and actually allow them to become the contextual and analytical mien.

A classical specimen of this credibility certification paradigm was the live tweeting of the Abbottabad raid by an insomniac social media buff. If there would have been a believability benchmark, the traditional media would possibly have picked it up and the world may just have watched it live. Traditional media organisations need to learn to live with the reality that they cannot be everywhere all the time.

Another structural issue that the traditional media has to cope with is how to democratise itself. The top down discourse where people have to suffer the agony of excruciating editorialites or anchorities on a daily basis, is passé. That is the reason why, despite having 400 odd news channels, they collectively account for only 7 per cent of total television viewership. The remaining 93 per cent is occupied by general entertainment channels. According to industry-accepted audience measurement indices, the largest Hindi news channel has a viewership that extends to 0.14 per cent of the populace and the biggest English news channel may just be circumscribed to 0.01 per cent of India's population. Despite a historical dominance stretching back three centuries to 1780, when James Hickey founded the bi-weekly *Bombay Gazette*, the biggest circulating Hindi newspaper reaches only 1.35 per cent of the people and the largest circulating English newspaper only 0.63 per cent of the public, while the analogous social media numbers are climbing exponentially.

The traditional media has a legacy of ownership issues going back to days of the Jute Press. The manner in which television licenses have been doled out over the past two decades is the most corrosive chapter in India's economic liberalisation story, despite the poster child status enjoyed by it. It has not led to market diversity but fragmentation compromising the independence of newsrooms.

The Chinese wall between boardrooms and editors' cabins has now morphed into a seamless funnel of synergy where the latter dictates the former in increasing if not domineering measure.

As the fabled editor of the *Patriot* newspaper, RK Mishra told the Rajya Sabha way back in 1974, " Now, where is the freedom of the press? What do we have? In India we have the freedom of the newspaper proprietor, and in some cases the delegated freedom which is enjoyed by newspaper managers."

The new and current affairs portals on the World Wide Web do not carry these legacy burdens. They are not publishing or streaming videos for an offline entity and then mutating it to fit an online paradigm. They can leverage the advantage that the democratised social media allows — to crowd source preferences and customise content accordingly. Not for very long can corporate agendas of media barons and the ideological predilections of editors hold sway.

If they do not change, they would perish and this is just the beginning with 4G, Long Term Evolution (LTE) and LTE-plus carriage technologies, coupled with artificial intelligence, transforming the new media on an everyday basis. The fun has just begun. This is a narration of just one out of the myriad trials that traditional media will have to surmount.

Rebooting Democracy

ONLY 57 PER cent of the electorate exercised their franchise in the first phase of the Bihar elections. Historically also, voter turnout in India has remained in the 50 to 60 per cent range. Given these numbers, the time has come for India and the world to consider— Can democracies move to voting on the Internet? Given the reality of 24x7 feedback on a range of issues, would the cyber interface rewire governance processes bottoms up? These were some of the interesting posers that came up for discussion at a conclave organised by a Washington-based think tank on—" The Future of Technology in Elections".

Borr in the Defense Advanced Research Projects Agency of the United States, the Internet represents the largest ungoverned space on planet Earth.

Today 3.22 billion people, out of the eight billion that inhabit the world, use the Internet. That accounts for 40 per cent of the world's population.

It was less than one per cent in 1995. The first billion was reached in 2005, the second billion in 2010 and the third in 2014. The Internet has changed the manner in which we consume information, order food, shop, ask for cabs and even do our banking. Trillions of dollars

The Asian Age, 17 October, 2015.

are transacted and moved by global banks everyday, over the secure and, at times, not so secure platforms.

The Internet has enabled the rise of a new form of media i.e. the social media or the fifth estate. It has democratised the discourse and made it horizontal, rather than the vertical paradigm it had been for thousands of years since the days of the town-crier. It has provided billions of people an opportunity to participate in public conversations on a second-to-second basis. It has made mainstream media barons look at the digital space to make their next billions. It has also revolutionised political communication. It has almost become obligatory for every public figure to be on Twitter, Facebook, Instagram and it's myriad variants. Increasingly, political campaigns are being run in the virtual space with political parties and candidates apportioning significant amounts of campaign resources to the "new media" that provides the channels of an interactive engagement as compared to the more expensive monologue of the print and the broadcasting medium.

Has the time then come to move to the next logical level i.e. vote on the Internet? There are countries like Estonia that conduct their elections and substantive parts of their national lives on the Internet, without fearing that the Russians would gerrymander with their nascent but blossomed democracy. Then why should the other large democracies not do the same?

Emerging nations like Brazil and India have successfully experimented with electronic voting machines (EVMs) for many election cycles now. Ironically, many European nations have rejected them as being unreliable and susceptible to manipulation. They have, instead, chosen to go back to paper ballots. Is it because they hold democracy in an exalted esteem, putting it on a hallowed pedestal, different from the various other transactions that underpin their daily existence? Do they consider this social contract to be too sacred to be left to the vagaries of machines? The answer, perhaps, is a no.

In India, the first pilot projects with the EVMs took place in the Assembly elections of 1998 when five constituencies each in Madhya Pradesh, Delhi and Rajasthan, got a chance to vote electronically, even though the first machines were manufactured and procured by the Election Commission of India way back in 1989-90. Though questions about the robustness of this process crop up from time to time, the experiment has by and large proven successful.

EVMs have been successful in mitigating the menace of ballot-stuffing and booth capturing. They have streamlined the counting procedure, with the results coming out in a few hours rather than taking a couple of days. The transactional cost of elections has come down as EVMs can be reused, unlike ballots that have to be printed afresh for each election. However, hackers have demonstrated that EVMs can be rigged even from a distance over the ether to produce a customised result. However, can this rigging be carried out on an industrial scale to make a substantive difference to the results is the million dollar question.

The average size of an Indian parliamentary constituency is between 1.5 to two million electors. Between 1500-2000 EVMs are deployed per constituency. If the number is multiplied by the 543 constituencies that make up the House of the people—the Lok Sabha—the figure comes upto to a mindboggling 1,086,000. That is a lot of machines to manipulate. Therefore, the security lies in numbers.

However, the ECI would be well served to emulate the example of the Superior Electoral Court of Brazil. As its President, Justice Jose Antonio Dias Toffoli explained at the conclave, they organise a "hack fest" (festival for hackers) annually, where they extend an open invitation to hackers from around the world to come and crack their electoral voting machines and manipulate them to produce a pre-ordained result. This helps the Brazilian Election Commission to keep making their own system more secure and tamper-proof.

Would the ECI have the guts to subject their machines to an open, transparent and public test? Or are they happy cocooned in their ostrich with the "head in the sand" attitude that bedevils our unelected institutions? It is a question that the ECI would need to ask itself at some point. Security in numbers is not enough. Even one machine, if it is corrupted, vitiates democracy.

Coming back to the more germane question, should India start a pilot project for voting on the Internet? What are the advantages and the pitfalls? There are 330 million Internet users in India at the last count. There are 960 million mobile phones out of which 140 million are smartphones and the figure is expected to reach 651 million by 2019. The total tele-density has reached 78.73 per cent with urban numbers touching 149.25 per cent and rural figures being 47.16 per cent. With this level of penetration, is it not the next logical step to take?

It could also commence with the diaspora that were given voting rights by the United Progressive Alliance government in 2011, and the ECI on the Supreme Court's prodding is exploring the E-Ballot voting option for them.

Not only would it make the whole process much simpler and in sync with the concurrent lifestyle, with people being able to vote from home or on the move, but it would also increase the participation of people in the democratic process, especially in the urban areas where the educated elite erroneously consider it beneath their dignity to stand in the polling booth line. They prefer to compromise with their democratic rights rather than their super-inflated egos.

The pitfalls are that the Internet still remains under the physical control of foreign Westphalian entities. All the root servers of the Internet are located in the United States except for one in Europe. The hardware of the Internet is under the physical control of private Internet service providers and the government controls national gateways. Moreover, there is no failsafe technology that can enable the elector to double-check, free from coercion or intimidation, that the vote has been recorded in the manner it has been cast.

The global conversation on agreed rules of engagement and the governance structure of the Internet is still meandering around in circles with multi-stakeholderism working to the disadvantage of countries that do not control the levers of the new economy, interface and the transformed social contract where the state is but one among the many entities that the citizen has to engage with. Undoubtedly, these are critical issues that need to be resolved, but, crucially, India needs to muster the conviction of courage to make that leap of faith to the next level of the people-technology interface.

Increasingly, governments are faced with the paradox of citizens talking to them in the language of the 21st century, with the governments absorbing those conversations in a 20th century mode and responding in an ossified 19th century manner. If governments have to keep pace with their own citizens they need to forever evolve both, institutionally and structurally. The empowerment that the Internet has provided to billions around the world must be leveraged to service the fundamental impulse of humankind—democracy through the exercise of franchise. It is an idea whose time has come.

Media ethics and self-regulation

AN INVITE to a discussion on the conundrum "Ombudsman: Media and social responsibility" triggered a thought. Implicit to the subject was the proposition that the media is obtuse to its obligations towards society. Could the institution of an ombudsman mitigate this delinquency?

The overarching problem of the media industry is flawed revenue models, which manifests itself in the form of paid news, private treaties, and surrogate political ownership of both content and distribution networks. Thus media outlets become insurance policies of large conglomerates. Then there's the quintessential question about the freedom of press vs freedom of the owner of the press.

On cross-media ownership, some in the industry strongly believe that any restrictions would be regressive while others believe that there should be no horizontal cross-media restrictions, but vertical ones are fine. But a lot of people in the public space hold the view that both horizontal and vertical restrictions are necessary.

Coming to the question of an ombudsman, the following facts need to be factored in to arrive at a proper understanding of this question: There is already a statutory regulator for the print media, i.e. the Press Council of India; in the electronic media space there is News

---

The Asian Age, 05 February, 2016

Broadcasting Standards Authority (NBSA) for news channels and the Broadcasting Content Complaints Council (BCCC) for entertainment or non-news and current affairs channels. In the advertising space, we have the Advertising Standards Council of India (ASCI). The government as the licenser has powers under various statutory enactments across the information, broadcasting and new-media space. It is an unwieldy arrangement, more like mosaic trying to establish a modicum of propriety on hundreds of 600-pound gorillas. Despite the clumsy structure, this task requires the circumspection and caution of a surgeon's scalpel and not a blacksmith's hammer that is much in vogue these days. It needs to be performed with utmost sensitivity to the fundamental freedoms delineated both in the Constitution and those available to humankind as a natural right.

As minister of information and broadcasting, I had studied the proceedings around the Broadcasting Services Regulation Bill (BSRB) proposed in 2007 by my predecessors ,at some length. Out of academic interest I followed the proceedings of the Leveson Inquiry in Britain, fairly closely throughout 2011-12. Concurrently, Justice Markandey Katju, the then chairperson of the Press Council of India, made a passionate case for converting the Press Council into the media council. The industry was experimenting with self-regulation paradigms and Parliament was up in arms demanding robust statutory regulation by an independent regulator of the entire media space. The Telecom Regulatory Authority of India as the regulator of the backend of the broadcasting sector was at war with the broadcast industry. The conflict between Article 19(1)(a) as caveated by Article 19(2) and Article 19(1)(g) as circumscribed by Article 19(6) could not have been more stark.

The question that I had to answer to the lawyer in me was whether the media was an institutionalised exercise in the freedom of speech and expression under Article 19(1)(a) or just another business in terms of Article 19(1)(g) for Article 19(1)(a) uses the expression: "All citizens shall have the right to freedom of speech and expression." Not all businesses shall have the right to freedom of speech and expression. Were media businesses then synonymous with citizens for the purposes of freedom of speech and expression?

The hard reality is that the media is a business. It has budgets, balance sheets, bottomlines and shareholders. Like any other industry, "honey it is about the money". However, unlike other conventional commerce ,the media business has extensive societal implications and impact. Jingoism of the variety that we see daily on prime time news, the 9 pm WWF, is perhaps the most in-your-face example of corrosiveness. On August 13, 2014, Trai made some far-reaching recommendations on issues relating to media ownership. The National Democratic Alliance government has not yet taken a view on these recommendations. Maybe because the corporate oligarchs that helped it come to power own substantial chunks of the media today. Maybe a concerned citizenry needs to move the appropriate court to direct the government to take a view on the Trai's recommendations, accepting or rejecting which could pave the way for further judicial consideration.

As I peruse, with much amusement, the complaint adjudication proceedings and decisions of the self-regulatory structures in the media and juxtapose them with powers the government has as a licenser, I wonder what would be the last straw that finally breaks the camel's back. Lest it be forgotten, the Trai has already recommended an omnibus independent regulator for the entire media industry, not once but twice over.

In August 2013, therefore, perhaps for the first time ever, all the statutory regulators and the chairs of self-regulating mechanisms, including the licenser came together on one platform. The ratio decidendi of the various opinions expressed leaned in favour of self-regulation underpinned by a statutory basis. Justice Lord Leveson, after a detailed inquiry recommended something similar for Great Britain. The reason why this model is preferable to an ombudsman is that till the time self-regulation is not embedded in a statutory framework, the doors of statutory regulation would always remain open. Media freedoms are too fragile and precious to be left to the tender mercies of the state. In fact, I would go so far as to state that a special article, notwithstanding all the aberrations that I have pointed out, must be included in the Constitution guaranteeing media freedoms and not leave it as a derivative of Article 19(1)(a).

For ,when the state starts drawing lines in the media space ,the spectre of intolerance becomes a chilling certainty. It would make whatever is happening appear like a children's tea party. In the case of the current government, even without any formal regulation of the thought space, protests against their anti-intellectual, anti-liberal and anti-creativity Orwellian mindset have already reached a crescendo —and the dance of fascism is yet to begin

JNU: Media is all about business

ONE OF the very curious collaterals of the JNU incident is the manner in which it has brought the dog-eat-dog divide within the media into the open. One evening, while surfing television to find my favourite cartoon channel, I paused for a couple of seconds on an English views channel that masquerades as a news and current affairs channel, for that is how they are licensed to operate.

I was amused to find the 'resident divinity' of that outfit virtually abusing the promoter of a media trust-funded independent news website for having ostensibly allegedly insinuated that the outfit in question had run a "fake video" of the incident in JNU. The promoter in question, in an earlier avatar was the editor of one of India's oldest and most respected paper.

Earlier, another 'deity' of another English TV views channel apparently dissected the Jawaharlal Nehru University (JNU) video to establish that it was morphed and that the voice was superimposed on the picture. Yet another English views channel took umbrage and as a counter to that deconstruction ran a full screen scroll across the plate accusing it of unethical journalism for suggesting that they had run a fake, morphed or doctored clip. It reminded me of the guy who called the police to say his friend 'everybody' was fighting his other friend

---

catchnews.com, website portal, 22 February, 2016

'nobody'. When the police personnel asked him, "Are you mad?" He said he was, for that was his name.

However, in the JNU affair, the shoe is on the other foot.

In another simultaneous aside, the Home Minister of India and the head honcho of Delhi Police tilted at their own windmills.

The first trotted out a tweet from a fake account to establish the ubiquitous Pakistan link to the *l'affaire* JNU while the latter tied himself up in knots while responding to a tweet from a parody account. It was the theatre of the absurd playing itself out in high season with free ringside tickets to boot.

It's not funny

All this would have been hilarious had the *dramatis personae* not been important stakeholders in our public dialogue and governance paradigm. It appeared to be inter-media rivalry or peer jealously among editors playing itself out in full public view.

The reason it is not funny is because of the manner in which each of the stakeholders, especially of television, have tried to mould public discourse, perhaps keeping a very narrow imperative in mind.

It is not a case of conceptual differences—that would have been acceptable. Ideological diversity in media is not new. The Indian media has provided working space to people with all shades of personal convictions from the ultra left to the extreme right. Their personal convictions and biases have always tinged the prism through which they have viewed people and events but that is human. However, that is not where the problem lies.

It's about money

The reality is that media is a business. The difficulty is that there is not enough money going around for everybody to get a piece of the action. There are flawed revenue models and the problem is most acute in the television industry.

The viewership is measured by a dubious currency called Television Rating Points (TRP's). In addition, they have to pay humungous carriage fee to the multi-system operators to carry their content to the viewer. If there would be no viewership there would be no inflow of money from the advertisers. The MSOs charge them carriage, for there is no demand from the people to watch these news channels.They carry entertainment channels free or even pay the entertainment channels for the privilege of carrying them in their distribution companies.

The business of TRPs was earlier run by a company called TAM, primarily an oversees entity held by people with fingers in both advertising and broadcasting businesses—a clear conflict of interest.

It meant 'you' were the index that you yourself used as an advertiser to decide which broadcaster to fund and you had stakes on the other side too. As the Minister for Information and Broadcasting, I came up with a policy guideline that required TV rating companies to publicly disclose their shareholding pattern.Sensing a difficulty, they moved the High Court and got some aspects of those guidelines stayed. The matter is still sub judice.

Meanwhile, the TV industry came up with its own measurement mechanism called the Broadcast Audience Research Council (BARC). However, rather than invest in putting up people's metres—the device that measures viewership—they decided to co-opt TAM's infrastructure.

So what you get now is TAM data put out by BARC and there remains one monopolistic entity that continues to do the ratings. Earlier it was TAM, now it is BARC.

It's not fair

There is no competition that can act as a double-check on the veracity and integrity of the viewership numbers being put out. Moreover, the spread of these peoples' metres is thin—30,000 to capture a universe of 168 million TV households.

That is where editorial checks become the casualty. In the mad rush to be the first to put out a story to grab eyeballs, no attention is paid either to its authenticity or genuineness.

If the story is something like the JNU video, (in this case, first put out by Akhil Bharti Vidyarthi Parishad, an RSS front), that appeals to the basest sentiments of the people—impetuous pulp patriotism—all the more better. For nothing sells better than jingoism masquerading as nationalism.

One of the most corrosive legacies of India's liberalisation has been the manner in which over the past 26 years we have handed out TV licences, especially to news channels virtually like toffees. It has not created diversity of views; it has led to market fragmentation and non-existent revenue models.

The mad rush to grab eyeballs has made the public discourse in India corrosive and gives WWF a run for it's money. Tomorrow, if it is established that the JNU video was morphed—a fake—would the 'eminences' that put it out take responsibility?

The answer is no, they would have moved on to the next byte of sensationalism for that is there bread—and there is no butter in the business.

Udta Punjab

THE BROUHAHA over the treatment of Udta Punjab by the Central Board of Film Certification has again focused attention on the arbitrary use of powers available under the Cinematograph Act 1952 and Cinematograph. (Certification) Rules 1983, and the rules made therein. The circumscription of creative licence has become the norm in the past two years of the BJP government. But before dealing with the constriction of India's liberal space by an obscurantist establishment, it may be worth examining how the process of certification/censorship plays itself out these days.

Article 19(1)(a) of the Constitution guarantees freedom of speech and expression to all citizens. There is a caveat in Article 19(2), however, that lets the State put reasonable restrictions on exercising this right. As the scope of these constraints are almost infinite, they were engrafted almost in toto in Section 5(B) of the Cinematograph Act. This virtually gives the censor board unbridled powers to refuse certification, impose arbitrary cuts, grant certificates ranging from U (universal) to S (specialised presentation). All this and more is done almost on a daily basis, supposedly to protect the sovereignty and integrity of India, security of the state, friendly relations with foreign nations, public order, decency, morality, defamation, contempt of court or even the incitement of an offence.

The Economic Times, 11 June, 2016

The power to certify a film is vested exclusively in the Centre under Article 246, entry 60 in the Union List of the Seventh Schedule. But state governments routinely misuse law and order powers and state laws promulgated under entry 33 of the State List to ban films that are granted certification by the CBFC.

A good example is the Tamil Nadu Cinemas (Regulation) Act 1955, that was invoked with Section 144 CrPC by the Tamil Nadu government to stop the screening of Kamal Hassan's *Vishwaroopam* in January 2013, despite it being cleared by the censor board. Under Rule 21 of the Film Certification Rules, a producer or his nominee applies for the certification of a film. It must be vetted in 21 days. This rule is routinely violated for big banners and major producers, ostensibly in the name of stopping piracy. It is then referred to an examining committee drawn from people on the advisory panel attached to every regional centre. The examining committee recommends how a film should be certified. If the producer or CBFC chairman is not satisfied with the committee's decision, it is referred to a revising committee. If the producer is unhappy with the revising committee's decision, he/she can appeal to the Film Certification Appellate Tribunal, after which a writ lies to the high court, then a special leave petition to the Supreme Court.

The fundamental point is that wide, arbitrary and almost draconian powers are vested in the CBFC that can drive even a conservative filmmaker around the bend. Given the huge financial investments in play, time is of the essence, which makes a producer a virtual puppet in the hands of the board. That is the reason why allegations of corruption, malfeasance and carnal favours are often rife. A command performance to deny certification at the Centre's behest is the easiest one-person act to perform.

If a filmmaker can navigate his/her way around this byzantine maze, state governments can always stop a film being screened there on the spurious ground of a threat to law and order, as happened in the case of *Vishwaroopam* in Tamil Nadu, *Sadda Haq* in Punjab and many other films along the way.

My experience in a former avatar with the functioning or rather malfunctioning of the CBFC convinced me that this institution should be abolished. I was trying to find a way to demolish this architecture. The opportunity came in the form of the Tamil Nadu government's move to ban Kamal Haasan's film. Oral instructions were issued to district collectors to halt advance bookings of the film, as it would ostensibly hurt the sentiments of one community. Despite my repeated public entreaties that this was wholly illegal, the state government wouldn't budge. It was clear there was a standoff. While the state government was bent on using its law and order powers to curb artistic freedom, the larger question was that if every state government took this route, where would it leave the Cinematograph Act, and, more important, would filmmakers be forced to run from state secretariat to state secretariat, hat in hand, to get their films exhibited, after spending huge sums to make the movie and then get all the requisite clearances as required by the law? The entire issue went far beyond the fate of just one movie.

On February 4, 2013, as the *Vishwaroopam* controversy was raging, I set up a committee with some of the most eminent and knowledgeable people to examine the issue. It included retired Punjab and Haryana high court chief justice Mukul Mudgal, FCAT chairman Lalit Bhasin, former CBFC chairperson Sharmila Tagore and Javed Akhtar, then an MP, and was tasked with reviewing the CBFC's mandate and functioning, and recommend steps, including statutory changes, to enable it to deal with the needs of a changing society. This would include the process of certification, the mechanism followed by the examining and revising committees, categories of certification, existing and proposed, including any special categories for broadcasting on television channels and radio stations, and finally to review FCAT's mandate to make it a more efficacious appellate body.

After wide consultations across the country, it submitted its report on October 9, 2013, and given that it included lawyers in addition to creative people it even drew up a model Cinematograph Bill. When the committee came to submit its report to me, the first question I asked was: have you recommended the scrapping of this whole silly censorship process masquerading as certification? The chairperson, Justice Mudgul, smiled back, saying we did not know that you wanted that. I reparteed back, saying it would have been wholly inappropriate for me to impose my subjective desires over your objective consideration.

It was another matter that, left to myself, I would have repealed the Cinematograph Act lock, stock and barrel and replaced it with statutory guidelines whose violation would entail hefty pecuniary consequences. If television can be beamed into people's bedrooms 24x7 regulated by only a programme code and advertising code, why have a censorship mechanism for films? It belongs to another time and place in history. Unlike TV, that someone may involuntarily be forced to watch, in case of a film you actually go to a theatre and buy a ticket to see a movie. There is no coercion involved in the process.

However, since it was late in the day and the process of inviting public comments and consultations with states would require time, I thought it prudent to put the whole report and the draft model bill in the public domain for people to peruse and react, hoping the next government would make it a legal reality. The BJP-led government, however, chose to cold shoulder this and set up another panel under top filmmaker Shyam Benegal to reinvent the wheel. Given this government's reactionary ethos, this committee was at best a tactic to divert the flak the government had been getting from the creative community over the spectre of intolerance that stalks the country today. Coming back to *Udta Punjab,* the mutilation of the film is undoubtedly a command performance as the Akali-BJP government is widely seen as either complicit or at least patronising of the drugs trade in Punjab that has ruined so many innocent lives. A movie that exposes the magnitude of the horror and monstrosity of the crime perpetrated on 30 million hapless people is obviously inconvenient to the powers-that-be and therefore must be discredited as propaganda, if not banned and consigned to the dustbin. This government and their trolls are giving even Josef Goebbels a run for his money. The fundamental problem is, however, institutional and structural. As long as the Cinematograph Act is not repealed, *Udta Punjab* will become the rule rather than the exception. Censorship must go, let freedom reign.

VI. Defence and Strategic Affairs

Growing India needs a permanent establishment

IN THE wake of the domestic fracas on the Iran vote at the IAEA, Dr Manmohan Singh recently bemoaned the lack of an "establishment" and a strategic culture in India that takes a long-term view of India's interests. This statement of the Prime Minister raises quite a few questions: What is an establishment? Does India need one? If it does, do we have one? If it does not, why does it not? And finally what should be its character and form?

Simply put, an establishment is a group of individuals/ organisations, essentially though not always outside the government, who can dispassionately take a long-term view of a nation's interests and are able to then exercise influence to steer the course of government and national policies towards those interests irrespective of the party in office at that point of time.

In Western democracies, the establishment has tended to consist of senior military, intelligence, diplomatic and political figures in conjunction with captains of the defence/nuclear/strategic industries, atomic scientists and strategic thinkers whose views on issues of national security have a certain common minimum consensus.

Moreover, as defence manufacturing in most of these nations tended to be or is in the private or public-private domain, there

---

The Tribune, 13 March, 2006

was a strong convergence of economic interests which created mini-oligarchies and banded them together.

The Pentagon Military Industrial Complexes combine with the recent co-option of the oil industry funded neo-con think tanks and the Wall Street-MNC combine are two examples of establishment in the US at the opposite ends of the national ideological paradigm.

They are not essentially large private interest groups but institutions that tend to best represent and promote the US worldview, with both balancing each other. The same pattern is there in Great Britain and France with the security establishments being dominant to a greater degree while in Russia and China, because of the totalitarian background, the establishment still consists primarily of the in-house atomic, intelligence, security and defence establishments.

In India, with defence manufacturing being totally in the government arena, and think tanks a recent phenomena, the establishment is really the status-quoist in-house or at best some retired military-diplomatic personnel. Most of these retired officers are also forever looking for post-retirement sinecures and, therefore, tend to align their views with that political group which is best placed to employ them. In that sense of the word, the Prime Minister is right—India has no establishment worth the name.

Does India need a truly non-partisan and independent establishment and what should be the shape and character of this establishment? Would it evolve on its own or does it need to be mid-wifed by the government?

Given the increasingly fractious nature of national politics and the decline of national party systems (howsoever undesirable they might be), juxtaposed with global challenges and India's own "great power" aspirations, a permanent establishment is a pre-requisite now. What would be its nature is something that needs to be widely debated.

In India today, business is perhaps the only driving force in our social milieu. However, it is still tiny and nascent by global standards. If an establishment has to emerge in India the defence Industry needs to be opened up to domestic players in the first instance so that a convergence of strategic and economic interests emerges in the medium term.

Think tanks and research organisations, not tied to the umbilical chord of the government, need to be listened to seriously by the government when they make policy recommendations. Big business by Indian standards, especially in the core and strategic sectors, needs to be co-opted into the process.

In other words, a grand coalition of forces has to be marshalled to act as a counterweight to the fractious and at times lunatic pulls of domestic politics that seriously threaten and undermine India's long-term interests.

This is necessary to bridge the gap in terms of time that it would take for a *genuine, respected and influential establishment to evolve and emerge.*

For an Indian military-industrial complex

ON JULY 25, 2001, replying to a question in the Lok Sabha, the then Defence Minister Jaswant Singh stated that, "the defence industry sector is opened up for participation by the Indian private sector up to 100 per cent of equity, with a foreign direct investment component of it being permissible up to 26 per cent." One decade down the road as foreign defence majors line up at the Defence-Expo 2010 to display their wares, it is time to take stock of the efficacy of this initiative and to the contribution of Indian industry to our defence effort. The defence ministry did take an interest in promoting the private sector to increase self-reliance in defence production. Myriad reform measures—the offset policy of 2006, the recent "Buy and Make (Indian)" provision, sharing a public version of the long-term plan of the armed forces with industry—were initiated. The results, unfortunately, have been disappointing.

Over the past decade, India has bought equipment worth $50 billion from foreign suppliers, and will likely spend more than $100 billion on weapons systems in the coming decade. The contribution of Indian private industry to this figure is miniscule, contrary to the claims of most industry associations. FDI is a mere $0.15 million, a fraction of the inflows into, say, the timber products sector. Even today, only 30 per cent of India's defence needs are indigenously met.

The Indian Express, 19February, 2010

Efforts at augmenting the private sector's contributions have only been incremental. Some were recommended by the Vijay Kelkar and the Prabir Sengupta committees; others resulted from offset provisions in foreign contracts with a value of Rs 300 crore and above. There have been policy roll-backs also—such as not nominating private Indian companies as "Raksha Udyog Ratnas" on the specious premise that it would discriminate against small and medium enterprises in defence production .

If there's one word to succinctly characterise the entire approach of the Indian establishment over the past decade in this sector, that word is "conservative". But caution must now give way to reforms that are visionary in scope, bold in character and sweeping in intent.

Government needs to leverage Indian corporate energy to create indigenous military-industrial complexes over the next two decades. This would have varied benefits: notably the incubation of a strategic culture which, as the PM rightly lamented four years ago, India sorely lacks. It would also invariably lead to the creation of privately-funded strategic think tanks which can engage in creative and independent thinking on a host of issues where India sorely lacks domain knowledge

But, fundamentally, government must make up its mind that Indian private industry be trusted in the true sense of the word. Oddly, while we trust foreign suppliers (essentially because there are few alternatives), governed as they are by their respective national laws that have in-built sanction mechanisms to restrict supplies in various situations, we have not extended the same trust quotient to Indian Industry.

Even now the private sector is at a distinct disadvantage vis-à-vis established defence public sector enterprises—the eight public sector units and 40 ordnance factories. IT struggles to push its interests through industry associations: the public sector has a non-competitive edge, because of its close proximity to the MoD. The role of the Department of Defence Production thus needs to be drastically retooled to evaluate India's requirements not in a public sector context but a larger India paradigm. The private sector is also inhibited by technical limitations primarily due to its late entry into the industry (a consequence of the policy regime and the government's years of investment, with questionable productivity, in its own companies). To catch up, the private sector needs to institutionalise joint ventures with established foreign defence majors—but the existing FDI cap, 26 per cent, doesn't help.

Essentially, a four-pronged initiative is needed. The licensing system needs to be liberalised. Except for very critical products, all other manufacturing needs must be put on the automatic approval route or approval should be simply done away with. Second, FDI limits must be enhanced to 49 per cent across the board; and, in non-sensitive areas raised to 76 or even 100 per cent. This would obviate the need for government to defray 80 per cent of the R&D costs, the centrepiece of its latest policy initiative, by positioning India, with its inherent cost advantages, as a manufacturing destination. Then, a level playing field must be provided to private industry in terms of the excise and custom regime. Finally, the government must seriously consider private equity participation in the defence-related public sector to unlock their potential and maximise returns on sovereign investment over the decades

In its second term, the UPA government must lay solid foundations so that in the decades to come a rising India is not scouring the world for military hardware. This trend needs to be reversed.

Clanking skeletons

PHILOSOPHER FRIEDRICH Nietzsche was oracular in his prophecy: "When we are tired, we are attacked by ideas we conquered long ago". Sixty-two years after the Sino-India border conflict, the Indian state remains obtusely paranoid about making the Henderson Brooks Report public.

The author of *India's China War*, Neville Maxwell, in a blog dated February 7, 2014 and titled *My Henderson Brooks Albatross*—accessible on www.indiandefencereview.com—put out in the public domain the version of the report available with him. The version underscores that the Henderson Brooks Report was an operational review instituted by the then Chief of the Army Staff on December 14, 1962, "to go into the reverses suffered by the Army, particularly in the Kameng Frontier Division of NEFA (now Arunachal Pradesh)".

The review was carried out by Lt Gen TB Henderson Brooks, assisted by Brig PS Bhagat. The terms of reference of the review were ostensibly to inquire into what went wrong with training, equipment, system of command, physical fitness of the troops and capacity of commanders at all levels to influence the men under their command. The review of the functioning of the Army Headquarters was purportedly not carried out on the advice of the Chief of the Army

The Asian Age, 26 July, 2014

Staff. This precluded the examination of the relationship between the defence ministry and Army Headquarters and the directions given by the former to the latter. The object perhaps being that Lt Gen Brooks could not have been expected to possibly evaluate the conduct of his superiors, eminently desirable, as it may have been. A perusal of the report even with pages 112-157 and the annexures omitted only underlines the fact that it was a professional exercise done without any predetermined intent to absolve some and blame others for the operational lapses that happened.

Yet, 58 years later, on April 19, 2010, in a reply to a question tabled in the Lok Sabha by the writer on making the report public, the then defence minister stated: "Henderson Brooks Report is a top-secret document based on an internal study by the Indian Army, contents of which are not only extremely sensitive but are of current operational value." Four years later, on July 8, 2014, the current defence minister, Arun Jaitley, responding to a similar question in the Rajya Sabha, stated, "This is a top-secret document and has not been declassified so far. Further release of this report, fully or partially, or disclosure of any information related to this report, would not be in national interest."

Paradoxically, on March 19, 2014, Mr Jaitley, then the Leader of the Opposition in the Rajya Sabha, made a strong pitch for making the report public in an article available on www.bjp.org. He wrote: "Are archival records to be kept away from public gaze indefinitely? If the document pertains to internal security there may be some public interest served in keeping them a secret for some time. However, to keep these documents 'top-secret' indefinitely may not be in public interest… The security relevance of a document loses its relevance in the long-term future… With the wisdom of hindsight, I am of the opinion that the report's contents could have been made public some decades ago." Yet, in four months, you see another about turn between the words and actions of the current dispensation. The core issue, however, is why is this hackneyed excuse of national security and strategic sacrosanctity trotted out by successive governments to deny access to archival material that can form the basis of informed analysis of our past actions?

India is not the only country that has national security forebodings. The United Kingdom has also evolved its position over the years. The Freedom of Information Act 2000 requires that information be disclosed unless there are sound reasons for confidentiality. Even the 30-year thumb rule for withholding Cabinet papers has been relaxed. In the United States, an executive order establishes the procedure for declassification of documents with a default date of 10 years, which is followed up with an automatic declassification review after 25, 50 and 75 years, respectively, with the provisions for keeping a document classified becoming exceptionally rigorous at each stage. In Australia, the threshold for declassification is 20 years, while Israel for non-security related documents has brought it down to 15 years while raising the bar on some defence-related documents to 70 years.

In the case of India, though Section 8(3) of the Right to Information Act mandates that information pertaining to events which occurred 20 years ago must be provided, the overarching exception clauses trip the entire purport of the provision insofar it pertains to the strategic domain. Almost any or all information can either be denied or stonewalled. Moreover, the Second Schedule of the Act puts a large number of intelligence and security organisations out of the purview of the Act. There is an urgent need to amend the Act, remove or narrow the exceptions to Section 8(3) and even fine-tune the kind of information that the organisations in the second schedule that are exempt from the purview of this Act can withhold. There is a requirement to repeal the antediluvian Official Secrets Act, 1923, and set up a National Declassification Authority that can, across the government, identify material for release.

Coming back to the Henderson Brooks Report, a lot of innuendo has been freely floating around for the past six decades with regard to the alleged accountability, culpability and malfeasance of certain individuals. Even Mr Jaitley in his critique makes an oblique insinuation: "It has been reported in the media that pages 112 to 157 are still not known. Is it because these pages contain material which can be embarrassing to those in power in 1962?" This needs to stop. If at all errors of judgment were made, India as a nation has the maturity to locate them in the correct context. It is, therefore, incumbent upon this government to walk the talk and put the Henderson Brooks Report with all the attendant material out in the public domain at the earliest. Don't we have the nerve to face our past squarely?

Chronic condescension

WHILE THE track record of DRDO may be a mixed bag open to critique, nothing can detract from the commitment of the talented professionals who serve it passionately and altruistically.

The reprehensible removal of Avinash Chander, the director general of the Defence Research and Development Organisation (DRDO) just months after his tenure was extended by the Bharatiya Janata Party-led government till May 2016 has once again focused attention on the imperious manner in which this government is trampling upon institutions.

It rekindles memories of the sordid events of December 30, 1998, when the Atal Behari Vajpayee-led government had unceremoniously sacked the Chief of the Naval Staff, Admiral Vishnu Bhagwat. Incidentally, two days before his unceremonious departure, Admiral Bhagwat had been elevated as chairperson of the Chiefs of Staff Committee. Are both instances an uncanny coincidence or incessant political arrogance of the same political dispensation separated by time and space only?

The reasons for the sacking in both instances are superfluous and fuzzy. While the Navy Chief is a uniformed officer, the crown of the DRDO is also the scientific adviser to the defence minister, a position

---

The Asian Age, 24 January, 2015

of enormous gravitas. Does this cavalier, if not callous attitude bode well for the higher defence management of the nation?

Unlike a number of countries around India, namely Pakistan, Bangladesh and Burma, the Indian armed forces have never crossed the sacred Rubicon and have always remained committed to the constitutional tenets that underpin the Indian state.

However, civil-military relations in India are not exactly the Shangri-la of bliss. On the contrary, the armed forces have been unremittingly exasperated with the civilian bureaucracy. They cogitate that it has a gratuitous pre-eminence in strategic affairs. Attempts to narrow the divergence and synchronise this dissonance have met with little or no success. In the aftermath of the conflict in Kargil, the government appointed a review committee under the leadership of former defence secretary, K Subrahmanyam, to examine the entire gamut of issues connected with the administration of India's defence. A group of ministers further deliberated upon the recommendations but nothing substantive came out of the whole exercise.

Subsequently, the Naresh Chandra Committee also went into the issue of defence reforms. They made apropos submissions that continue to linger in suspended animation. The fundamental enigma is who is statutorily charged with the responsibility for defence of India. The rules of business mandate that it is the defence secretary who is charged with the remit. The service chiefs are kept at an arm's length from the realm of policy formulation, though they provide the necessary input and discernibly implement the decisions arrived at. Coupled with this is the malady that service headquarters are not integrated into the defence ministry and function as an entity extrinsic to the rarefied echelons of the state.

The question that requires to be answered is what do we mean by civilian control of the defence establishment? Does it mean superintendence by the political executive or subordination to the bureaucracy? Has this subordination impacted India's defence preparedness and its ability to surmount the myriad challenges—both in the region as well as beyond, as India widens its strategic horizons.

Repeatedly, it has been recommended that the government should appoint a Chief of the Defence Staff (CDS) who should be the single point military adviser to the government. But successive governments have been chary about making this leap of faith.

What is, therefore, left with the armed forces and various other bodies that form the larger defence fraternity are the values of honour and respect, the imperative of being treated with due regard for the perilous duties they perform.

A case in point was the issue of former Army Chief Gen. VK Singh's date of birth. He articulated it as a matter of honour. Whether it was or not is debatable. He took the government to the Supreme Court and then had to withdraw the petition after the court refused to entertain it.

It was unprecedented that a serving chief takes the government of the day to court, thereby clearly indicating that he had lost confidence in the ability of the government to redress his grievances. The government would have been well within its rights to ask the chief to go because a lack of trust and faith is a two-way affair. Adding to the spectre of distrust were bizarre rumours of alleged unauthorised troop movements and deployment of mobile communication interceptors in Delhi.

However, rather than asking him to either step down or resort to anything more knee-jerk, the United Progressive Alliance government acted with maturity and restraint. It allowed him to complete his tenure and retire gracefully. What probably weighed with the government was the negative impact it would have on the armed forces as an institution had the government chosen to act in a churlish manner in order to validate the maxim of civilian dominance.

Run-ins between the civilian authorities and military personnel are not confined to India alone. Enough has been written about how both, Presidents Bush and Obama, were exasperated with their military commanders talking out of turn. Both in Iraq and Afghanistan, top military commanders were replaced or shuffled, but it was done with dignity and decorum.

Even during the Second World War, President Roosevelt and Prime Minister Churchill repeatedly transferred battlefield commanders, but it was done without rancour.

Despite being a one party state, the rulers of China are extremely meticulous as to how they treat the ranking apparatchiks of the People's Liberation Army though the general secretary of the Chinese Communist Party doubles up as the chairperson of the Central Military Commission. Deng Xiaoping had famously advised his successor Jiang Zemin, "Out of five working days spend four with the top brass."

While the DRDO may not be a uniformed service in the strict sense of the word, it draws into its fold personnel from the uniformed services also. While the track record of the organisation may be a mixed bag open to critique, nothing can detract from the commitment of the talented professionals who serve it passionately and altruistically. Many of them can easily get a quantum jump in their emoluments were they to move to the "civvie" street.

Rather than indulging in cosmetic histrionics, the government should try and understand the innate dynamics of the defence establishment. The battles that may have to be fought are outside, but that cannot be achieved by starting a war within.

Loose lips sink ships

ON THE EVE of President Barack Obama's visit to New Delhi, the defence minister of India, Manohar Parrikar, made a rather zany proclamation. Some Prime Ministers, he said, had compromised the country's "deep assets". He further decreed that he would not name the former Prime Ministers though "many people know".

Fourteen Prime Ministers have served India, 1947 onwards. Notwithstanding the partisan divide, each of them has had years of public service behind them. The defence minister's ambivalence opened the doors and windows to a frenzied bout of speculation. The social media, where everybody and their grandmother is a broadcaster, became the arena for many hard-won reputations with years of public service behind them to be slandered with impunity. Some sections of mainstream media also reproduced the innuendo without compunction. With one bald conjecture, Mr Parrikar bade to raise misgivings on the conduct of one or more of India's leaders. An outraged former Prime Minister HD Deve Gowda retorted, "There are only two Prime Ministers now who can react to it. Vajpayeeji is not well. I am saying, I am prepared to go through any kind of investigation or trial to see what happened during my tenure." He went on to question the Prime Minister, stating, "It is for Prime Minister

The Asian Age, 07 February, 2015

Narendra Modi now to specify the charges made by his minister and whether it is proper for him to make such remarks."

"Deep assets" is the most deliciously woolly term. It can mean everything and nothing. Was Mr Parrikar referring to covert intelligence assets or the strategic programme? Was he alluding to the alleged lack of apex-level attention that may have bedeviled our indigenous defence programme since the Bharatiya Janata Party government recently sacked the director-general of the Defence Research and Development Organisation? This is not the first time that BJP leaders have indulged in such sensational susurration. Way back in 2006, Jaswant Singh in his book, *A Call to Honour*, had alluded that there was a mole in the Prime Minister's Office during Prime Minister PV Narasimha Rao's regime. When challenged by the then Prime Minister, Manmohan Singh, on the floor of the Upper House to reveal the name of the mole, he backtracked and was unable to substantiate the claim.

Another glaring example of such insouciance is provided by Major General VK Singh in his book, *India's External Intelligence*. He describes how the then National Democratic Alliance government had compromised a very vital "deep communication asset" by making the conversation between Pakistan's Army Chief, Pervez Musharraf and his Chief of Staff Lt Gen Mohammed Aziz public to prove Pakistan's complicity in the Kargil War. Pakistan became wise to the circumstance that the Research and Analysis Wing (R&AW) was intercepting a particular satellite link between Beijing and Islamabad, leading to its immediate closure. Had the then NDA government handled the dissemination of information more skillfully and safeguarded the technical asset, the link would have proved to be the mother lode of information for India. Rumours have been doing the rounds for decades now as to how the alleged indiscreet slip by a former Prime Minister compromised Indian assets in the Pakistani nuclear programme. There is yet another one which slyly insinuates that a Prime Minister ordered the winding up of ostensible covert operations in a neighbouring country.

For all you know these could just be vile lies spread by jealous rivals or even malevolent creatures for the sake of sadistic pleasure. After all, rumour unfortunately is humour in India. For the defence minister of the country to buy into these conspiracy theories is a bit of a stretch. If Mr Parrikar does have any substantive evidence, then he is duty bound to put all the facts in the public space because the subtext of his statement is portentous. He is accusing some people who have been at the helm of affairs of being virtually anti-national.

In addition to the collateral damage caused by such assertions, there are implications of such rash flippancy on India's national security also. At a point in time when foreign direct investment caps in defence have been upped from 26 to 49 per cent, and the BJP government has promoted this initiative as the centerpiece of its "Make in India" initiative, what is the message that you are sending to countries and potential investors? That India cannot be trusted to maintain confidentiality, therefore, sensitive defence technology on which billions have been spent in research and development should not be shared with or transferred to the Indian government or companies?

The one country that India has been desperately wooing is the United States of America. US interlocutors have been privately seeking assurances that their intellectual property would be secure, not because they are scared of leaks, peeps and squeaks, but because we are generally perceived to be of a permissive ethos. Nations such as the US have been nurtured in the adage "loose lips sink ships". Where then does this go from here? The usual Indian attitude would lend itself to a let-it-be attitude. Given that the defence minister is relatively new to Delhi, perhaps he does not realise or understand the full import of his utterances. The other way would be to confront him on the floor of the House, just as Dr Manmohan Singh had locked horns with Jaswant Singh on the "mole" matter, and compel Mr Parrikar to either substantiate his statement or withdraw it and tender an unconditional apology.

The honour and dignity of former Prime Ministers is not a matter intrinsic to them, their families or their legacy alone. It is a matter connected with what defines us as a nation. Are we a country that cynically suspects or is skeptical of its leaders and tends to imagine that there can be no smoke without a fire? Conversely, do we as a democracy consider that we have at least, over the years, elected patriotic people to lead us irrespective of their politics or other shortcomings? Would it not be the appropriate thing to do, that if anyone questions the nationalism or commitment of our Prime Ministers to the nation, they must be put to the strict burden of proof?

VII. Doodling about Things

Corporate India defeated Congress

WINSTON CHURCHILL had aptly remarked, "If we open a quarrel between past and present we shall find that we have lost the future". However, there is another adage that states that those who forget history are condemned to repeat it. Therefore, it is both obligatory and imperative to objectively, if not critically, analyse the past 10 years of the Congress-led United Progressive Alliance administration and then try and discern the way forward for it.

The India that the UPA inherited in 2004 was deeply insecure and communally divided as a result of the wider ramifications of the Gujarat pogrom and a growth model which, since the advent of liberalisation, ostensibly delivered for the affluent and the upwardly mobile, but not the poor or the marginalized.

The UPA government, given the complexities of India, gauged the pulse of the people correctly when it conceptualised the paradigm of equity with growth. From 2004 to 2008, an innovative model of socio-economic inclusion was institutionalised that included but was not limited to an ambitious school lunch initiative catering to more than 139 million children daily, guaranteed hundred days of employment to the rural poor, and a holistic loan waiver to the farming community. During these four years, the economy also grew at an impressive rate

---

The Asian Age, 14 June, 2014

of 8.5-9 per cent and corporate bottom lines were robust and in the black. Coupled with this, the Indo-US civil nuclear engagement created a feel good excitement across the middle class as a signal went out that two estranged democracies were now engaging with each other across a broad spectrum of issues. It seemed that there was finally utopia in Shangri-La. However, the apparitions of the global economic meltdown were lurking ominously over the horizon. India was able to surmount the storm as its economic fundamentals were healthy and timely counter-cyclical measures were put in place. All this enabled the Congress and the UPA to increase its tally impressively in 2009.

However, the second term of the UPA government started inopportunely, if not inauspiciously. Right in the beginning, the unfounded trepidation regarding Prime Minister Manmohan Singh's Sharm el-Sheikh initiative on Pakistan sent out a signal of confusion and division, both within the government and between the party and the government. In 2009, the American surge in Pakistan was under contemplation. The Taliban had made deep inroads into Pakistan right up to the Swat Valley. Pakistan was perhaps at its most vulnerable and the unnecessary brouhaha about the inclusion of Balochistan in the agenda for future talks, which incidentally would have been to India's advantage, was totally avoidable. In terms of realpolitik, Sharm el-Sheikh was a golden opportunity that became a casualty of myopic domestic paranoia.

Moving back to the domestic context—while on one hand the government phased out the economic counter-cyclical measures rather prematurely when domestic industry had yet not recovered from the ravages of the economic meltdown, food inflation remained at a stubborn high as a consequence of the change in consumption patterns, especially across rural India, where the rights-based entitlement programs had started making a qualitative difference to the lives of the people, but more so because of the lackadaisical approach of state governments in checking hoarding and profiteering in commodities.

By 2010, the euphoria of 2009 had started turning to sullenness, especially among the middle-class that had overwhelmingly voted for the Congress and now had to bear the brunt of high food prices. Amidst all this, the controversy surrounding the Commonwealth

Games commenced and the telecom wars peaked in the form of a Comptroller and Auditor General of India report, which coined a new terminology "presumptive loss" and put a bizarre figure of 1,766.45 billion as loss to the exchequer as a result of the decision to award licences on a first-come-first-served basis rather than auctioning them.

This was crunch time, the quintessential inflection moment that dealt a deathblow to the credibility of the government from which it never could recover. After the report came into the public domain, the inability of the government or the parties in the UPA to formulate, enunciate and convincingly put forth facts in the correct perspective only inflamed the already simmering surliness among people who were reeling under the impact of high food prices. The Joint Parliamentary Committee Report on telecom matters adopted by a majority of 14 to 11 and tabled in Parliament on December 9, 2013, demolished the disingenuity of the "presumptive loss" theory. But, by then, the damage had been done and a noxious mood against the UPA had already coalesced across the nation. The JPC report sank without a trace.

The Eurozone crisis had kicked in and the Indian economy had started to sputter. From 2009 to 2012, when the focus of the government should have been on revving up the economy by kick-starting the second generation of economic reforms, it harked back to the erstwhile socialist era, the retrospective taxation in the Vodafone case perhaps being the most damaging signal that India could have sent to foreign investors about the fairness of its tax regime and the sacrosanctity of its judicial pronouncements. In many ways, 2009 to 2012 were the locust years of the Indian economy.

Meanwhile, the government continued to push its rights-based entitlement programmes with free and compulsory education, food security and land acquisition being added to the welfare architecture. Time will vindicate that these were steps in the right direction, but to a corporate India, whose bottomlines were bleeding, overdue loan repayments had turned accounts into non-performing assets; it was like showing a red rag to a bull. The intricate balance between equity and growth that characterised the first term of the UPA was lost somewhere along the way. Corporate India individually and collectively started feeling that the emphasis, whether in terms of incentives, concessions or palliatives, should have been on the industry rather than the disempowered, the marginalised and the poor.

What the UPA failed to discern was that the balance of power had shifted from government to corporate India. The first economic power shift that commenced with liberalisation in 1991 had fructified by the second decade of the 21st century. More than 75 per cent of the 2 trillion Indian economy was now privately controlled. Coupled with this, the instruments of information dissemination were also now corporate controlled. The print media had historically been owned by corporate barons, but from 1991 to 2014, they collectively acquired control over 415 news and current affairs channels which were streaming 24x7 into people's drawing rooms and bedrooms. The middle class had got empowered by the new media, with social media platforms giving people the ability to put their most vitriolic thoughts in public space, at times without restraint or responsibility. This was perhaps the most critical misjudgment that the UPA made about the power of corporate India and the newfound muscle of the middle class.

In the midst of all this, the chief minister of Gujarat won a third term in December 2012. Corporate India thought they had discovered their nemesis. While the facts are still hazy and will emerge over time, perhaps a spoken or unspoken consensus emerged across influential sections of corporate India that a second power shift must take place. It was Bombay Club version 2.0 at play. After acquiring the levers of economic power they made a decisive bid for political power. It was the Rockefeller moment of Indian politics. They put their bets not on a party but on an individual. An across the board effort was unleashed to successfully bring a second power shift to fruition. An irate middle class was the veritable canon fodder available to successfully execute this project. Sadly for India and democracy, they succeeded. Corporate India defeated the Congress Party.

The politico-economic history of myriad nations testifies to the corrosive effect of malevolent corporate influence on public policy and political processes. The long-term implications are portentous for India. What is the way forward for the Congress? While the introspection process would meander along at its own pace, what needs to be evaluated is why those sections of society for whom the entire rights-based architecture was created did not vote for the Congress? In 2005, the population living in poverty was as high as 37.2 per cent. By 2014, this number had dropped to 21.3 per cent. The UPA government was successful in bringing about a drop of 15.9 per cent in just one decade. In the past 10 years 190 million people were lifted out of poverty irrespective of the criterion or benchmark that you apply.

The alienation of the middle class is understandable, but why the party fared badly across rural India is not clear. Had it missed a fundamental change that India had moved from a welfare ethos howsoever it be packaged, to an aspirational one? The children of MGNREGA no longer sought subsistence but were itching to claim their place in middle- class India, interring the tendency to slot them into religious or caste denominations. This fact alone if properly evaluated without ideological biases would be the most important determinant in the course-correction exercise.

An argument has been put forth that the reverses were due to the inability to convey policies, programmes and achievements to the people. It must be remembered that perception is the alter ego of reality, and if the underlying conditions are unfavourable, facts cannot be spun beyond a point. Such naive assessments tantamount to shooting the messenger rather than decoding the message. It was a crisis of credibility and not of communication.

In conclusion, a few words about the diarchy of power between Dr Singh and Congress president Sonia Gandhi: Time will judge it to be a wise arrangement and history will vindicate its astuteness. While Mrs Gandhi managed the party and the politics of the UPA, she left the Prime Minister free to concentrate on governance. For 10 years it was the raison d'être of the UPA. Yes, the UPA lost rather badly but as Winston Churchill had said, "Success is not final, failure is not fatal: It is the courage to continue that counts".

The Rockefeller Moment

OVER THE PAST one year, the term "Rockefeller moment" has often been used to describe the genesis and trajectory of the current Bharatiya Janata Party-led National Democratic Alliance government. What does it really mean?

It was in the year of the Lord 1888 that US President Grover Cleveland, concerned over the pernicious influence of corporate enterprises, asserted, "Corporations which should be carefully restrained creatures of the law and servants of the people, are fast becoming the people's masters." In early 2008, after winning the Iowa caucus, Senator Barack Obama declared that he would free the US once and for all from the "tyranny of oil".

For over a century since, what egalitarians have been fighting is not a commodity but a maleficent tendency that has elevated brazen racketeering through the manipulation of public policy to a fine art. As one of Big Oil's notorious enforcers once remarked, "We make money by procuring policy". J Paul Getty of Getty Oil supplemented, "Money is like manure. You have to spread it around or it smells".

John DRockefeller founded the Standard Oil Company in 1870. In a decade, Standard Oil controlled 90 per cent of all refining in the US, 80 per cent of the marketing of oil products, a quarter of the

The Asian Age, 30 May, 2015

country's total crude output and, in that pre-automobile era, produced more than a quarter of the world's total supply of kerosene.

A broadsheet caricature from that era best crystallises the preponderant cronyism. It portrays the US Senate. Looming above the seated senators, three times their individual size, stand vulgarly corpulent men representing the corporations. Each one is dressed in top hat and tails. Standard Oil, the most overriding, is the only company depicted by name among the copper, iron, coal and railroad companies. Above them is a sign: "This is a senate of the monopolists, by the monopolists and for the monopolists". In one spot a miniscule sign reads "People's Entrance" below which is a padlocked gate marked "Closed".

Such was the all-encompassing embrace of these corporations that a legal text book from the time, *Leading Cases Simplified*, warned students, "Do not pay much head to the decisions of the courts of Pennsylvania—at least during the past 10 or 15 years. The Pennsylvania Railroad appears to run the tribunals with the same success that it does its own trains". An overwhelming groundswell of people's action mobilised itself against the maleficent ways of the corporations and the first anti-trust laws were forged.

Explaining the rationale of the Antitrust Act on the Senate floor, Senator Sherman of Ohio, whose name the Act carried, declared, "If we will not endure a king as a political power, we should not endure a king over the production, transportation and the sale of any of the necessities of life. If we would not submit to an emperor, we should not submit to an autocrat of trade, with power to prevent competition and to fix the price of any commodity... The inequality of condition, of wealth and opportunity has grown within a single generation out of the concentration of capital into vast combinations to control production and breakdown competition. The people of the United States as well as other countries are feeling the power and grasp of these combinations, and are demanding of every legislature a remedy of this evil..." Senator George Hoar of Massachusetts opined that the gravest evil of our times is the accumulation of vast fortunes and properties in single hands.

The Sherman Antitrust Act was enacted as an explicit response to concerns that humungous business interests were emasculating government. It was therefore designed to restrain economic wealth from becoming political power. In 1911, the US government, exercising powers under the Sherman Antitrust Act broke up Standard Oil into 34 separate companies. Now cut to India of 2015. Does the context not ring a bell? Isn't the government of the corporates, for the corporates, by the corporates well and truly here? India's Rockefeller moment has arrived, 135 years later, riding on the coattails of 25 years of economic liberalisation that has created evil empires that span the length and breadth of the mercantile expanse. India is exactly where the US was at the turn of the 19th century.

The most discernible anecdotal evidence of this is the fact that senior government functionaries are now invariably seen pontificating from corporate platforms. Rarely do we see them on the stage of a people's movement or even a public university. A new belief system seems to be taking root in the current political dispensation—that corporates with their moneybags and control over instruments of information dissemination can make or mar governments.

Notwithstanding the results of the Assembly elections in Delhi, the pendulum is still swinging in favour of corporate benefaction. What this does is that it changes the reference point of decision-makers. No longer do the concerns of the common man remain the focus in designing policy or legislation; it is the preponderance of converged corporate interests that are regarded as ultimate. The sovereign in the process is relegated to the margins.

The second and the most lethal stage of the corporatisation of a government is the movement from lobbying to legislating. This happens through the placement of key personnel in government and then the entire institutional clock starts ticking to an entirely new and different rhythm. Listen carefully. The carpetbaggers are at the door, not desperate to get their crooked feet in, but to stamp their entire grotesque persona across the government space.

During the Bush-Cheney years, Big Oil was able to wangle its appointees into even the environmental bodies, notwithstanding the fact that it is the Earth's biggest polluter. Compare that with the systematic destruction of environmental safeguards that has been taking place over the past one year in the name of development by the BJP government. Distilled environmental jurisprudence is being thrown to the wolves. Another manifestation of this is not just the substance of some of the government's recent decisions, but even the style. The manner in which ordinances are being re-promulgated is as much to gerrymander the legislative processes, as it is to placate the impatient corporate sponsors.

The flak that the government has been receiving recently is not so much a measure of the disillusionment of the people, who in any case realise that they have been sold a pup, it is, in fact, the capitalists firing a warning shot. Getting restless to taste the carrots dangled prior to the elections, their message is stark: if we could make you, we can also break you. Civil associations that tell the truth to power are being emasculated through every legal and extra-legal measure, whether it is the Foreign Contribution Regulation Act, 2010 (FCRA) or the denial of the right to travel that is an inalienable part of the right to life guaranteed by Article 21 of the Constitution. What is unfolding is extremely dangerous for any democracy. When corporates overtly begin taking sides in politics, they do not remain companies. They become politicians and a different set of rules needs to be applied to them. The time has come for India to seriously think of an innovative variant of antitrust measures to preclude financial muscle from acquiring political supremacy. Conglomerates must be brought to heel.

Antitrust is very different from the Competition Act, 2002, that created the Competition Commission India. The mandate of the commission is to keep the market at an even keel by regulating anti-competitive agreements, abuse of dominant position by enterprises and merger and acquisition processes. What gives corporations political and financial muscle is their sheer size, the horizontal and vertical crossholdings across the expanse of business space. It brings with it delusions of grandeur in most cases.

They need to be broken down into manageable entities so that while they are free to engage in entrepreneurial activity, they do not threaten democracy. Just as Standard Oil was broken up in 1911 and the Bell system in the telecom arena in 1982, India needs to seriously look across the conglomerate realm and identify those whose insolence would make even Rockefeller turn in his grave. Any guesses who the Indian Rockefeller is?

The Bose enigma

THE JAWAHARLAL NEHRU government spied on Netaji Subhas Chandra Bose's family for 20 years has been the refrain for the past week. This hypothesis rests on the presumption that the Nehru government and its successors were not convinced about Bose's death and, therefore, insecure about his return to India. The evidence that has been put forth in the public domain about Nehru's individual interest in the matter is a note from the then Prime Minister dated November 25, 1957, addressed to the then foreign secretary, Subimal Dutt, enquiring about the activities of Bose's nephew, Amiya Nath Bose in Japan.

A dispassionate examination of the facts and then the conjectures may be in order. On the night of January 16-17, 1941, Bose escaped from his home in Calcutta and reached Berlin on April 3, 1941, to seek the support of the Nazis for India's liberation. At the time of his departure, relations between Bose and the Congress leadership were at the nadir. He had resigned as the president of the Congress on April 29, 1939, and later formed the Forward Bloc that really did not take off as he had expected. After staying in Germany for two years, he left empty-handed for Japan in February 1943. He was unable to persuade Adolf Hitler to issue a declaration recognising the right of

---

The Asian Age, 18 April, 2015

the Indian people to full and complete independence. In the July of 1943, he took over the reins of the Indian National Army (INA) that had been created a year earlier by Gen Mohan Singh and his associates after the British surrendered Singapore to the Japanese.

While Bose was in Berlin attempting to persuade the Nazis about the legitimacy of Indian aspirations and his centrality in realising them, events in the Allied camp were moving rapidly. Desperate for American assistance in the fight against the Axis powers, the British Prime Minister, Winston Churchill, was compelled by the American President, Franklin Delano Roosevelt, to sign the Atlantic Charter on August 12, 1941, that inter alia recognised the right of all peoples to choose the form of government under which they would live. This was widely seen as an outright negation of the imperialistic and colonialist practices of even those European powers that were fighting against the German-Italian and later Japanese Axis.

In fact, President Roosevelt wrote two very compelling letters to Prime Minister Churchill on March 11 and April 12, 1942, urging him to hand over the reins of India to the Indians. In the latter communication, following the British chicanery over the Cripps Mission that provided the trigger for the Quit India Movement, Roosevelt chastised Churchill stating, "The feeling is held almost universally that the deadlock has been due to the British government's unwillingness to concede the right of self-government to the Indians notwithstanding the willingness of the Indians to entrust to the competent British authorities, technical, military and naval defence control." These letters are reproduced in Churchill's six-volume history of the Second World War. The significance of these developments would not have been lost on Bose.

Moving back to the INA, the only significant action it saw in the Indian context was in the battles of Imphal and Kohima in April 1944. Though the Indian forces were able to plant the national flag at Moirang, soon they had to retreat and Bose was constrained to announce the failure of the Imphal offensive by a radio broadcast from Rangoon on August 21, 1944. Also, the personnel of the INA were not treated well by the Japanese. But the tide of war was turning against the Axis powers. In May 1945, Germany surrendered, and in August

Japan too capitulated after two atomic bomb attacks that destroyed the cities of Hiroshima and Nagasaki. Thus, Bose found himself on the side of the vanquished.

Now let us turn to the conjectures. For the sake of argument, if it is assumed that after dissolving the INA on August 17, 1945, as per some historical accounts, Bose had come back to India, what may have happened? He, perhaps, would have been another important player on India's political firmament, especially since he would have been the lead defendant in the INA trails.

However, it may be worth recalling that the Forward Bloc that he had started was unsuccessful in even uniting all the radicals and Left groups—all of whom preferred to maintain their distinct identities. The best that was achieved was a Left coordination committee of which Bose became the chairperson before he escaped from his home in Calcutta in 1941 and arrived in Berlin via Kabul and Moscow. It, therefore, may be a bit of a stretch to assume that Messers Nehru, Gandhi and the Congress felt threatened or insecure about Bose and, therefore, put his family under surveillance after his whereabouts became enigmatic. After all, they all had dealt with and had a fair sense of each other's respective strengths and weaknesses. In any case, Bose's real difference of opinion was with Gandhi and not so much with Nehru.

Even if it were presumed that the plane crash in Taipei on August 18 was a smoke screen to facilitate his escape and he was indeed headed to the Soviet Union to resurrect the struggle, Bose would have been aware of the Soviet attitude towards him. In his book, *Nehru and Bose: Parallel Lives*, Rudrangshu Mukherjee writes: "Berlin was not Subhas's first choice. On Subhas's arrival in Kabul, Talwar who was with him, made attempts to contact the Soviet ambassador but failed. It was then that Subhas gatecrashed into the German embassy. He had a better reception there." Mukherjee further elaborates, "After what for Subhas was an agonising wait, he left Kabul on March 18, 1941, for Moscow en route to Berlin. He arrived in Moscow on March 31 and left for Berlin the same day." It is evident that Bose had no expectations from the Soviet Union and had no relationship with the Soviet leadership.

After the invasion of the Soviet Union by Germany on June 22, 1941, when Bose was in Berlin, and the subsequent declaration of war by the Soviet Union even on Japan on August 8, 1945, merely 10 days before the purported air crash, Bose would have been well aware that he would perhaps not be very welcome in the Soviet Union which had by then lost 26.6 million people in the war. Even his exertions to establish contact with the Soviet ambassador in Tokyo, Jacob Malik, were thwarted by the Japanese. Thus, if he was indeed travelling to Dairen in Manchuria, then Bose was flying in the fog of war.

There is another tittle-tattle that has been spread—that the Congress leadership prevailed on Joseph Stalin to neutralise Bose. In the years before and immediately after India's Independence, Stalin had a very low estimation of the Indian nationalist leadership. He would use colourful epithets like "running dogs of imperialism" to describe them. He believed that both India and Pakistan were appendages of Anglo-American imperialism. In fact, chroniclers recount that Stalin ostensibly refused to grant an audience to free India's first representative to the Soviet Union, Vijaya Lakshmi Pandit, who was Nehru's real sister. Under these circumstances, even such a charge can only be termed as comical.

Finally, why should Nehru have been interested in Amiya Bose's activities in Japan? Like Germany, Japan also carried the "war guilt" heavily on its conscience. The atrocities perpetrated by the marauding Japanese during the Second World War still touch a raw nerve in large parts of Southeast Asia. For a country that was attempting to shake off that legacy, it is unlikely that it wanted to be reminded of its war associations. Moreover, on October 19, 1956, Japan had re-established diplomatic relations with the Soviet Union and was demanding the reversion of Okinawa and Bonin islands that were under US control. There were also issues about war criminals convicted in the Tokyo trials. Nehru, who was attempting to structure a third way away from Bloc politics and believed in Asian solidarity, possibly saw an opportunity to bring the Japanese within his ambit. He, therefore, may have been apprehensive of any Indian activity that delved into a past that Japan was attempting to surmount. The reason for the query could be as innocuous as this. Whatever the real story, time has come to declassify all files pertaining to Bose so that blasts from the past finally stop feeding fevered imaginations.

A flawed re-discovery of India

AS THE EVENTS around Jawaharlal Nehru's 125th birth anniversary draw to a close, it is perhaps an appropriate occasion to revisit the Nehruvian construct and understand why it is under a sustained assault today.

The genesis of the Nehruvian construct lies in the Indian liberation struggle, a battle that led to Nehru's incarceration for close to a decade and, perhaps, provided him with the time and space to write some great books. The ideology that underpinned that battle rested on three pillars: sovereignty rooted in anti-imperialism, commitment to a secular and inclusive democracy and an economic vision that embraced the emancipation of the last person in the last row. Taken together they constitute what is referred to as "the idea of India".

The India that Nehru inherited in 1947 was in a global context, where on one hand imperialism and colonialism were being swept away by the tide of liberation, with over 150-odd countries becoming independent in Fifties and Sixties, while on the other, 51 member states that founded the United Nations in 1945 were, within one year, with the onset of the Cold war, united in blocs rather than peace. This reality was underpropped by a nuclear holocaust in Japan that signposted the pecking order post World War II.

The Asian Age, 14 November, 2015

Nehru chose the non-alignment paradigm as it organically grew out of the rejection of the dominance model that had characterised India's quest for Independence. Not only did it provide India a platform to emerge as a leader of the new world, but the large swathe of newly emerged Asian and African nations provided a counterbalance to the Euro-centricity of global affairs.

From the Asian Relations conference in 1947 till this moment in time, non-alignment has provided us with the flexibility of taking positions based upon "enlightened" national interest. From the treaty with the Soviet Union in 1971 to the US civil nuclear deal of 2008, this policy has stood India in good stead. As the world moves towards multi-polarity and India has to nimbly navigate a conundrum of conflicting interests on issues like climate change, the mayhem in West Asia and belligerence in the South China Sea, it helps not being tied to a bloc.

The economy that Nehru inherited had had virtually zero per cent growth from 1900 to 1947. Per capita income had shrunk by 0.2 per cent, agricultural output by 0.72 per cent and foodgrain production by 11.4 per cent on an annual basis between 1917 and 1947.

Three million people had perished in a famine in undivided Bengal alone. The British rulers diverted grain to the war zones during the Second World War without trepidation for the starvation and suffering that it caused in India. In 1947, the illiteracy rate was 84 per cent, and higher at 92 per cent among women. The average life expectancy was about 30 years and the poor died younger. At the time of Independence, 90 per cent of machines and machine tools were being imported from abroad.

What did the Fabian Socialist Nehru achieve? Between 1951 and 1965, the Indian economy grew at an average of 4.10 per cent annually. During the same period that coincided with the three Five-Year plans, industry grew at 7.1 per cent per annum. The Index of Industrial Production grew three-fold between 1951 and 1969. There was a 70 per cent increase in the consumer goods industry, quadrupling of intermediate goods and a tenfold increase in the output of capital goods in that decade and a half. Social development and human life indices also started a positive march. These numbers are perhaps a fitting riposte to all those neo-liberal economists who preach that the first 40 years of Independence were the locust years.

How did India remain democratic when a bulk of the newly Independent states of Asia, Africa, and even Latin and South America, either fell victim to a military dictatorship or the tutelage of one party rule? While the flame of democracy burnt bright in the souls of the leadership of the Indian liberation movement, Nehru, as Prime Minister, set an example by showing exemplary tolerance to criticism by his parliamentary and other peers both in the Opposition and within the party. That India did not become a Hindu Pakistan after Partition is perhaps best summed up by Nehru himself in his very first letter to the Prime Ministers (Chief as they were then called) of the provinces on October 13, 1947, while the nation was still engulfed in a communal cauldron.

Nehru wrote: "I know there is a certain amount of feeling in the country—how strong it is in your province you can judge better than I can—that the Central government has somehow or other been weak and following a policy of appeasement towards Muslims. This, of course, is complete nonsense. There is no question of weakness or appeasement. We have a Muslim minority who are so large in numbers that they cannot, even if they want to, go anywhere else. They have got to live in India. That is a basic fact about which there can be no argument. Whatever the provocation from Pakistan and whatever the indignities and horrors inflicted on non-Muslims there, we have got to deal with this minority in a civilised manner. We must give them security and the rights of citizens in a democratic state. If we fail to do so, we shall have a festering sore which will eventually poison the whole body politic and probably destroy it."

Nehru was a pragmatist. He understood that given the sheer demographics, if some lunatic wanted India to become a "Hindu Rashtra", it would be at the cost of a bloodbath that would make the horrors of Partition look like a picnic. Moreover, though he may have acquiesced to a communal Partition, he was intellectually opposed to the idea that religion was anything more than a private space activity. His definition of secularism began and ended with the strict separation of the church and state unlike the fuzzy "Sarv Dharm Sambhav" that it morphed into and which became the cause of a lot of India's problems subsequently.

It is often overlooked, that far from being a Muslim appeaser, Nehru was the one who had opposed the appointment of only Muslims belonging to the Muslim League as ministers in the Provincial governments in 1936. Many believe that this became the trigger for the subsequent Partition of India. For Nehru this was an article of creed, of not conceding a veto over public affairs to religious bigotry represented at that point in time by political Islam. This is the Nehruvian narrative that has held the field for the past 67 years that is now under a systematic, calibrated, sustained and diabolical assault by the present dispensation, which believes that history began the day they assumed office on May 26, 2014. In its place the National Democratic Alliance/ Bharatiya Janata Party government, and their ideological mentors and fellow travellers want to establish a historical narrative which emphasises that the Aryans, Harappans included, were Indians and they did not come from Central Asia.

They want to delegitimise adivasis—the eternal inhabitants of this ancient land—by turning them into Vanvasis (forest people), thereby creating a quixotic mythology of evolution. This is in direct contra-distinction to the historical narrative of India articulated by Nehru in his book *The Discovery of India,* and other distinguished historians who have written about South Asia.They want to cast Indian nationalism in a uni-racial, uni-lingual and uni-religious framework that challenges the diversity and plurality of India and its struggle for Independence which was a multi-religious and multi-ethnic affair.

They want to create a clash of religions by making common cause between Hinduism and the so-called Indic religion and juxtapose them against Islam and Christianity. A "Clash of Civilisations"—indigenised. They want to unify the Hindu faith by de-emphasising caste differences by changing the basis of affirmative action, while foregrounding Sanskrit as the mother of all languages, thereby creating linguistic hegemony, completely overlooking that some of the south Indian languages like Tamil, Malayalam, etc., may even predate Sanskrit.

The shrill and sharp conflict in the public discourse over intolerance is, in fact, the public manifestation of a confrontation against a larger and more insidious agenda that is to change the basic ethos and storyline of India. From a liberal, pluralistic, tolerant and inclusive ethos to a majoritarian, intolerant, misogynist and exclusivist social more.

In the coming three and a half years, the Nehruvian narrative will face a robust challenge. The tragedy, unfortunately, is that many of the defenders of Nehru's legacy, his ideological inheritors, have not cared to read, much less understand and absorb, Nehru's beliefs.

Pulp patriotism

ON THE EVENING of April 7, 1775, the British man of letters Samuel Johnson made a rather prophetic assertion. He said and I quote: "Patriotism is the last refuge of a scoundrel." The statement was about the false use of the term "patriotism" by William Pitt, the first Earl of Chatham (the patriot minister) and his supporters. The context is apt to describe the trigger happy response of the Central government to l'affaire Jawaharlal Nehru University.

While the slogans raised by a bunch of students to mark the third anniversary of the implementation of capital punishment awarded to Afzal Guru are certainly undesirable, by no stretch of the law do they constitute criminality, much less sedition. It has been over 11 days since the said incident took place and the Centre is still scrambling for evidence to substantiate the sedition charge that was levelled against Kanhaiya Kumar, the president of the JNU students' union, who continues to be wrongfully incarcerated. For the law on sedition as laid down by the Supreme Court in a catena of judgments from Kehar Singh to Shreya Singhal is very clear. Allegedly seditious speech and expression may be punished only if the speech is an incitement to violence or public disorder. In fact, in the latter case that struck down Section 66A of the Information Technology Act, 2000, the Supreme

The Asian Age, 20 February, 2016

Court even drew a distinction between "advocacy and incitement". In the JNU matter there was no encouragement to violence or even provocation to create disorder. That begs a fundamental question as to why did the Centre resort to the use of the most draconian section in Indian criminal law — a provision that none other than Mahatma Gandhi described as the "prince among the political sections of the Indian Penal Code designed to suppress the liberty of the citizen".

For if the pulp patriotism of the Bharatiya Janata Party was indeed something more than chicanery, then they should break their alliance with the Akali Dal in Punjab as the current Chief Minister Parkash Singh Badal's political party was routinely involved in burning of the Indian Constitution in the early '80s. In fact, on February 27, 1984, Mr Badal personally led a band of protesters who burnt copies of Article 25(2)(b) of the Indian Constitution outside Parliament — an offence far more heinous than raising anti-India slogans. Similarly, in Assam, the party that the BJP was negotiating to tie up with, the Asom Gana Parishad (AGP), had on August 19, burnt copies of the 119th Constitutional Amendment Bill to protest against the Land Boundary Agreement with Bangladesh that Mr Modi now claims as a feather in his cap. Earlier, during the Assam agitation in the early'80s, the All Assam Students Union, the progenitor of the AGP, was equally creative in its protests.

Similarly, the People's Democratic Party (PDP), with whom the BJP was running an alliance government in J&K till yesterday ,had, as late as March 3, 2015, in a written statement declared: "PDP has always maintained that late Afzal Guru's hanging was a travesty of justice and constitutional requirements and process was not followed in hanging him out of turn… PDP stands by the demand for return of his (Guru's) mortal remains, and the party promises to follow vigorously for the return of the mortal remains. We believe that the resolution brought by Engineer Rashid to seek clemency for late Afzal Guru was justified and should have been adopted by the house at that time."

It is typical of the BJP to have one standard in Delhi and another in Srinagar. However, what is far more portentous is the flimflam of the BJP-led National Democratic Alliance government. While it has no hesitation in sending its police into women's hostels in JNU, ostensibly searching for anti-national elements, it is equally blasé about announcing half-baked accords like the one with the National Socialist Council of Nagaland (Isak-Muivah) in August 2015. The NSCN(IM) has been waging a war against the Indian state for decades. If the government has such a huge problem with slogans shouted by some students, how is it so nonchalant about negotiating with armed insurgents?

However, what took the cake was home minister Rajnath Singh saying that there was a Lashkar-e-Tayyaba (LeT) link to the incident in the JNU. It was based upon certain tweets emanating from the account of Hafiz Saeed, the godfather of all Punjab-based terrorist groups in Pakistan, that have a purely India focus. Saeed later disowned the tweets as well as the account itself. Having served in the United Progressive Alliance government, I am well aware that the government has the capacity to track social media. It can not be the case that officials would not have informed Mr Singh about the veracity of the account that he decided to use to point a finger at non-state actors in Pakistan.

Given all these apparent contradictions, why is it that the government tried to frame the entire issue in the nationalist qua traitor paradigm. First and foremost, the progenitor of the BJP, the Rashtriya Swayamsevak Sangh, has a visceral hatred for the JNU. Many RSS and BJP leaders have used the choicest epithets to describe the university with one "eminence" of the RSS labelling it as the Centre of intellectual terrorism in a TV debate with me on February 18. If the RSS has its way, it would shut the university down, lock stock and barrel and throw the keys into the Bay of Bengal.

Second, the Centre believes that by taking the low road of jingoism it can label every censure of the government, not as anti-BJP or anti-NDA, but as anti-national. Anybody with even a nodding acquaintance with the consolidation of Nazism is Germany between 1933 and 1936 after Adolf Hitler seized power would see the same pattern playing itself out in India over the past 20 months. For the first thing that the thugs of the Waffen-SS did was to go after every writer, teacher, playwright, filmmaker, and any other intellectual, that it considered hostile to the ideological mould they wanted to cast Germany in.

The third, and perhaps the most important, is that the RSS-BJP feels that this is the one chance that they have got after 67 years of

Independence to change the fundamental narrative of India. Since 1947, there have been two competing visions of India. The liberal, progressive, pluralist idea of India as articulated and implemented by the founding fathers of the Indian Constitution and the majoritarian, theocratic and obscurantist worldview that seeks to convert India into a monolithic "Hindu Rashtra" conveniently ignoring the intrinsic diversity of the Hindu faith. The appointment of fellow travellers to institutions like the Central Board of Film Certification, the Film and Television Institute of India, the Indian Council of Historical Research, despite stiff opposition from the stakeholders ,and the hounding of a young student to suicide on the campus of Hyderabad University are but manifestations of this insidious design.

However, the intrinsic lack of sophistication in implementing a devious project of transforming the basis of a nation exposes their ineptitude as nothing else does, making them objects of ridicule if not mirth. For example, the knee-jerk diktat by the "highly academically qualified" human resource development minister Smriti Irani in response to the developments in JNU. Ms Irani directed that the national flag must be flown in all Central universities as if it did not earlier. Perhaps, it would have been better if the government had advised the RSS to unfurl the Tricolour once in a while at their headquarters in Nagpur or in their offices across India.

In November 2013, at the International Film Festival of India in Goa, I had cautioned the creative community that the ominous drumbeats of fascism are growing louder and a great evil would soon stalk our land. They would squeeze the liberal spaces in the country, stamp out the right to dissent and crush the alternative narrative by misusing the instrumentalities of the state. The prophecy is unfortunately coming true. For when you sow the wind you reap the whirlwind and stopping this pulp patriotism from consuming India would require a lot of good men and women to step up to the plate.

On the brink of an abyss

IN A YEAR from now the border state of Punjab would be in the midst of its most crucial electoral battle, a fight that would determine whether the state would embark on a long haul for returning to the path of holistic governance or descend into further chaos. Political change in the state is almost a given now after the coming elections, but the nature of that change is critical for various reasons. However, before talking about the alternatives for the state, it may be much more appropriate to remind readers the reasons for the collapse of the state under the Akali-BJP government that has been ruling it for the last decade.

First, the economic and fiscal crisis has turned Punjab into one of the most indebted and debt-stressed states in the country. By the end of 2015-16, the state would be in debt to the tune of $18.79 billion (1 dollar=Rs 66) approximately. Ten years ago, in the last year of the then Congress government, it stood at $7.73 billion.

The debt constitutes over 30% of the Gross State Domestic Product. Twenty-one per cent of all revenue receipts go towards servicing it. While the government would like to blame it on the legacy liability of fighting terrorism, it needs to be remembered that active militancy in the state ended way back in 1995. The current situation is a result of

---

The Hindustan Times, 05 January, 2016

economic mismanagement, financial licentiousness and crass populism over the past decade. With a committed interest liability of $1.5 billion per year, Punjab is caught in a debt trap. This has demolished business sentiment, leading to a flight of capital from the state.

Second, the agrarian crisis. Agriculture, the principal occupation of the people, is no longer a remunerative vocation. As I had earlier pointed out conventional wisdom holds that 84% of the farmers own less than five acres of land. A family of four or five toiling ceaselessly on a three-acre plot of land can in a good year at best make about Rs 19,350 per month but if there is any unnatural occurrence, there can be a severe drop in income for farmers. A recent example is the whitefly pest attack in southern Punjab that led to dozens of cotton farmers committing suicide.

Third is the narcotisation of the state that has wiped out a generation of young adults. Punjab lost a generation to terror between 1980 and 1995 and is now losing another to drugs. The state apparatus, from the highest echelons to the lowest functionaries are allegedly deeply entrenched in the production, sale and proliferation of synthetic drugs. Over 75% of the youth in the state are addicted to one fatal psychotropic substance or the other.

The fourth is the complete subversion of the law enforcement machinery of the state. It started with police sub-divisions being made congruent to assembly constituencies and the in-charge of the sub-division (usually a deputy superintendent of police) being appointed on the recommendation of the ruling party MLA, or its defeated candidates designated as the constituency in-charge. The police hierarchy has been obliterated with the deputy chief minister, who is also the scion of the ruling oligarchy, giving instructions directly to police station heads who are usually in the rank of assistant sub-inspectors of police. This subversion of the structure of the uniformed forces has converted the Punjab Police into a virtual front organisation for the Akali Dal-BJP government.

Latest reports suggest even development funding is now being arbitrarily outsourced to elected and defeated political activists of the ruling combine, bypassing all established channels of the civil administration.

The fifth challenge is the sudden resurgence of the separatist fringe in the state. The mishandling of the sacrilege issue as well as the controversy on the question of a religious pardon granted to the head of Dera Sacha Sauda has provided space to the hardliners to reassert themselves. There has always been a minuscule but vocal minority that has clung to the dream of a separate Sikh homeland, mistakenly believing and erroneously propagating that when India was partitioned in 1947, the Hindus got Hindustan, the Muslims got Pakistan but the Sikhs got a raw deal. Their intermittent dormancy should not be misconstrued as permanent redundancy as they have a resonance with some influential elements of the Sikh diaspora that provide both moral and material support to their activities. This phenomenon will be more visibly seen this time around.

Sixth, recent revelations about alleged fake encounters during the decade-and-a-half of extremism that point a finger at certain officers of the Punjab Police. If these revelations are correct, then those involved would have to face the legal system because state terrorism cannot be accepted. It is a travesty that officers facing heinous criminal charges for gross human rights abuse continue to occupy the highest positions in the state police. In addition to the domestic turmoil, Punjab is also a frontline border state that is always in Pakistan's cross hairs, as can be seen in the Pathankot outrage.

What Punjab requires at the moment is resuscitation of the normal governance processes. It can ill afford to experiment with the AAP's ochlocracy that is on display in Delhi. There is only one template for decent governance in Punjab: A competent administrator that can run the state and impartially protect its interests.

PART B

India and the World: Issues and Challenges

I. A Problem called Pakistan

The Baloch question

WITH THE foreign secretary level talks between India and Pakistan being iced due to the meeting between Kashmiri separatists and the Pakistani high commissioner, it may be worth recalling an episode from contemporaneous history. On July 16, 2009, at Sharm el-Sheikh in Egypt, one line in a joint statement issued after the meeting of former Prime Minister Manmohan Singh with his Pakistani counterpart, Syed Yousaf Raza Gilani, set off a firestorm in India. The line read as follows: "Prime Minister Gilani mentioned that Pakistan had some information on threats in Balochistan and other areas".

All manner of adjectives were mobilised to characterise this inclusion in the joint statement as a sell out. It was alleged that India had allowed Pakistan's proxy war in Jammu and Kashmir be equated with Pakistan's oblique insinuation about purported Indian meddling in Balochistan. Interestingly, the ubiquitous "K" word was not even mentioned in the joint statement except a rather ambiguous reference to all outstanding issues. In fact, India should have seized the opening provided by Pakistan as it is in India's interest to discuss the situation in Balochistan. This region bestrides three countries—Pakistan, Iran and Afghanistan—all of whom are of strategic consequence to India.

A historical overview of the Baloch question may be in order to provide perspective to the issues involved. Informed opinion suggests

---

The Asian Age, 23 August, 2014

that the Baloch Nationalist Movement has an antiquity that dates back two millennia. However, analysts put the origins of the struggle down to the late 19th century when the rivalry between the British and the Russian imperialists impelled the first British invasion of Afghanistan between 1839 and 1842. This brought the British in contact with the princely state of Kalat that comprises modern day Balochistan.

However, the British were rather prudent though persnickety about prying into the internal affairs of princely states and it was only on August 15, 1947, when the Khan of Kalat declared his independence from the state of Pakistan that had come into existence a day earlier, that trouble really commenced. Pakistan, of course, rejected the declaration ,and nine months later Kalat was forcibly appropriated into Pakistan. Baloch nationalists did not take this annexation kindly. In 1948, and then again in 1958 and 1962, encounters of fluctuating force took place between the Pakistani state and Baloch autonomists.

However, from 2005 onwards, a full-scale unrest commenced, triggered by the rape of a doctor, Shazia Khalid, allegedly by Pakistani security forces in the town of Sui, where the provinces of Punjab, Sind and Balochistan meet. The Pakistani state reacted to the insurrection in the same manner as it had attempted to stamp out the Bangladeshi liberation struggle in 1971. Alleged "kill and dump" operations, as they are colloquially referred to, let loose a wave of oppression and repression. Enforced disappearances became the norm rather than the exception. The killing of Akbar Bugti, the leader of the Baloch Republican Party by the Pakistani Army in 2006, is a poignant case in point. Nasrullah Baloch, the chairperson of the Voice for Balochistan Missing Persons, puts the number of missing persons at 23,000 according to a statement attributed to him on the South Asian Terrorism Portal, though the portal, based on partial data compiled by it, puts the civilian fatalities at 3,073 since 2004.

The moot point being that the human rights of the Baloch people are being seriously trampled upon by the Pakistani state. When India can host the Tibetan government in exile in Dharamsala, express solidarity with Aung San Suu Kyi, vote for the Tamil minorities in Sri Lanka and the Palestinians at the UNHRC, should the Baloch people be treated differently? Should India at least not bilaterally raise it with Pakistan if not at multilateral settings?

Even from a purely strategic perspective, Balochistan is also home to the port of Gwadar that lies at the mouth of the Persian Gulf just outside the Straits of Hormuz. On February 18, 2013, Pakistan transferred the control of this strategic asset to China, giving it the ability to project power and, if required, even dominate the Sea Lines of Commerce through which the bulk of the world's energy supplies transit.

The Chinese are already contemplating building an LNG terminal with pipelines from Gwadar to MP 250, a point on the Iran-Pakistan border, and Gwadar to Kashgar in western China. The latter pipeline is ostensibly supposed to transit through those parts of the state of J&K that are in illegitimate possession of Pakistan and further unlawfully ceded to China. The proposed pipeline notwithstanding, the technological challenges would allow China to simultaneously surmount both the Hormuz and Malacca "dilemmas" and would add another dimension to the already complex strategic situation in the Sino-Pak-India triangulation. Does this not warrant a discussion with Pakistan and, for that matter, even with China as to what would be the implications of these developments on India?

With triple transitions at play in Afghanistan, chaos and the rise of radicalism in Balochistan would have a direct impact on the two most fragile provinces of Afghanistan—Helmand and Kandahar that adjoin it. This is a consequence of a policy of years of Islamisation followed by the Pakistani state's attempt to erase the Baloch identity and overlay it with an Islamic one. A large number of sectarian and terrorist outfits are not only active but are now based there, riding on the back of a string of madrasas, especially on the borders. They include, and are not limited to, the Lashkar-e-Jhangvi, Sipah-e-Muhammad, the Tablighi Jamaat and both the Afghan and Pakistan Taliban, all of whom have a pernicious Pan-Islamic agenda. Since India has a stake in a stable and peaceful Afghanistan, is it not imperative that in conjunction with other stakeholders who have similar priorities, there be a sombre conversation with Pakistan as to how its internal dynamics can potentially destabilise efforts of the international community in securing Afghanistan?

While it needs to be made abundantly clear that India does not have even the remotest interest in the secession of Balochistan, the fact is that, contrary to all allegations that have been levelled till now, Pakistan has not been able to furnish evidence of any Indian involvement to that effect. In retrospect, was Sharm el-Sheikh then not a missed opportunity to put Balochistan on the table? Does obtuse opposition not jeopardise national interest? Should Balochistan not figure on the agenda in the Indo-Pak dialogue?

PS: This was written two full years before the Prime Minister of India chose to raise the Baloch issue from the ramparts of the Red Fort on 15 August, 2016.

Pakistanisation of India

ARE THERE ANY takeaways for India from the sickening slaughter of hundreds of innocent school children, teachers and other enablers at the Army school in Peshawar? Was it an act of utter depravity by the Tehrik-e-Taliban Pakistan which underscores that no abomination is beyond them? Was it unfortunately a cataclysm waiting to happen with the cycle of violence becoming all the more brutal in Pakistan? To answer these questions one has to take a step back into history. A recap is imperative to contextualise the chronicle.

It all began four decades ago, after the liberation of Bangladesh in 1971. Pakistan, that had been formed in the name of religion, tore itself apart in the name of ethnicity. The West Pakistani Punjabi was not able to accommodate the East Pakistani Bengali. The flower of the Pakistani Army—90,000 officers and men became Indian prisoners of war. The largest number in any single conflict, post the Second World War. Pakistan was aching for revenge.

Fully cognisant that India held the strategic advantage in conventional military terms around the middle of the Seventies, Pakistan honed a three-pronged approach. The first was the quest to acquire nuclear arms ominously articulated in the words of late Zulifkar Ali Bhutto: "Pakistanis will eat grass but we will get a nuclear

---

The Asian Age, 27 December, 2014

bomb". The second was the journey to Islamise the Pakistani armed forces and the larger social milieu in an attempt to define the identity of Pakistan by Gen Zia-ul-Haq. The third was the mission to bleed India with a thousand cuts.

By the beginning of the Eighties, all three projects were well underway. AQ Khan, ably assisted by the Pakistani intelligence services, was stealing nuclear technology wherever it could be purloined from. The transformation of the Pakistani armed forces from an institution incubated in British traditions to an Islamic military was on a roll. A proxy war against India, first targeting Punjab and, by the late Eighties, encompassing Jammu and Kashmir was being implemented.

What proved to be providential for the Pakistani establishment through the Eighties and later became their Achilles' heal was its voluntary enrolment as a frontline cat's-paw in the West's cold -hot war against the Soviet occupation of Afghanistan ubiquitously referred to as the "Afghan jihad".

Advantageous—because it gave Pakistan access to billions of dollars and sophisticated weaponry that it was able to divert into funding and equipping its proxy war with India. Expedient—because it provided the human resource in the form of internally displaced Afghans who had crossed over from Afghanistan to Pakistan to execute its diabolical agenda. Disastrous—because the legacy of those years—the use of religious institutions to radicalise young minds to keep the human resource for the Afghan jihad and the proxy war against India flowing, coupled with the adoption of terror as an instrument of state policy has brought Pakistan to the state it finds itself in today.

By the end of the Eighties, the Cold War had ended,. The Soviets went back over the Amu Darya, but Pakistan could not dismount the tiger it had willingly straddled petrified that it would devour it. Pakistan, therefore, did what it thought would provide it strategic depth: unleashing the Taliban on the war ravaged people of Afghanistan and broadening the proxy war with terrorist strikes deep into Indian mainland.

By the time the millennium turned, the Al Qaeda had already attacked American assets worldwide from its safe havens in Afghanistan.

On September 11, 2001, Al Qaeda launched the most audacious outrage on the American mainland that dwarfed even Pearl Harbour. The Americans came back to the Afghanistan they had abandoned a decade ago. Pakistan, under the threat of being bombed back to the Stone Age, was again a frontline state in the notorious "war against terror", overcharging and shortchanging its allies simultaneously.

In this process, the major fatality was the collective ethos of Pakistan. To sustain these multiple conflicts, Pakistan had to demonise other nations and peoples, especially India. It had to patronise multiple terrorist groups. What it did not perhaps visualise is that when hate and negative energy begin to override national impulses, then all that you are doing is traipsing on the edges of a catastrophe. That is the tale of Pakistan over the past four decades.

This is exactly the tutorial that the Bharatiya Janata Party government, its fellow travellers and doctrinal mentors need to absorb. Ever since this government came into existence, it has left no stone unturned to polarise society. From "love jihad" to religious conversions they have run the entire gauntlet. What is playing out is a very insidious attempt at the "Pakistanisation" of India. Just as in the late Seventies, President Zia-ul-Haq erroneously thought that the idea of Pakistan should begin and end with a strictly circumscribed Islamic identity, similarly, our home grown zealots speciously think that the philosophical postulate that should underpin the Indian identity should be that of a "Hindu rashtra".

The reason why the idea of India survived and has thrived in the past 67 years is primarily because of its holistic and pluralistic conception, what is often referred to in a dismissive manner as pseudo-secularism nowadays. This perhaps is the most vital ingredient that has held India together, notwithstanding the multiple stresses and strains on its substance and structure.

The cause for Pakistan to go belly up was the proclivity to move away from the conception of Pakistan as envisaged by its founder Muhammad Ali Jinnah, howsoever hypocritical it may have been, to the vision of Zia-ul-Haq. Just as in the Eighties and the Nineties, the toxic hot mix of the politics of identity and religion—the ubiquitous "Mandal and Mandir", left in its wake a noxious legacy whose after-affects the nation has to still contend with. The attempt to equate national identity with a undenominational religious identity is a very hazardous hand to play.

If there is one message that the Peshawar massacre sends out, it is that a radicalised society, a polarised nation and a myopic notion of national priorities eventually debases populaces, leading to the basic tenets of humanity being cynically sacrificed for objectives wrongly interpreted as being divinely ordained. Social conflict is the bane of national security. The BJP should reflect on this before leading India down that path.

India, Pak & the nuclear threat

IT IS IN India's interest to work multilaterally with other global powers to eliminate battlefield nuclear weapons. Its continuance, rather than preventing conflict, is the perfect recipe for a nuclear Armageddon. General Khalid Kidwai, who headed the Strategic Plans Division (SPD) of Pakistan's Nuclear Command Authority for 15 long years, laid out the doctrinal basis of Pakistan's nuclear programme during an expansive interaction in Washington, DC, recently.

The General said that the rationale for developing tactical nuclear weapons, including the nuclear missile Nasr, that has a range of 37 miles, is to respond to India's Cold Start doctrine. The ostensive Cold Start doctrine that has not been officially acknowledged by India envisages a blitzkrieg of a number of armoured battle groups simultaneously attacking Pakistan after being mobilised in 48 to 72 hours. Clearly, conceding the asymmetry between conventional forces of India and Pakistan, he preached that battlefield nuclear weapons would deter India from probing for gaps in Pakistani nuclear deterrence to find space for a conventional war under a nuclear overhang. (After the Kargil War, a theory was propounded by Indian strategists that there is space for a conventional war with Pakistan despite the nuclear equation. That is the rationale that Pakistan extends for battlefield

---

The Asian Age, 04 April, 2015

nuclear weapons to stop Cold Start.) If strategic nuclear weapons had kept the peace for four decades in South Asia since 1971, tactical weapons would only perpetuate it further, he argued.

He further delineated that the logic of the Shaheen-III nuclear missiles, that have a range of 2,750 kilometres, was to knock out India's second-strike capability even if it was located on the islands of Andaman and Nicobar. It would neutralise India's bluster by conveying that any use of nuclear weapons of any kind would invite massive retaliation. He also acknowledged that Pakistan was well on its way to developing a submarine-based nuclear capability as a second strike option, thereby completing the nuclear triad.

Gen Kidwai was rather candid in implicitly acknowledging that Pakistan uses terrorist organisations as an instrument of state policy, though he blamed the Kashmir and Afghanistan bogey that Pakistan keeps raising to try and justify its actions.

Before contemplating the implications of these grandiloquent pronouncements, it would be worth recapitulating that Pakistan's nuclear programme emerged as a consequence of the liberation of East Pakistan as the independent nation of Bangladesh. The Pakistani establishment was mortally petrified that if India could dismember their country in two, tomorrow they may split what remained into four. Goaded by Zulfikar Ali Bhutto, the Pakistani nuclear establishment—led by the proliferator AQ Khan—stole nuclear technology from around the world and succeeded in developing an indigenous capability.

It did not take them long to threaten India. In 1990, the United States picked up intelligence that Pakistan was on the verge of deploying nuclear weapons, prompting the then US deputy national security adviser, Robert Gates, to travel to both Islamabad and New Delhi to urge restraint. Both countries and the dramatis persona involved denied that this was the case. But then, given that neither Pakistan nor India declare how many weapons they have, that was expected. It would be relevant to remember that India had conducted a peaceful nuclear explosion in 1974, when Pakistan's capabilities were still shrouded in secrecy.

In May 1998, all that changed when both India and Pakistan set off a series of nuclear explosions, freezing the power balance in South Asia into perpetuity. It has never been dissected whether from India's perspective those tests made strategic sense as they allowed Pakistan's nuclear programme to crawl out of the woodwork and blunt the conventional advantage India had. To even suggest an evaluation is considered blasphemy. The contra argument is, of course, that it merely converted the de facto into de jure.

Coming back to the present—what does Pakistan's policy of full spectrum deterrence mean for the stability of South Asia and, more specifically, the security of India? To start with, the development of battlefield-level nuclear weapons and their intermixing with conventional weapons raises the risk of nuclear war, over-extended command and control systems leading to oversight, the possibility of nuclear weapons falling into terrorist hands and the spectre of foolish adventurism by an overzealous combat commander increases exponentially.

It, therefore, is in India's interest to work multilaterally with other global powers to eliminate battlefield nuclear weapons. Its continuance, rather than preventing conflict, is the perfect recipe for a nuclear Armageddon. Specifically, how must India deal with Shaheen-III and other such capabilities that threaten to counteract India's massive retaliation philosophy? Should India seriously consider revisiting its "no first use" policy given the ominous developments in the neighbourhood? What would be its implication qua China that has a similar no first use principle? India's nuclear deterrent is both a hedge against China as well as Pakistan and the Indian nuclear military programme was a response to Chinese tests at Lop Nur commencing on October 16, 1964.

The other option is to engage bilaterally with the Pakistanis on nuclear issues. Would that be interpreted as a sign of weakness on the part of India or an acknowledgement of a reality that has to be managed? At the height of the Cold War, there was a regular interaction between the strategic force commanders of the United States and the erstwhile USSR. Notwithstanding the "mutually assured destruction" doctrine, missile-flying time between the two Cold War adversaries provided a sliver of space to ascertain a launch and interdict it.

However, the deployment of Soviet missiles in Cuba stood the mutually assured destruction doctrine on its head because Cuba is a mere 90 miles from American mainland. If one reviews the literature of the Cuban missile crisis in October 1962, when the US and the USSR were a heartbeat away from a nuclear exchange, what is alarming are the number of dangerous moments catalogued in those 13 days. They range from Soviet submarine commanders calibrating a nuclear torpedo for battle readiness to American pilots possessing the ability to drop their thermo-nuclear weapons without seeking a green signal from the ground. The reason why this predicament is germane to India and Pakistan is not only because we are immediate neighbours, but because missile flying time may be three minutes or less.

It, therefore, is important that despite the "off and on talks" between India and Pakistan, there must be a full spectrum uninterrupted dialogue on nuclear issues between the two. Confidence building measures with regard to the efficacy of command and control systems is an inexorable imperative. The margin of error is non-existent to prevent a nuclear apocalypse.

Perks of being normal

A DINNER table conversation about the Nobel Prize-winning conundrum called India-Pakistan provoked a think—Is there a way out of this frozen turbulence? To establish a "new normal" between India and Pakistan, the first question that India should ask itself is: Do we gain anything by normalising relations with Pakistan? The second query is: What does normalisation mean for India? The third is, what is it that India is prepared to do or even give to achieve this objective?

What does India gain by establishing a "new normal" with Pakistan? If you take a long lens view of Asia from Turkey in the west and Japan in the east, you discern three historical choke points on the continent: Israel-Palestine, India-Pakistan and North-South Korea. Though myriad other conflicts are also festering in Asia, what is unique about these antagonisms is that they have a nuclear dimension to them. Israel's de facto nuclear weapon state status is troublesome for West Asia. The opacity of the Indo-Pakistani nuclear programme has its own implications for South Asia, while the erratic regime in North Korea is a toxic dynamic for north and northeast Asia.

Put together, these three historical choke points have been responsible for institutionalising "big power" presence in the region. There is, of course, an equally cogent argument—that these conflicts

---

The Asian Age, 30 April, 2015

have been deliberately nurtured by the neo-imperialists to legitimise their presence in Asia. All the more reason that Asians should unplug these choke points.

The peculiarity of the Indo-Pak hostility is that since South Asia lies at the junction of west, central and east Asia, it inhibits the various regions from actualising their full potential. While regional groupings like the Gulf Cooperation Council (GCC) in West Asia, Association of Southeast Asian Nations (Asean) in Southeast Asia, Eurasian Economic Community (EurAsEC) in Central Asia and a host of other bewildering acronyms have taken off, the South Asian Association for Regional Cooperation (Saarc) has proven to be a virtual non-starter. Other South Asian nations, exasperated by the Indo-Pak asphyxiation of this grouping, are now seeking bilateral space within this multilateral arrangement.

South Asia is the extended land bridge that can connect the various regions of Asia to each other and act as an economic multiplier. Regrettably, its corrosive geo-politics—from Afghanistan right up to Myanmar—acts as an inhibitor for other regions to enter into seamless cooperation. Thus, from a pan-Asian perspective, the India-Pakistan stand off in the heart of South Asia could not have more portentous portents.

Notwithstanding the traumatic past, and perhaps because of it, normalisation, i.e. bridging the divide between people on both sides of the Indo-Pak border, would bring a semblance of emotional equilibrium to the Indian subcontinent. And it could also, perhaps, divert a substantial portion of Rs 3,95,796 crore budgeted for defence and another Rs 62,124 crore allocated for internal security in the 2015-16 fiscal in India alone, towards more productive purposes. The prime minister of India would also not be compelled to buy warplanes on the hop. Every country that has aspirations of becoming a great power needs space for consolidation—a relatively calm period of time when it can focus on surmounting its internal challenges. For that a peaceful periphery is a pre-requisite.

A classic example being the transition of China from the Mao Zedong to the Deng Xiaoping era when the latter ordained that China requires 30 years of peace to develop. In pursuit of this philosophy, China settled all its land boundary disputes, except with India and Bhutan. Though six of its maritime disputes are still outstanding, they are more about hydrocarbons in the waters around China subterfuged as territorial issues. It, therefore, is in India's interest to establish the "new normal" with Pakistan. India owes it to Asia, too. What does normalisation mean from India's perspective. Substantively it means only one thing: Export of terror by Pakistan into India must stop. Given that Pakistan has large ungoverned spaces where militant Islam is nurtured, what is the guarantee that even if the Pakistani establishment were to eschew terror as an instrument of state policy, attacks against India would cease? And if they do not, what then would be India's response to Pakistan?

This is not an insurmountable issue. India and Pakistan could put into place protocols and mechanisms to deal with terror if it is indeed conveyed through deeds that the Pakistani establishment has finally realised the perils of nurturing snakes in their backyard. They have created mayhem in Pakistan also. What that "deed" should be that wins India's confidence is for the Pakistani leadership to figure out. If the Pakistani establishment were to continue its policy of bleeding India with a thousand cuts, would it still make sense for India to have a relationship with Pakistan? Are there any positive spin-offs of absorbing terror attacks emanating from Pakistan and still continuing to talk, trade and have people to people contact? No argument to support this preposition manifests.

What then is India prepared to give in return to Pakistan for this normalisation? What is that we are prepared to put on the table to ensure an end to terror? Is there a grand gesture that India can make, one that could transcend the corrosiveness of the past six decades and open up vistas for a new future? Yes.

First, Pakistan has to be consciously made a non-issue in India's domestic discourse. A debate on probable solutions is imperative in the public discourse for credibility, but not the high-decibel nuclear wars fought on TV by ostensibly inebriated warmongers on both sides and mediated by unwitting slaves to the tyranny of television ratings. Closet consultations are condemned as perfidy by hawks.

And second, it requires two prime ministers and a general armed with the conviction that it is their manifest destiny to liberate both nations from the servitude of history, notwithstanding the obstacles and the possibility that it may render them one-term Gorbachevs. Resolution of conflicts involves audacity to make concessions, including territorial swaps by both sides. Status quoists do not build futures. You cannot invest in the rhetoric of war and pray for peace.

Let the imagined wars begin

WITH THE national security adviser talks between India and Pakistan being called off late on Saturday night, despite tensions on the borders at a zenith, it may be worthwhile simulating a war game between the two countries.

It is the autumn of 2018. The Union government has lost a string of state Assembly elections since November 2015. The government, despite having the numbers in Lok Sabha, is at sixes and sevens. Social cohesion is at a nadir as a consequence of the politics of polarisation pursued by the ruling party. The economy is sluggish with a flight of domestic capital and an erosion of confidence among foreign investors. Foreign and strategic policy has been reduced to high-decibel verbiage dished out to captive NRI audiences in foreign capitals.

The internal security situation has deteriorated. Maoist insurgency has bared its nasty fangs menacingly across the Red Corridor. What, however, is really undermining the credibility of the government are repeated terrorist strikes from across the western border. In the salubrious climes of a holy shrine tucked away in the high Himalayas, as devotees congregate for the evening prayer at about 7.30 pm, the calm is shattered by a burst of gunfire from a group of heavily armed terrorists. Instantly, a hundred odd people are killed. In minutes,

---

The Asian Age, 23 August, 2015

pictures of the carnage go viral and are amplified and beamed to 160 million television homes across India. In New Delhi, the Indian and Pakistani NSAs are just settling down to dinner. Their friendly banter is cut short by news of the terrorist attack. Both the NSAs hurry out of the exclusive dining suite.

At the Prime Minister's residence the members of the Cabinet Committee on Security (CCS) go into a huddle. The Pakistani NSA en-route to IGI airport briefs the Pakistani prime minister on a secure satellite phone. The Pakistani prime minister instructs the NSA to brief the army chief so that the Pakistani forces can go on alert.

At the CCS meeting the atmosphere is surcharged. Crowds have started gathering across India. The first lot of injured and dead have started pouring into the base camp at the foot of the mountain as the first media crews arrive. Raw emotions and blood lust are being let loose on live television without restraint. In Delhi, calls for action grow. CCS members remind the Prime Minister that the first right-wing Hindu government since 1952 cannot be a mute spectator to this latest outrage. The Kargil victory is recalled. The general elections, now barely seven months away, are looming.

The service chiefs, now accustomed to political hyperventilation, are circumspect about any knee-jerk action. When asked why India should not take out the 40-odd terrorist camps in Pakistan-Occupied Kashmir (PoK), they point out that these are not permanent camps. They are mobile. Egged on by his pugnacious but ignoramus colleagues in the CCS that demonstrable action must be taken against Pakistan, and in the teeth of military advice to the contrary, the Prime Minister instructs the Air Force to take out the Lashkar-e-Tayyaba (LeT) office in Muzzafrabad.

In a midnight strike, two Halwara based Su-30s flying at tree-top level take out the LeT office in Muzzafrabad. Using the customised Indian version of the Over the Horizon Promis software that can pinpoint a target 40 miles away, they do not cross the Line of Control as they fire their missiles. The missiles strike home and the building is obliterated with the minimal of collateral damage.

At about 12.30 am past midnight, while the defence minister is briefing the media, a slip of paper is handed over to him. Indian satellites have picked up frenetic activity on Pakistani airbases. All Indian civil and military airports are put on high alert and aircraft patrols are scrambled. The first armoured division of the Ambala based Kharga core is ordered to go into the Cold Start mode. Indian submarines in the Arabian Sea are instructed to stake out the Karachi harbour. Barely two hours later the Pakistanis hit back. Using over-the-horizon technology and long-range missiles of their Chinese-supplied Shenyang J-16 fighters, they flatten a government building in the heart of Jammu. Though the damage is minimal as the building was devoid of people, the point has been made.

In the intervening hours between the Indian strike and the Pakistani retaliation, the global leadership has got into the act. Calls are made to both the Prime Ministers of India and Pakistan. All available spatial resources are re-tasked over the subcontinent. Every centimetre of land and sea is under continuous satellite watch. It is 5pm in the evening on that very day in New York. The United Nations Security Council goes into a hurriedly convened session to discuss the conflagration between the two nuclear-armed states. The Security Council unanimously passes a resolution holding India responsible for initiating hostilities. In the meanwhile, the advance of the first armoured in the Hindumalkot area of Rajasthan and of the Multan-based Pakistan's Army Reserve South is picked up by satellites.

At 4 am in the morning, the President of China makes a tough conference call to both the Prime Ministers of India and Pakistan. He has the President of the US and Russia also on the line. Both India and Pakistan are warned that any further escalation would be met with a coercive response from the space based military platforms of all three countries. Already the higher command and control systems of both the defence establishments have been rendered redundant by white noise. Through interdiction of the up linking beams, Russian military satellites have commandeered every major TV and radio stations in both countries. They are now broadcasting programmes in Russian only.

Both the prime ministers are pilloried to fly to Honk Kong pronto for a working summit later that very day. It is indicative of the shift in the global power balance to Asia. At 5 am hostilities cease with both sides declaring victory in a zero sum game without the nuclear threshold being reached. Thus ends the frenzied one nightstand between the two nuclear-armed neighbours.

Given that a war between the two countries would be adventurism of an insane degree and talks with Pakistan tantamount to a dialogue with the deaf, what are the options for India? Pakistan will not desist from exporting terror as its India policy is controlled by a defence establishment that still wakes up in a sweat from its Bangladesh nightmare.

The only option for India is to transform itself into a fortress with stouter intelligence, analysis and interdiction capability. It needs to export its ideas of democracy, entitlement constructs, women's empowerment and federalism into Pakistan to strengthen the liberal element in their polity.

The NSA-level talks are an exercise in futility as they only serve to hyphenate India and Pakistan—a construct repudiated with much effort during the United Progressive Alliance years. It exposes the current government's lack of coherence, consistency and even control over its Pakistan policy.

Talking some sense into the talks

WHAT DOES India want from Pakistan? While the answer to this question should be fairly linear, it has defied a succession of Indian governments over the past four decades because the reality is deeply convoluted.

The genesis of the current state of affairs between the two nations lies in the Bangladesh war of 1971. A country that was created in the name of religion in 1947, split in the name of language in 1971, primarily because of its inability to handle its own contradictions. The Punjabi Muslim could not countenance being ruled by the Bengali Muslim. India, unfortunately, got drawn into an internal affair primarily because the political disagreement between the two halves of Pakistan soon turned into a full scale genocide with the overwhelmingly Punjabised army of West Pakistan turning on their East Bengali brethren. The viciousness and brutality that followed shamed humanity, compelling India to intervene and the rest is history. Some would argue that given the moth-eaten geography of Pakistan, what happened was but inevitable.

However, the liberation of Bangladesh left an ineffaceable scar on the psyche of the Pakistani defence and security establishment. In addition to demolishing the obtuse martial race theory, it led to

---

The Asian Age, 12 December, 2015

paranoia—that if India can cleave our country into two, then what prevents it from carving the remaining part into four. The trajectory that Pakistan followed, 1971 onwards, is impelled by these impulses: Proximity to China, military relations with Nato, nuclearisation, cross-border terrorism and becoming frontline undertaker for Western powers in Afghanistan, both in the Eighties and in the first decade of the 21st century.

Former foreign minister of Pakistan Khurshid Mahmud Kasuri, in his book *Neither a Hawk nor a Dove*, writes: "Like most professional institutions the Army has an operational code that most officers are taught and meant to subscribe to. The code can be summarised as follows: Avoid a war with India, without yielding to Indian pressure on vital issues; Support the Kashmir cause but not to the point where it leads to an open confrontation with India; Attempt at maintaining positive relations with the major Islamic States in order to broaden the base of economic and potential military support, and to avoid the appearance of tilting towards one or the other, thereby triggering sectarian conflicts within Pakistan itself; Maintain and expand the nuclear program, but without risking Pakistan's relationship with the United States and other anti-proliferation states; Avoid a too dependent relationship with the US, the state that has let Pakistan down many times in the past but remain close enough to make Pakistan's case in Washington and to balance India's influence; Do whatever is possible to hold together Pakistan's most important proto alliance with China."

Quoting Stephen Cohen, an academic who has written prolifically on Pakistan, Mr Kasuri further states: "The excellent army sees Pakistan as a threatened, peace loving and a status quo power pursuing a defensive strategy heavily dependent upon the support of friends and allies of uncertain reliability… Kashmir is not considered as an international issue as much as an extension of domestic politics and the remnants of a flawed Partition."

He rounds it up by saying, "Stephan Cohen reproduced the code in 1998 and significant changes have since then taken place. The code could nevertheless be regarded as an accurate reflection of the mindset of the Pakistani Army." Mark the phrase "mindset of the Pakistani

Army". Lest it be forgotten that since the early 1950s Pakistan has been run by three As: Allah, America and the Army. Herein lies the conundrum. If you start decoding the cryptogram, it simply deciphers as follows—Do not yield to Indian pressure to stop the myriad Punjab based terrorist outfits like the Jamat-ul-Dawa, Lashkar-e-Tayyaba, Jaish-e-Mohammad from attacking India. Patronise the Khalistanis and every other insurgent who is willing to take up arms against the Indian state. Do not stop supporting the All-Party Hurriyat Conference and every other separatist strain in Jammu and Kashmir. Miniaturise, tacticalise and expand the nuclear arsenal using India's cold start doctrine as a bogey for that purpose, for this would keep India off balance. Last, but not the least, consolidate the relationship with China for that is the bug bear that can keep India contained with its string of pearls and "one belt, one road" (OBOR) paradigms.

As long as this code continues to be the directorial principle of the Pakistani Army, no amount of engagement is going to produce any substantive results. The track of Indo- Pakistani relations over the past 40 years underscores this reality abundantly. The key, therefore, to a substantive, result-oriented conversation lies in convincing the Pakistani defence establishment that India is not an existential threat to Pakistan. That Bangladesh was the net result of Pakistan's own follies. However, even if the above two postulates are surmounted, how does India address the shame that the Pakistani Army has internalised into its collective psyche about being decisively routed in Bangladesh. That the flower of their army, 91,000 soldiers, were taken prisoners of war, including many of its generals who have shaped Pakistan's military doctrines over the years.

The desperation to get but a sliver of Indian territory that can then become the totem pole for the collective catharsis is the overriding yearning that drives the Pakistani security and strategic mindset. Along the way a lot of economic and commercial interests have also evolved that allow the Pakistani defence forces to appropriate a large share of the national budget by keeping the India threat in play.

It is for this reason that Bangkok and even the visit of the foreign minister to Islamabad is a bad idea. The spectacle of the Indian foreign minister, who till yesterday was playing verbal kabbadi over the airwaves with her Pakistani counterpart, addressing a press conference in Islamabad resplendent in a green sari, reminiscent of the colours of the Pakistani flag, announcing the resumption of the composite dialogue process was the most pathetic commentary on the lack of even a coherent strategy, much less a policy, that the BJP government has qua Pakistan. Similarly, the decision to hold national security adviser talks in a third country may just become a precursor to inject third party mediation into the Indo-Pakistani dynamic. After all, if India is all right with a third country as a "neutral" venue for bilateral party talks, then influential players in the international community can legitimately ask why does India have a problem with third party mediation. Ten years ago, while returning from an Indo-Pakistan track two event in Muscat, I asked one of the finest practitioners of diplomacy that the Indian Foreign Service has ever produced as to what is the best case scenario for India- Pakistan relations. He replied, "The situation as it stands today—no war, but no peace." Those words have proven to be prophetic, for nothing has changed between the two countries.

But are we going to bequeath this toxic hot mix to our children or is there a real way out to solve the problem called relations or the lack of them between India and Pakistan?

As a retired Pakistani general told me recently over a couple of rounds of good single malt one balmy evening, "A day will come when that disgrace would be redressed even if it takes a thousand years. We shall patiently prepare for it. For revenge is a dish that tastes the best when it is cold, to quote the Godfather." If India feels that it is in its larger interest to make peace with Pakistan and as the bigger nation it must take the initiative, then it must put its best minds to crack the riddle as to how we can mollify the dreads of the Pakistani establishment, and what can be done about Pakistan's deep craving for retribution since the Bangladesh war, for that is where the adventurism of Kargil and state-sponsored terrorism stems from. Whether the Indian government is willing to do this or not will answer the question posed at the beginning: What does India want from Pakistan?

The geopolitics of Pathankot

WHY WAS UFA followed by Gurdaspur and Lahore by Pathankot in double quick time? The easy answer is that the permanent establishment in Pakistan does not want peace with India for a variety of reasons that have been analysed to death. However, the more important question is what emboldens the generals in Pakistan to act with such impunity. The key lies in the changed geopolitics of the region. But before this, it is important to unscramble as to how Pakistan had everything to gain by walking away from Ufa and why diplomacy on the hop is not a great idea.

For 10 long years ,the Bharatiya Janata Party was in the Opposition and it kept saying that terror and talks couldn't go hand in hand. It strongly critiqued every attempt that its predecessor government made to engage with Pakistan—be it in Havana in 2006 or Sharm el-Sheikh in 2009, or even thereafter. As the wheel of electoral fortune turned, the BJP came into government on its own in 2014. Pakistan, that loves to portray itself as a victim of terror notwithstanding that it is the principal exporter of terror, sensed an opportunity to insidiously obtain equivalence with India on this issue. The previous government had smartly denied Pakistan this congruence for long by promising to engage across a spectrum of outstanding bilateral issues, but caveating

---

The Asian Age, 23 January, 2016

it by insisting that the export of terror from Pakistan would have primacy in the pecking order of subjects on the table.

To get out of this box that Pakistan found itself in, especially after the 26/11 terror attacks in Mumbai in 2008, it sold the Government of India a pup by offering an exclusive format of talking primarily about terror in Ufa, Russia. Without looking at the teeth of the gift horse on offer, the BJP government accepted it. With one stroke, Pakistan achieved its strategic objective of changing the BJP's position from no talks till terror abates, to talking about terror.

In 2006, the joint anti-terror dialogue was pegged at the level of additional secretaries in the ministry of external affairs of both the nations. The NDA government elevated it to the level of national security advisers, thereby giving it a far higher profile. Having got equivalence on the question of terror, Pakistan had nothing further to gain from Ufa and, therefore, even before the ink had dried on the joint statement, Pakistan trashed the follow up process and consigned the document to the dustbin of history. To make sure that the phantom of Ufa did not resurface, Pakistan buried it by ordering their proxies to perpetrate the attack in Gurdaspur.

The Indian Prime Minister should have realised that his government has been played for a song and should have been more careful the second time around before embarking on the Lahore trip. Again, the only objective behind this entrapment by holding out the bait of "out of box" diplomacy was to get an Indian Prime Minister to visit Pakistan—something that had not happened in the past 10 years. For such a visit provides a semblance of respectability that Pakistan desperately craves. This myth of differences between the civilian government and the military establishment in Pakistan is a "good cop, bad cop" act that Pakistan has perfected to play the international community and blindside India. The empirical evidence of this, over the decade, is too overwhelming to ignore. All that is required is to connect the dots.

What gives Pakistan the confidence to carry out this duplicity? It is the changed international environment in the region. Despite American anger at the harboring of Osama bin Laden, Mullah Omar and other leaders of the Quetta Shura, support to the Afghan Taliban, the Haqqani network and other Mujahideen groups, America figured out that it needs to keep Pakistan on its side if it does not want Afghanistan to slide into a morass like Iraq, Syria and Libya, post its withdrawal from that country. Realpolitik dictated that they needed to deal with the Pakistan Army. That is the reason why Americans rolled out the red carpet for Pakistan Army Chief Gen Raheel Sharif when he visited Washington DC some months ago. For they knew that he is the real "sheriff" in Pakistan.

China has a long-standing relationship with Pakistan. In fact, the kernel of the relationship is between the People's Liberation Army of China and the Pakistani Army. The recent pronouncement by China to make Pakistan an integral part of the "one belt one road" (OBOR) initiative, by committing to invest $46 billion in Pakistan, has only consolidated the relationship further.

Even Russia—that till not very long ago had a non-existent relationship with Pakistan—has not only made overtures at the highest level, but even reversed its long-standing embargo with regard to arms sales to Pakistan. India should have read the tea leaves when it was offered membership of the Shanghai Cooperation Organisation (SCO) along with Pakistan, thereby demolishing the construct of de-hyphenation that India had assiduously attempted to cultivate over all these years. Even the Ashraf Ghani-Abdullah Abdullah combine in Afghanistan has been warmer to Pakistan by taking a different line from the one espoused earlier by former President Hamid Karzai. It is only recently that the tilt is being partially corrected, though even today India remains a non-player in Afghanistan.

All this deludes Pakistan into believing that from a geo-strategic standpoint, it is in an exceptional sweet spot. Something that is a far cry from the pariah status it had achieved post-9/11 when Americans threatened to bomb Pakistan back to the Stone Age. This villainy only got reinforced after the Abbottabad raid that killed Bin Laden.

Because of these transformed geopolitical imperatives, the Pakistani establishment feels reassured that it can continue to indulge in its game of bleeding India with a thousand cuts without any hindrance, while outwardly presenting a veneer of eagerness to extend the dubious hand of friendship.

It is this altered power dynamic that gave Pakistan the temerity to follow up Narendra Modi's Lahore visit with the Pathankot attack. It is much like the nuclear tests of 1998 which led to the freezing of power balance in South Asia into perpetuity and encouraged Pakistan to follow former Prime Minister Atal Behari Vajpayee's Lahore visit with Kargil. For Pathankot, Pakistan deliberately chose Jaish-e-Mohammed to do the evil deed for its founder, Maulana Masood Azar, is a special red rag to some influential eminences in this government. Exactly 15 years ago, they were witness to the ignominy of the then minister of external affairs, Jaswant Singh, having to escort this terrorist to Kandahar to secure the safe release of passengers of the hijacked Indian Airlines flight IC-814 as they stood helplessly on the desolate tarmac of that godforsaken airport.

India would have to work at transforming this geopolitical landscape if it wants any forward movement with Pakistan. For notwithstanding the attack on the Army public school in Peshawar last year, and the January 20 attack on Bacha Khan University in Charsadda, Khyber Pakhtunkhwa, both of which left scores of innocent students and teachers dead, Pakistan continues to be hell bent upon nurturing snakes in its backyard.

Siachen and the lines that divide

THE TRAGIC death of 10 Indian soldiers in February on the Siachen Glacier has once again drawn attention to the world's highest battlefield. In April 2012, 138 Pakistani soldiers had also died in an avalanche in Siachen. The then Chief of the Pakistani army, General Ashfaq Parvez Kayani stated that India and Pakistan must live in peaceful co-existence as defence without development is neither viable nor acceptable. However, he had added an expected caveat stating, "everyone knows why the army is here... because in 1984, the Indian army occupied the area and in response to that the Pakistan army was sent in". In the context of this assertion, it may be worthwhile to examine the historical genesis of this dispute.

The first question that needs to be answered is: What was the position on and off the glacier prior to 1984 when Indian troops moved in pre-emptively to foil a Pakistani attempt to occupy Siachen? The crucial date for determining that is July 29, 1949, when a ceasefire agreement was signed in Karachi by ranking military representatives of India and Pakistan and the UN Military Observer Group.

A meeting was held in Karachi from July 18-27, 1949, to establish "a ceasefire line" (CFL) in the state of Jammu and Kashmir. Major-General WJ Cawthorn, Major-General Nazir Ahmad, Brigadier

---

The Asian Age, 02 April, 2016

Sher Khan and some observers represented Pakistan at the Karachi Conference. On behalf of India ,Lieutenant-General SM Shrinagesh, Major-General KS Thimayya, Brigadier Sam Manekshaw, with HM Patel and Vishnu Sahay as observers participated. The ceasefire line delineated and demarcated the lines separating the two sides following the pause in hostilities in Jammu and Kashmir under the auspices of the United Nations on January 1, 1949. The July 29 Karachi Agreement delimited the entire ceasefire line defining over 740 km on the ground. Where then did the northern-most fringe of the ceasefire line lie? When the line started running through high mountains and glaciated areas as it panned north, it habitually started following an indicative route in the absence of clear landmarks on the ground. Its two penultimate and then the final benchmark became "Chalunka (on the Shyok River), Khor, thence North to the glaciers" transiting through grid reference NJ 9842.

However, the delineation of the northern-most segment of the ceasefire line was definite: NJ 9842, "thence north to the glaciers". If every one of 30 or more earlier directional commands were fastidiously followed in tracing the ceasefire line, there was no reason whatsoever for any departure from this norm in the case of the very last markers. "Thence North", could only mean due north to wherever the boundary of the erstwhile princely state of Jammu and Kashmir state lay. The Karachi Agreement directed that "the ceasefire line described above" be drawn "so as to eliminate any no man's land".

The ceasefire line was ratified by both sides and placed with the United Nations Commission on India and Pakistan. It was revalidated as the Line of Control (LoC) by the Suchetgarh Agreement of December 1972, in accordance with the explicit intention of the Simla Conference earlier that year to move from a military conflict towards a political solution in Jammu and Kashmir. The LoC assimilated military advances made by either side in Jammu and Kashmir in the 1971 war. Thus, in the Kargil-Siachen sector, all territorial gains went entirely to India which acquired the 254 square mile Turtok salient, comprising five villages (Chalunka, Thang, Tyakshi, Pharol and Turtok) just south and west of NJ 9842.

This modest but vital military acquirement provided India a supplementary territorial defence against hostile cartographic or physical claims on Siachen. Thus, there was a CFL that was established in 1949 that after the Simla Agreement morphed into the LoC. After 1984, as India acquired tactical dominance of the area, it established an Actual Ground Position line (AGPL) that outlines its physical presence on the ground today. That has been the progression in defining India's borders in its northern-most reaches.

Therefore, to interpret NJ 9842, thence north to the glaciers, as meaning northeast as the Pakistanis do is to give up the accuracy of the Karachi/Suchetgarh Agreements for any one of the many subjective interpretations that can then be given to this operative phrase. Historic realities cannot be sacrificed at the altar of strategic fantasies of General Headquarters (GHQ) in Rawalpindi. Pakistan consistently insists that "north" here really means northeast to the Karakoram Pass.

All United Nations global and even Pakistani maps illustrated the CFL objectively and properly till approximately 1964-72. However, between 1964 and 1972, the US defence mapping agency, a global benchmark for cartography, began depicting the CFL as extending from NJ 9842 to a point just west of the Karakoram Pass. This emboldened Pakistan to commence eastward on their atlases also. World atlases followed suit, portraying the line drawn from NJ 9842 northeast to the Karakoram Pass as the authentic and internationally accepted CFL-LoC, backed by mountaineering legends. India unfortunately did little to rebut or put in context. Pakistan appreciatively accepted these counterfeit universal testimonials and thereafter initiated moves to occupy Siachen. Precisely what motivated this cartographic (and from the Indian point of view, disconcerting) aggression is not clear. Incontrovertibly backing these moves were specious depictions of the CFL-LoC on some authoritative maps produced by instrumentalities of the US administration.

Under these circumstances, any unreserved relocation from the Siachen glacier without affirming the precise delimitation of the CFL-LoC from NJ 9842 "thence north to the glaciers", will mean accepting the Pakistan claim and throwing the August 1948 UN Resolution and derivative 1949 Karachi Agreement into the dustbin. This omnibus resolution on Jammu and Kashmir explicitly establishes Pakistan as the antagonist and trespasser. It necessitated that Pakistan's military regiments and tribal irregulars leave the state forthwith, and upheld India's de jure sovereignty over the entire state even while preparations were made for a plebiscite.

The only lasting solution to this impasse in Siachen that is needlessly costing human lives is to get the LoC firmly anchored to a northern terminus. If it continues to dangle loosely creating contested zones open to subjective interpretation, it will always remain a source of conflict and confrontation. The glacier would see an augmentation of military presence rather than the other way around.

The only way forward is, therefore, the mutual authentication of the AGPL on established cartographic principles outlined earlier. This should be merged with a covenant on a correct interpretation of "NJ 9842 thence north to the glaciers" leaving no room for creating any no man's land thus clearly marking a firm boundary running from NJ 9842 thence north to the glaciers. That is the only starting point of any substantive dialogue with Pakistan for disengagement, relocation and the eventual demilitarisation of the Siachen glacier that is in the interests of both the nations. Would Pakistan bite the bullet?

Sir Creek begs joint resolution

I HAD EARLIER described the wrangle between India and Pakistan in the icy wastes of the Siachen glacier. Let us now examine another dispute between the two neighbours. This one in the balmy waters of the west coast of India, namely, Sir Creek. Not many would recall that in the days leading up to the Gujarat Assembly elections in December 2012, the then chief minister of Gujarat, Narendra Modi, had created a minor storm in the teacup by alleging that Sir Creek was being handed over to Pakistan by the then United Progressive Alliance government. Nothing was farther from the truth. There could never have been any such move but it is typical of Mr Modi, now the Prime Minister, to mix metaphors, especially national security and politics, to score odd and rather misconceived brownie points.

What is Sir Creek? It is a 96 km-long tidal estuary on the western border of the two countries. It empties itself out into the Arabian Sea. Colloquially referred to as Baan Ganga, it derives it's present name from a British gent who was ostensibly tasked to resolve a dispute between the erstwhile ruler of Sindh and the Rao of Kutch over a pile of firewood lying on the banks of a concurrent body of water called the Kori Creek.

What is the quarrel then? Is it about firewood again? Unfortunately, no. It is centered around the interpretation of the frontier between

---

The Asian Age, 16 April, 2016

the erstwhile states of Kutch and Sindh. After Independence, Sindh became a part of Pakistan and Kutch was amalgamated into the present state of Gujarat. Therefore, the dispute is about delineating the borders of India and Pakistan.

In 1914, a Bombay government resolution between the government of Sindh and the erstwhile ruler of Kutch demarcated the frontiers of the two territories by delineating the eastern flank of the creek as the boundary line. This ipso facto put Sir Creek in the territory of the province of Sindh and, therefore, according to Pakistan now in its territory.

This boundary line, also referred to as the Green Line, is disputed by India. It bases its claim on two constructs. The first is based upon a map dating back to 1925 that shows the boundary lies in the middle of the channel as delineated by the installation of mid-channel pillars dating back to the same time. The second asserts that the Green Line is only an indicative line also referred to as the "ribbon line" in procedural gobbledygook. Moreover, the Thalweg doctrine of international law asserts that the boundaries between two states can, by mutual consent, be delimited in the middle of river channels.

It would be instructive to note that all these claims and counter claims based upon historical records pre-date the birth of two sovereign nations i.e. India and Pakistan. India was partitioned based upon lines drawn across the map of the subcontinent by a British barrister Sir Cyril Radcliffe who had never ever visited India before he embarked on his fortuitous mission. What needs to be done is that a physical demarcation needs to be made by both the countries from the mouth of Sir Creek to it's very top and then eastwards to a point on the line designated on the Western Terminus. From this point, "thence onwards" the tribunal award of 1968 crystalises the boundary between the two countries.

Why is it proving to be difficult to draw this line? It has less to do with some territory gained or lost in marshy wastes of the Rann of Kutch —through which the Sir Creek runs—and more to do with the fact that the delineation would define the land and sea terminus that then actually determines the acreage of the exclusive economic zone under the United Nations Convention on the Law of the Sea. Pakistan has been contending that should it accept the Indian interpretation that the boundary between the two countries lies in the middle of the Creek, it would loose several thousand kilometers of its exclusive economic zone. India's assertion is to the converse: Were it to accept the Pakistani claim it would be similarly disadvantaged.

For the last 47 years, many rounds of negotiations between India and Pakistan have yielded no result in terms of an abiding resolution to the dispute. Like in the case of Siachen, it is linked to the larger problems that bedevil the two countries. From India's point of view it is terrorism and from Pakistan's standpoint it is Kashmir. As territorial readjustment of boundaries in the context of the Indian subcontinent is both an emotive and a cultural issue, any give or take that involves the loss or gain of territory just does not seem possible. While loss of human lives is acceptable, the loss of territory or even a territorial swap is a non sequitur.

In the wake of the attack on the Indian Parliament on December 13, 2001, at the height of Operation Parakram, the largest mobilisation of the Indian armed forces after the 1971 war, General Pervez Musharraf, the then President and Army Chief of Pakistan, asked one of the foremost foreign strategic analysts of South Asian affairs, for a read on Indian intentions. The analyst ostensibly told Gen Musharraf that India would do nothing for India fights over territory and not people. It factors in the casualties as the price of living in a bad neighbourhood and moves on. His incisive insight into the collective Indian psychological matrix proved to be prophetic. Operation Parakram ended in a whimper and even subsequent terrorist attacks by Pakistan-backed semi-state actors, including 26/11, were absorbed by India without a robust and befitting response. The bogey trotted out for this inaction is that both are nuclear weapon states and any coercive reaction can lead to disastrous consequences. However, this claim is belied by the Kargil episode when Pakistan intruded in Indian territory and, throwing all caution to the winds, the retaliation by India was swift, furious and befitting. Given this peculiar angularity in our psyche, India would not accept any international arbitration on the premise that disputes should be resolved bilaterally, and Pakistan, in turn, would not accept the Indian proposal for a demarcation of the maritime boundary under the aegis of the technical aspects of the law of the sea. It is, therefore, a stalemate much like Siachen.

What complicates matters is the perception that the area is oil, gas and mineral rich and, therefore, umbilically tied to the energy security imperatives of both the countries. This could prove to be the proverbial gamechanger. However, here lies the crucial distinction between Siachen and Sir Creek. If the latter has oil, gas and minerals in the wider continental shelf and the disputed economic zone to be delineated in terms of how the land/sea terminus is determined, perhaps it makes a case for a joint endeavour between India and Pakistan. The two, through their respective government or public sector entities, can demarcate acreage for joint exploration. Public sector is the key because private money is a coward and likes to find the safest harbour.

A case is repeatedly made in the Track one and a half to Track five between India and Pakistan that economic linkages, if sufficiently developed, can surmount the political and military differences between the two countries. The undefined seascape around Sir Creek could be a place to test out this claim by evolving a template. Though this idea may sound fuzzy at the moment but as the adage goes—confusion is the first stage of resolution.

News diplomacy

THE PARALLEL accounts put out by both the sides of what transpired at the meeting between the foreign secretaries of India and Pakistan and the media spin on it in respective countries has once again underscored a fundamental query: How corrosive is the role of the prevailing narrative in adding to the bitterness and vitriol between India and Pakistan? A gentleman who works on South Asia at a think tank was curious to know.

Some people who watch the World Wrestling Entertainment histrionics, that pass off as prime-time debate on Indian television, are regularly subjected to a set of eminences from either country—some seem positively inebriated hurling high decibel invectives at each other. As an aside, it is widely rumoured that some of these Pakistani prima donna's are handsomely remunerated for the theatrics they perform on Indian news channels. Some years back, while surfing to find my favourite cartoon channel, I happened to pause on a "views" channel that masquerades as "news and current affairs" channel. One Pakistani panelist was screaming: "In 1971, we bombarded Dwarka."An Indian panelist retorted: "We gave it back to you in Karachi by shelling your harbour." Till this point, the hysterics were droll but then it got ugly. The Pakistani yelled that that was 1971—now his country had nukes

---

The Asian Age, 30 April, 2016

and they could take out New Delhi. Another Indian shrieked that India had a second-strike capability and could wipe out Lahore and Rawalpindi. The nuclear armageddon on TV was perturbing. I called up one of my colleagues and requested her to advise all the "views" channels that there would be statutory implications that they would need to factor in for orchestrating this dramaturgy of the absurd.

The advice worked but only for a few days. Soon, they were back at it. The question that kept niggling was: Does this poisonous dialogue for the sake of television rating points, tap into the very fertile soil of hate and odium that is a part of our unhappy legacy? Conversely, does it exacerbate the climate of distrust and animosity that then becomes an insurmountable obstacle in the search for even a sliver of common ground between the two countries? On balance, is it a bit of both?

India-Pakistan relations are a complex, nuanced and a layered cookie. At the very base is the warmth and camaraderie of Indians and Pakistanis when they encounter each other. There are stories galore from Lucknow to Lahore of "the human connect playing itself out in myriad drawing rooms and bazaars of both the nations". On top of it is the institutional hostility that establishments in both countries have towards each other. Then there is the cricketing rivalry where every match is a metaphoric war between the two. Supplementing all this are the myriad diplomacy tracks where policy wonks, retired officials and civil society bleeding hearts attempt to find solutions.

Finally, there is the pacifist impulse in the political establishment on both sides that manifests itself periodically, perhaps prodded by international powers who are petrified that these crazy South Asians may just blow themselves up. Here, also, there is a split between the print media that is broadly sober even in its criticism in either country—except for certain vernaculars, especially in Pakistan (pardon the Indian bias). Television is generally hyper and social media is downright vicious in both the countries. Can a change in the prevailing narrative to a conversation focusing on the positives help in changing the ambience? If so, how? Or is it that the structural fault lines between the two countries run so deep that even an improvement in the atmospherics would not resolve or put on the backburner the contentiousness between the two countries. Irrespective of the outcome, this is an endeavour worth pursuing. It would only get off the ground if media barons on either side see an economic opportunity in terms of a market for their respective media products across the border. The real meat, of course, lies in entertainment where there is a ready appetite to consume each other's music, films, theatre, animation and even television. Regular concerts by artists from each side notwithstanding, the loony fringe in both the countries is a market that has been tapped into in the past as well, but never exploited to its full potential. A lot of this is already happening but via other countries and needs to be institutionalised.

Even in the news and current affairs genre, allowing the respective public broadcasters to uninterruptedly downlink their content onto distribution platforms in either nation, albeit governed by a mutually-negotiated programme and advertising code, could be a first step and an appropriate confidence building measure. Hypothetically speaking, if private newspapers of both countries are allowed to distribute—whereby they start earning revenue on both subscription and over the medium term even on advertising—would that moderate the vitriol? The answer is "yes". In any case, they are freely available on the Internet but the reason why the content in some of them remains vitriolic is simply because there is no revenue imperative for moderation.

Similarly, if news channels realise that there is subscription and advertising revenue that they can earn in either country, despite the tyranny of carriage fee in India and the corresponding ogre in Pakistan, it would defiantly tamper down on the staple violent sensationalism on either side. For the media, at the end of the day, is a business. It is about the money, honey; and if media czars start seeing that there is even a sliver of silver to be made, they would start looking at the India-Pakistan equation through a totally different prism.

It would make eminent sense to put together a quiet retreat for the big media owners from either side to kickstart the process. Improved acoustics would definitely help in creating a better ecosystem that could have a spillover effect in other spaces too.

II. The Canker of Terrorism

Fighting terrorism under a nuclear umbrella

AS INDIA and Pakistan decide to resume the composite dialogue helped along by Pakistan acquiescing to an anti-terror mechanism, it may be worth recalling that negotiations on the Draft Articles of a Comprehensive Convention on International Terrorism have been on hold by a group of nations led by Pakistan on the central issue of a "legal definition of terrorism". India had proposed the treaty in 1996.

There is a fundamental disconnect between India's definition of terrorism and Pakistan's. The basic assessment that we need to make is whether exporting terrorism to India is, or is not, a part of Pakistan's State policy. The foreign secretary-designate says that "Terrorism was a threat to Pakistan and its leaders as well". Can an inference be drawn that the Pakistani establishment is no longer culpable? Is it our assessment now that the terror organisations are not working on the instructions of the ISI and other Pakistani covert agencies?

Does this mean that the Pakistani leadership has decided to eschew its policy of bleeding India with a thousand cuts? Does this mean the mastermind of Kargil has changed his spots? Gen Musharraf said enroute to Havana: "I think our relationship with India has never been this good." This is a sentiment nobody in India would endorse, given the bombings in Mumbai and Malegaon.

Tehelka.com-the People's Paper, 23 September, 2006

It has been clear that while Pakistan's tactics may change, its core strategy remains constant. The Pakistani establishment believes that its desire for regional hegemony can never be realised till India is split into several separate nation states. The intrusions in Kargil were not only payback for Siachen but part of a calibrated attempt to sever Ladakh from the rest of India. This is precisely the reason why Pakistani covert agencies have a hand in fomenting violence from Punjab and Kashmir in the North-west to Nagaland, Manipur and Assam in the Northeast.

Following the transformation of both India and Pakistan into de jure nuclear weapon states in 1998, the global hawkeye has been focused on South Asia. India's response to the attack on Parliament—the ill-fated Operation Parakram launched in January 2003—rattled strategic thinkers and decision makers around the world just about enough into believing that these "mad South Asians" would unleash a nuclear holocaust. The spectre of a possible nuclear exchange has emboldened Pakistan, sanguine in the knowledge that unlike in 1999 when the Indian response to the Kargil intrusions caught the world unawares, global pressure would never allow a repeat.

The question that arises then is—how do we combat terrorism being perpetrated under the cover of a nuclear umbrella? Would resolving the Kashmir question to the satisfaction of the jehadis help? Would bringing the perpetrators of the Gujarat pogrom to justice help? Would rebuilding the Babri mosque help? In simple words, what is the price of peace?

To answer this question, it is important to know whether those responsible for terror attacks are our own 'boys' or foreign mercenaries. Or, if it is a combination of the two, can these strands be unravelled and dealt with separately?

Notwithstanding the answer to this question, the Indian State—democratic and based upon the rule of law as it is—must bring the perpetrators of the Gujarat carnage to justice and voluntarily rebuild the Babri Masjid, at the same site or a couple of hundred feet away, depending upon the outcome of the litigation. This will send a clear message that in India, mobocracy can never be the order of the day. Coming back to the question, there should be no doubt in anybody's mind that India is now in the vortex of the global jehadi campaign.

Even if Kashmir is resolved to the satisfaction of the militants — and that cannot even be an option on the table—it still would not free India from the scourge of terrorism. Pakistan would only shift its attention to another part of India and attempt to hack it limb by limb.

It is time the Indian leadership figured out an innovative plan for combating Pakistan. The plan must ensure that the Taliban does not re-emerge in Afghanistan, to deny Pakistan strategic depth. The oppressed people of the Northern Territories must be helped to find their voice. The situation in Baluchistan only exemplifies the artificial union called the Republic of Pakistan. The illusion, that a democratic Pakistan would be better for India than a benign or authoritarian military dictator, should be discarded from our strategic calculus once and for all.

The Nuclear Tests of 1998 froze the power balance in South Asia into perpetuity. It blunted the conventional advantage that India had over Pakistan in purely military terms. This has further emboldened Pakistan.

The case for a hard line on terrorism

TERRORISM TODAY poses the gravest threat to India's sovereignty and integrity. It subverts the fundamental Rule of Law, denies rights to the citizens, endangers the social fabric, and threatens political and economic stability. This should not be allowed to happen. The state must deny operating space to terrorists and their supporters, deter them from carrying out terrorist acts, ensure the basic rights of the people, and uphold the Fundamental Rights enshrined in the Constitution.

When terrorists target the Parliament in Delhi, temples in Jaipur and Varanasi, mosques in Ajmer and Hydrabad, trains in Mumbai, Courts of Law in Uttar Pradesh, Indian Institute of Science in Bangalore, State Assembly in Jammu & Kashmir; an armed forces camp in Kalchuk or Rampur they are neither attacking a particular state or its government nor are they attacking a specific para-military or military battalion. They are attacking India. By hitting at symbols, infrastructure and the heritage of the Indian state at places and times of their choosing, terrorists repeatedly underscore their pan- national designs and the extent of their reach. A distinguished analyst of South Asian affairs was asked by the Pakistani government for a reading of the Indian intentions in the wake of the attack on

---

Condensed version was published under the heading,
'India must respond to Jaipur', *The Indian Express*, 29 May, 2008

the Indian Parliament. He told the Pakistanis not to worry, as India would do nothing. His logic was very simple: "India does not react to the loss of people. They have just too many. India only reacts to the loss of territory."

Why is India unable to pre-empt and prevent terrorist attacks? Why is India unable to hit back at terrorists and their masters? These are the twin questions that come to the mind whenever terrorists kill and maim innocent civilians, bloody India's nose and walk away with impunity. The same pacifist headlines repeat themselves with monotonous regularity. *Mumbai bounces back, Terrorist plans to ferment communal tension in Jaipur foiled. Hundreds line up to donate blood in Delhi, Inter-faith candle lit vigil for the dead in Varanasi.* Ever wondered why you have never ever read a headline that says *Precision strike takes out a terrorist den, Terrorists apprehended—Plot to attack Parliament foiled.* Security experts tell you that terror groups have become extremely sophisticated at their business and correspondingly India's operational capacities to pre-empt and impose a punitive cost on them have not been upgraded at the same pace over an extended period of time. Intriguing, considering India was subjected to the most vicious terrorist onslaught over that very time scale. If this is correct we have something to be worried about?

Despite being subjected to 60 years of insurgency in the North East, 28 years of terrorism in the North West (Punjab & Kashmir) and over 18 years of Naxal violence in Central India, there has been no policy and consistency in strategy to deal with the various dimensions of terrorism. Political consensus is missing even today. Public debates have often turned into slanging matches with political and communal overtones. Coalition politics has only made matters worse. The political leadership must send out a strong message of zero tolerance to terrorism.

The high decibel campaign by bleeding hearts for wrong causes killed two anti-terror laws, Terrorists and Disruptive Activities (Prevention) Act, 1985, 1987 (TADA) and Prevention of Terrorism Act, 2002 (POTA). Despite being upheld, with modifications, by the Supreme Court of India, while TADA was allowed to lapse, POTA was repealed. Repeal or lapsing of laws is seen as weakness on the part of the state by non State actors seeking to overawe the State through violence. TADA, 1987, faced unprecedented protests from civil rights groups. They said the law violated fundamental rights and gave police unbridled powers with little accountability. In 1994, the Supreme Court, however, upheld the provisions of the law (Kartar Singh v State of Punjab 1994 SCC Cr 899), stating "freedom of individual must take second place to the requirement of safety of citizens". The court directed specific modifications to temper the law. An important direction was the constitution of Screening or Review Committees to periodically scrutinize cases registered under the Act. Despite these safeguards, there were allegations of abuse of law by the executive (police) from different parts of the country, including from states not affected by terrorism.

It took fifteen years of unabated terrorism across India, the cataclysmic attack on the World Trade Center in New York on September 11, 2001, and no less a brazen attack on the Indian Parliament on December 13, 2001 for the missing lines. Like TADA, the new legislation, too, attracted volumes of protests from various quarters. A civil rights organisation, People's Union for Civil Liberties (PUCL), challenged its constitutionality before the Supreme Court. The Court upheld the constitutional validity of POTA but with several caveats to check its possible arbitrary use by police. The court held that the "protection and promotion of human rights under the rule of law is essential in the prevention of terrorism", involving "court's responsibility", and that if human rights are violated in the process, it will be "self-defeating". The judgement pointed out that "lack of hope for justice provides breeding grounds for terrorism" and, therefore, in the fight against terrorism "human rights" will have to be respected. In the wake of allegations of misuse and abuse of POTA and an electoral promise by the INC ,the law was repealed on September 21, 2004.

It is fallacious to argue that existing laws are sufficient to deal with acts of terror. The Indian Penal Code (IPC), for instance, was conceived to deal with individual acts of crime and not terrorist activity. Although there are a plethora of laws to deal with specific instances of militancy and violence—for example, The Armed Forces

(Assam & Manipur) Special Powers Act (1958); Anti- Hijacking Act (1982) and Maharashtra Control of Organised Crime Act (1999)—none of them are equipped to deal with acts of terror committed by terrorist groups supported by foreign nations and entities.

Knee-jerk and ad hoc responses to what is now established as a consistent onslaught on India's secular, plural character by terrorist groups should be dispensed with. Laxity in counter-terrorism efforts, including framing legal measures, belittles Indian demands for action by the world community against cross-border terrorism. A comprehensive counter-terrorism legislation that provides ample safeguards against its abuse, therefore, cannot be delayed any further. In the past few years, India has been hit by a series of terrorist attacks which are aimed at expanding Islamist terror across India, causing communal violence, economic loss, enlarging the support base for terrorists, attracting potential recruits and influencing foreign policy options. These attacks reveal the increasing influence of Al-Qaeda on the terrorist leaders and supporters, a factor that has the potential of radicalizing a section of the 140 million-strong Muslim population which may unravel six decades of communal harmony and pluralism.

India's battle with terrorism, especially in the North West, can be divided into two phases. 1980-2001—when the world never took notice of our protests that India is being subjected to a low-cost high intensity proxy war supported, organised and executed by Pakistan. After 9/11, when the global war on terror commenced, it changed a lot of things for a lot of people around the globe.

It changed things for India also in terms of the fact that we at least started getting lip service of sympathy from the western alliance. The irony, however, is that the fountainhead of terrorism as far as India is concerned, was co-opted by the US as a frontline ally in the battle against terrorism. The US candidly admits that its interests come first and therefore it has no problem in having one approach to terrorism on Pakistan's western border and a completely different approach on the eastern border. It is high time India realised that it would get no help in this fight from anyone. It has to fight alone if it wants to survive as a nation, keeping its political and territorial integrity intact. This issue has to be divorced from partisan party politics. If some civil liberties get curtailed in the process, we have to learn to live with it.

The government ,in turn ,needs to follow the example of Israel and Russia. A well-trained, appropriately armed, elite anti-terrorist force has to be created. Backed by top-notch intelligence and appropriate legal immunity, it must be mandated to operate across state and national boundaries against the enemies of the Indian State. The apex leadership of terrorist organisations needs to be told that they would be made to pay the price for their actions, irrespective of whether they live in Karachi, Dubai, Dhaka, the mountains of Afghanistan or the lowlands of Myanmar. They must be made to realise that the world is equally unsafe for them. Legal processes also need to be fast-tracked so that trials do not carry on interminably for decades, as has happened in the 1993 Mumbai bomb blasts case.

The real threat to India comes from the smaller groups which remain below the radar scans of intelligence agencies by their sheer autonomy and number. These groups, as revealed in the attacks since 2005 in Kashmir and outside, are capable of causing immense damage to the country, its economy, its image, its pluralist character by calculated terrorist attacks in specific centers. Terror is not the only agenda these groups profess. As revealed in attacks in market places in Delhi, Varanasi, Ayodhya and Mumbai, the primary objective has been to trigger communal riots and widen the historical divide and suspicion which has existed, at subliminal level, between Hindus and Muslims.

Another development that has tested the counter-terrorism effort in India, in recent times is the profile of terror leaders and operatives. Today, the terror coalition constitutes professionals—businessmen and IT workers who live in mixed residential colonies and lead a normal middle-class existence. They act more like sleeper agents and their leaders are often recruited to the cause by operational commanders of Let or HuJI who are based in Bangladesh, Pakistan or west Asian countries. These groups of men are neither indoctrinated nor recruited in a traditional manner but nevertheless are willing to cause death and destruction in the name of religion. India cannot afford to ignore the perils of chemical, biological and nuclear attacks by terrorist groups. Terrorist groups the world over have been desperately hunting for nuclear or radio active materials to cause maximum damage to life and property in select countries. India is one of the primary targets of Al-Qaeda and its affiliated groups like LeT, HuJI and JeM. Besides the real threat of radioactive materials falling into the hands of terrorist groups, there is even greater threat of terror attacks on nuclear installations. In fact, two years ago, troops were moved to protect nuclear installations in southern India. Interrogation of some terrorists caught in the Bangalore and Mumbai attacks, had reportedly revealed plans of launching suicide attacks (truck bombing) on nuclear reactors. There are now indications that these groups, particularly LeT, might enter the political arena through proxy candidates. There are reports of LeT sympathizers in political parties operating in Kashmir. In the past two years, some of them have been discovered and arrested. LeT and other groups have also been instigating protests and dharnas in Kashmir, particularly against the security forces. The email sent to different television channels five minutes before the serial blasts in Uttar Pradesh on November 23, 2007 indicate the political agenda of the groups.

There is a growing perception that the UPA Government was soft on terror. This is despite the fact that the Indian National Congress, which is the Principal component of UPA Alliance, lost the maximum number of cadres and leaders to the fight against terrorism, whether in North-East, Punjab or Jammu & Kashmir, including two of its Prime Ministers. There is an urgent need to take proactive steps to both fight terrorism effectively and dispel this impression. It would not be out of place to mention that the situation in our neighbourhood is deteriorating rapidly. Pakistan is in a mess, Bangladesh in ferment, Nepal going the Maoist way, the LTTE situation continuing in Sri Lanka. All these would increase pressures on different points of vulnerability within the Indian State. As pointed out earlier, the Naxal situation in Central India has added an entirely new dimension to this challenge.

In the last 3 decades, terrorism has become globalized. It cannot be fought with a moffusil mindset. Every law enacted to deal with terrorism only serves the purpose of an effective postmortem of the crime. It does not prevent it. In any case, terrorists who kill and maim innocent people do not do so after reading the IPC, CRPC, TADA, POTA and whatever other laws you may enact. Starting here and now, let us take a stand. Let the terrorists and their masters know that we can give as hard as we get. If we are serious about playing a meaningful role in global affairs, let us rid ourselves of this wimp image as a nation and let the world know that we are capable of taking care of ourselves.

Robust security response necessary

IT IS INDEED comic that CPI(M) general secretary, Prakash Karat, opposed the decision of the government of India to declare the CPI (Maoist) as a terrorist organisation under the Unlawful Activities (Prevention) Amendment Act, (UAPA Act).

In fact, what the declaration did was only to remove an ambiguity by putting the new hybrid called the CPI (Maoist) into the schedule of terrorist organisations that came into existence as a consequence of the merger of the Peoples War Group (PWG) and the Maoist Communist Centre (MCC). Both these organisations were already in the schedule of terrorist organisations at numbers 24 and 25 in terms of Section 18 of the UAPA Act. What the CPI(M) general secretary must understand is that the fight against terror, be it of any shade ,saffron, red or green, is a continuous battle of attrition. Like amoeba, terrorist organisations continuously keep mutating to avoid the rigours that the legal architecture of rule based societies impose to deny them both safe havens and public space, thereby pre-empting and preventing their activities, which pose a clear and present danger to nation states.

India faces an existential threat from a host of internal actors. Left wing extremism ranks fairly high on the list. From 53 districts across

The Economic Times, 28 June, 2009

nine states in 2001, the virus has rapidly spread to 252 districts across eighteen states in a short span of eight years.

India has 533 tribes comprising 88.3 million people. This translates into 8.6% of our population. 85% of this population lives in central and peninsular India that is in the active command area of the Maoist movement.

Unlike other extremist/separatist movements in Punjab or Jammu & Kashmir or insurgencies in the North East, left wing extremism is not a rim land insurgency but more in the nature of a heartland rebellion.

A bulk of our mineral resources are concentrated in this region. While a mere listing in the terrorist schedule would not resolve the problem, it does give the states concerned the flexibility of a robust security response that is also a necessity.

A solid sense of security

THE PROTEST by eight chief ministers, characterising the Union government's decision to give powers of search and arrest to the National Counter Terrorism Centre (NCTC) under Section 43 (a) of the Unlawful Activities Prevention Act 1967, as an assault on federalism, comes in the wake of a "sticky bomb" attack that injured an Israeli diplomat in the high-security Lutyens Delhi. The attack, perhaps, is a precursor to the export of a new wave of terror to India. In any other democracy, both the decision and the attack would have triggered a larger debate about the nature and functioning of our law enforcement and intelligence structures.

India's counter-terrorism structures and operational capacities to pre-empt and prevent terror attacks suffer from both design flaws and capacity constraints. The complete absence of a consensus on national security issues turns debates into slanging matches, replete with political and communal overtones. It is not surprising, then, that the rhetoric of zero tolerance against terror has never turned into an operational reality. In sharp contrast, a survey of global counter-terrorism efforts reveals that nothing has been allowed to stand in the way of crafting an effective pre-emptive response to terror. After the Munich Olympics outrage, counter-terrorism through the use of

---

The Indian Express, 21February, 2012

military, law enforcement, intelligence and other resources to identify, circumvent and neutralise terrorist groups has been among the principal security concerns of Germany. The counter-terrorism effort in Germany is directed by the federal coordinator for intelligence, who reports directly to the German chancellor.

In the wake of the 9/11 attacks, a national counter-terrorism centre was created at the federal level by the US government, with the 2004 intelligence reform legislation, to serve as the primary organisation responsible for the war on terror. Its objective was straightforward — ensure that terrorists do not strike again. The rationale — focus all elements of national power in the fight against terror by clearly delineating national priorities, breaking down inter-agency barriers and overriding federal qua state jurisdictional issues.

Similarly, Spain in the wake of the Madrid train bombings in 2004, and Britain after the London bus bombings in 2005, have substantially beefed up their counter-terrorism structures. Britain has an organisation called National Counter Terrorism Security office, exclusively dedicated to this purpose. In Russia, the National Counter-terrorism Committee (NAK) is tasked with coordinating all federal-level anti-terrorism policies and operations with the powers to intervene at the federal, regional or even municipal level. Even Sweden has designated its security police as the lead agency in the fight against terrorism. Most of these countries, in addition to being democratic, have strong federalist impulses.

What was required was a national organisation, exclusively tasked with confronting every part of the terrorists' life cycle—from radicalisation to recruitment, financing to training for an attack. The decision, therefore, to establish the NCTC by drawing executive power from Article 72 of the Constitution and empowering it under the UAPA, needs to be understood and located in this security environment. However, the decision to create such an institution through an executive order and locate it within the Intelligence Bureau (IB) does raise certain valid concerns, given the tenuous legal basis of our intelligence structures, the lack of an independent oversight mechanism and the atmosphere of permanent political distrust in a polarised polity.

In response to a Parliament question in July 2009 pertaining to the legislative act from which the Intelligence Bureau draws its right to function, the government came up with this: "The Intelligence Bureau figures in Schedule 7 of the Constitution under the Union list". When pressed that this may not be an appropriate answer, the government emphatically reiterated: "The Intelligence Bureau finds mention at S NO 8 in the Union list under the 7th Schedule of the Constitution of India".

Entry 8 in the Union list enunciated in the government's response merely gives it the legislative power to enact a statute to bring a Central Bureau of Intelligence to be called by whatever name (IB or BI) into existence. A mere mention of a subject in the laundry list of legislative powers neither gives an organisation life nor legitimacy. Unfortunately, no such law has ever been enacted by successive governments since the commencement of the Constitution.

Similar is the case of India's external intelligence service, the Research and Analysis Wing (R&AW). Responding to a Parliament question about the law/statute which enables the R&AW, the government admitted that there is no specific statute governing its functions or mandate. However, a formal charter listing the scope and mandate of the R&AW governs its functioning. Contrast this with the position in other countries. The Central Intelligence Agency (CIA) was created by the National Security Act of 1947 and is empowered by the Central Intelligence Agency Act of 1949. MI5, the domestic intelligence service of the United Kingdom, draws its legal authority from the Security Services Act 1989, and its sister organisation MI6, or the SIS, from the 1994 Intelligence Services Act, thereby subjecting its activities to the scrutiny of the British Parliament's Intelligence and Security Committee. The Foreign Intelligence Service of Russia draws its legal basis from the Law on Foreign Intelligence Organs 1996. The German Federal Intelligence Service Bundesnachrichtendienst (BND) draws its legal sustenance from the Federal Intelligence Service Law 1990. Its activities are supervised by the Parliamentary Control Commission (PKK) for intelligence services, which in turn is empowered by the law over the Parliamentary Control of Intelligence Activities 1978.

The current challenge should be turned into an opportunity, both by the government and by Parliament, to provide a statutory basis and an oversight mechanism for our intelligence agencies. A template in the form of a private member's bill introduced by me in the Lok Sabha entitled "The Intelligence Services (Powers and Regulations) Bill 2011" already exists. The NCTC can be incorporated in omnibus treasury legislation with statutory safeguards that clearly delineate the role of state governments in this existential struggle. This should be in addition to the operational standing council the NCTC order 2012 seeks to create. This would prevent the bogey of federalism from derailing the fight against terror.

Playing with fire

THE ISLAMIC State of Iraq and Syria (ISIS) or the Islamic State (IS), as it currently calls itself, controls hundreds of kilometres of territory from Syria's Mediterranean coast to the south of Baghdad. It is a chilling reminder that even in today's day and age a non-state actor can physically capture and hold territory while ignoring or erasing national distinctions.

However, what is more perturbing is the radical Islamic theology that underscores its ideological basis that makes it an existential threat to European multi-culturalism to its West and the syncretic Indian ethos to the East. For many centuries, ascetic forms of Islam have held sway across the desert lands of the Greater Middle East. They were unable to spread beyond its territorial confines as there were strong civilisational buffers on either side, in addition to the moderating and modernising impulses at play within the region itself. However, the desire of the Western powers to once again re-order the Middle East has bared the deep faultlines that run through the region. It has allowed the lava of religious and sectarian differences to violently bubble up to the surface.

In the process, a number of European countries, with predominantly Muslim populations, have estranged themselves from

---

The Asian Age, 08 October, 2014

public opinion as a consequence of their participation in operations in Afghanistan, Iraq, other parts of the Middle East and North Africa. Muslim citizens have not taken very kindly to these engagements. Evidence of this is emerging in the form of sporadic attacks in various countries. The attack on the Jewish Museum of Belgium, in Brussels, by a terrorist who had returned from Syria is a case in point.

The German Federal Office for the Protection of the Constitution estimates that over 300 Islamists from that country alone have gone to Syria. A number of them have returned with combat experience. Nato ally Turkey is also in the cross hairs of the ISIS. With Al Qaeda veterans from Afghanistan and Pakistan regrouping in Syria under the tutelage of the so-called Khorasan group, the possibility of high visibility terrorist assaults has increased significantly. The European Union has started conferring as to how border controls within the Schengen zone can be beefed up to screen travellers. It invited representatives of social networking companies, including Twitter, Facebook and Google, to the EU interior minister's meeting in Luxembourg to help develop a counter narrative that can deprive the ISIS of its exceedingly effectual and exploitative use of the Internet. There is a growing realisation that the most effective ballast to radicalisation is the prevention of further alienation, especially among minority populations.

Moving towards the East, India was able to withstand three decades of proxy war unleashed by Pakistan because the bonds and threads between communities remained strong notwithstanding the stresses and strains that cross-border terrorism imposed upon them. However, even these ties have now started wilting and falling apart at the seams. The principle reason is that three decades of the politics of polarisation has now come home to roost. It all commenced way back in the second half of the Eighties, with the campaign started by the current ruling party to demolish the Babri Mosque and build a temple in its place. A climate of hate and distrust was perpetrated. It culminated in the demolition of the Babri Masjid in December 1992. These actions laid the foundations of estrangement, alienation and polarisation and not essentially in that order.

While wounds of the Eighties and Nineties were still raw, the Gujarat pogrom of 2002 was unleashed on a hapless minority with the active collusion of the then state government. This was followed by the killings of innocent Muslim boys and girls in police encounters—encounters admitted to as fake by the Gujarat government in affidavits before the highest court of the land. The silver lining on this otherwise ominous cloud was that there was a secular government in office for 10 years at the Centre. It gave a sense of reassurance to the minorities that there was an institutional commitment to the doctrine of pluralism and equality. This changed in the May of 2014, with the emergence of India's first Right-wing government since Independence that is wedded to the politics of revivalism. From the day it assumed office, the Bharatiya Janata Party has been attempting to instil a sense of insecurity among the minorities in an orchestrated and calibrated manner. Whether it is articulating the need for the repeal of Article 370, exhortations for a Uniform Civil Code, statements that minorities should consider themselves as second-rate citizens, or the vile campaign against "love jihad"—all are attempts to morph India into a de facto Hindu state. What the government and its politico-cultural instrumentalities seem to be oblivious of is the extremely radicalised region we live in and that their rhetoric is no longer perceived as the raving and ranting of a fringe but has the force of the state behind it. Each utterance, therefore, only reinforces the sense of estrangement among the minorities.

This is where the ISIS fits in and why it may pose a real existential threat to India unlike in the past when Pakistan's proxy war, the Al Qaeda or even the Indian Mujahideen all failed. Given the reach and the efficacious use of the Internet as a conscripting tool by terrorist organisations, it becomes easy to influence impressionable young minds when they juxtapose the narrative of persecution and ignominy with the bigoted and prejudiced approach of this government in an ostensibly representative democracy. A decade earlier, in 2001, the US went after Al Qaeda in Afghanistan. But it will not pull the chestnuts out of the fire by going after the ISIS. Its attempts to de-fang the ISIS will be at best half-hearted, if not perfunctory. As things stand, the ISIS would continue to hold large areas of ungoverned space that would provide both the launch pad and a safe haven for terrorists and their operations.

Unlike Europe that is walking the extra mile to rejuvenate the culture of pluralism, the current Indian government is falling over itself to enhance alienation, thereby providing a fertile ground to every extremist who wants to tear the idea of India asunder. This government is sowing the wind; the nation will have to reap the whirlwind.

III. Creative Cartography

The China conundrum

THE STRATEGIC implications of the Middle kingdom's economic trajectory on regional and global stability is an enigmatic riddle that defies linear answers. It was the subject of an animated discussion on the sidelines of an International Conference of Asian political parties (ICAPP) on poverty alleviation attended by senior functionaries of 55 political parties from 28 countries holding leadership positions in party hierarchies and government structures at Kunming in South Western China and later Beijing.

With a USD 4 trillion economy and laudable efforts at lifting 300 million people out of poverty, China today looks more socially cohesive than ever before notwithstanding the reports about wage riots and subterranean tensions that economic prosperity juxtaposed against the absence of political freedom in a one party state. However ,with an economic model that continues to be export driven with foreign trade accounting for 68.5% of the GDP at 2008 WTO numbers, the consequences of a still sluggish American economy and some serious belt tightening in the Eurozone begs the obvious question—Does China have the internal capacity to absorb the output of its production processes given the continuing slow down in the western economies coupled with an intrinsic thrift milieu and comparatively moderate wage structure.

An abridged version of this article was published under the title 'Sweet and sour menu', *The Hindustan Times,* 29 July, 2010

While analysts contend that China may see an opportunity in the economic meltdown to further its G-2 aspirations, given its aggressively expanding footprint of economic acquisitions across South America, Africa and all the way back again to Asia, the highest echelons of the Chinese leadership goes to great lengths to emphasize that China continues to be a developing country that has profound developmental challenges to surmount. In an interaction with the delegates to the ICAAP conference ,the Vice President of China, Mr Xi Jinping widely considered to be the heir apparent to President Hu Jintao, eloquently articulated that China's priorities lie in eradicating poverty by 2020 in line with the Millennium Development goals (MGD) of the United Nations and augmenting existing infrastructural capability by 2050 to truly emerge as a developed country in the OCED league.

The sub -text of the Vice President's assertions was to assure the widely representative and observant Asian audience that China's rise is absolutely peaceful and that the Asian nations would only benefit from the mutual synergies that this growth would continue to unleash. Senior functionaries of the Chinese Communist Party (CPC) tasked with economic and foreign policy responsibilities also strove to drive home this point in their presentations and private interactions in and around the conference. The inherent contradiction manifests itself when the development narrative is contrasted with China's burgeoning defense budget and the aggressive search for equity oil and natural resources around the world thereby raising red flags in establishments charged with assessing the direction of Chinese Comprehensive National Power.

If independent assesments are anything to go by, China's defense budget for the fiscal 2010 is most probably in the range of 90 to 120 Billion USD, substantially more than the official figure of 77.95 billion US dollars. Even if one was to go by the official Chinese numbers the budget is up by 7.5% over the 2009 figure which just can't be put down to a factor of inflation in today's economic scenario. Moreover ,the Chinese armed forces have an active strength of two million, one hundred and five thousand active personnel making it among the largest standing defense forces in the world. However, if you evaluate the regional landscape from a threat perception point of view there is nothing substantive that can validate such a defense dynamic especially when the leadership emphasizes that developmental priorities are uppermost in the pecking order.

Does then India have anything to be concerned about given the differing perceptions on a host of issues? Viewed from strictly a geo-strategic perspective there is the obvious spectre of existing and prospective Chinese naval and submarine bases stretching from Sanya in the South China Sea, 1200 nautical miles from the Straits of Mallaca, traversing Hambantota in Sri Lanka , Marao in Maldives right up to Gwadar in Pakistan situated 100 kms east of the Mouth of Hormuz—the ubiquitous string of pearls encircling India. These naval bases effectively can exercise oversight over the Sea Lanes of Commerce that are pathways of Intra-Asian energy flows from the West to the east. Given that China is the largest consumer of oil in the world and it would remain dependent on Hydro-carbons till 2020 at the least, therefore it cannot completely wish away the import of the sea routes though it is going to considerable lengths to surmount its Malacca dilemma. Coupled with the reported up -gradation of its surveillance capabilities in the great coco-islands of Myanmar, it would create natural points of inflection in areas critical to both India and China's blue water strategic interests stretching from the South China Sea to the Persian Gulf.

Evaluated in the context of the conceptual shift outlined in the 6th Chinese white paper on defense, released in January 2009, from strategic counter attacks to strategic projection operations ,it does raise the obvious question . Does this heightened presence underscore just energy security anxieties or is it reflective of China desiring to acquire strategic dominance of the SLOC or a more visible presence outside its sphere of conventional interest.

While enhancing trade to 80-100 billion USD by 2020 and increasing civilizational equities and other multilateral linkages in the region may create both a robust hedge and a sense of equilibrium to offset divergent strategic and tactical priorities, China would continue to remain among India's foremost strategic dilemmas in the twenty first century. Does India have the intellectual capacity and structures to engage in the rigors of a dynamic, multilayered and nuanced relationship?

China's art of wars

WHY DID THE Chinese-government approved Hunan Map Press and the Hubei Bureau of Surveying Mapping and Geo-Information suddenly decide to issue a map that shows Arunachal Pradesh, Aksai Chin and parts of the Karakorum tracts as integral parts of China?

The fact that the atlas was issued when a delegation led by the vice-president of India was in that country to commemorate the 60th anniversary of Panchsheel, the five principles of peaceful co-existence, makes it all the more disquieting. Concurrently, China violated Indian land and airspace in Pangong Tso and Chushul region of Ladakh respectively. An infelicitous coincidence or a deliberate design?

Provocation and harmony cannot go in tandem. However, as the Chinese philosopher Sun Tzu said, "The supreme art of war is to subdue the enemy without fighting". It is not the first time that the Chinese leadership has shown utter disregard for Indian sensitivities. Way back in 1979, while the then external affairs minister Atal Behari Vajpayee was on a visit to that country, China invaded Vietnam, compelling Mr Vajpayee to cancel his visit and return home. Intriguingly, in June this year, another Chinese mapping authority, Sino Mass Press, ostensibly issued a new map of that country showing 80 per cent of the South China Sea as internal Chinese waters. Earlier,

---

The Asian Age, 12 July, 2014

in 1995, in pursuit of historical if not mythological claims, China had occupied Mischief Reef, and in 2012 it had seized Scarborough shoal both in the South China Sea and regarded as Philippines territory. The hard ball it played with Japan in September 2010 on the Senkaku/ Diaoyutai Islands dispute still riles the region.

Why do nations indulge in creative cartography? Maps denote the renewal of a nation's persona and identity. In the case of China, the politico-strategic leadership has always believed that the past two centuries, because of the imperial occupation of large parts of Asia, do not represent the natural order of things. It, therefore, invokes annals and ancient narratives to lay substantial claims on foreign territories. This is then further reinforced by conjectural cartography that bestows upon itself expansive latitude in delineating national boundaries to substantiate these abstract entitlements. Not only do they celebrate the extent of China's eminent domain, but also mourn the loss of national territories. With the economic rise of China and the consequential influence it wields, even militarily, in the region, it has developed a hazardous propensity to try and correct perceived historical injustices. While rewriting history has its own perils, gerrymandering is a sure recipe for disaster. However, the Chinese leadership has demonstrated the will, erroneously, to leverage its comprehensive national power and ignore international opprobrium in pursuit of its territorial designs. The power play in the South & East China Sea cannot but help the obvious conclusion that map making in China is a precursor to the more ominous actions that follow.

What are the lessons that India ought to draw from this latest provocation as well as the continual stand off on the border question over the decades? To understand the issue beyond the fact that the Line of Actual Control (LAC) is repeatedly transgressed under the subterfuge that it is inconsistent with the perception line that both the countries have of their respective borders, a peep into the past to discern mindsets shaped by national narratives is imperative. Both India and China, in their current avatars ,came into existence in 1947 and 1949 respectively. While Indian Independence was the result of a pacifist struggle against imperialism led by Mahatma Gandhi and his colleagues, the Chinese state was born out of a violent and protracted armed struggle led by Mao Zedong and his comrades. Though the Mao years were repudiated by Deng Xiaoping in 1978, the fundamental reality that got embedded in the Chinese psyche was deference and reverence for strength. While there may be a lot of economic liberalism on display—it is glorious to be rich, and have Weibo, the Chinese Twitter—at its core China remains a hard state. Historical mores and contemporary milieus shape the worldview of nation states. They invariably view other countries through that prism.

A classic manifestation of this truism is that notwithstanding the magniloquence that Asian affairs should be left to Asians, China has never challenged the claim of the United States of being an Asian power. China recognises that with its hub and spoke network of military alliances and now the Asian pivot, the US is the balancer of the first and last resort in the Asia-Pacific region. Strength begets respect.

It therefore, should come as no surprise that whenever a change of government takes place in New Delhi, the Chinese state would be tempted to probe the temperament, will and resolve of the new dispensation, especially now since the current Prime Minister had stated during the parliamentary election campaign in Pasighat, Arunachal Pradesh, that "no power on earth can take away even an inch from India. Moreover the present world does not accept an expansionist attitude. Times have changed; China should give up its expansionist attitude and adopt a developmental mindset". Now contrast this with the rather lackadaisical response of the new government to the cartographic aggression stating, "Cartographic depictions do not change the reality on the ground". Can it then be concluded that the BJP government is nonchalant about misrepresentation of Indian territory on the atlases of the world?

Coupled with this is the fact that no firm message was given by the new government to the visiting Chinese foreign minister, despite the bombast of the BJP while in Opposition, on the issue of border intrusions, stapled visas etc. This, perhaps, served to consolidate the impression in the minds of our north-eastern neighbour that this government is unwilling to walk its tough talk. This would have implications in the immediate future on a broad range of bilateral and multilateral issues germane to both the countries. Nothing can be more damaging than the impression that the party in government is blasé about its past utterances. In addition to the international repercussions, back home it only reinforces the growing perception that the words and actions of this government are two parallel tracks not destined to meet.

IV. Nuclear Concerns

The nuclear deal is not just about energy security

IF NUCLEAR energy is going to constitute only 8 per cent of our energy mix by the year 2020, and 20 per cent by 2050, then why is the UPA prepared to stake its government on the Indo-US nuclear deal? Why do the NDA and the Left find themselves on the same side as Pakistan and China in opposing and expressing reservations on the deal?

The operationalisation of the deal would not take place before the end of 2008 going by even the most optimistic time frame. That is subject to protocols still to be negotiated with the International Atomic Energy Agency (IAEA), the Nuclear Suppliers Group (NSG) and finally a vote by the US Congress. The Hyde Act is only a waiver from the provisions of Section 123 of the US Atomic Energy Act permitting the US administration to arrive at an agreed bilateral framework with India for cooperation in the field of civil nuclear energy.

The nuclear deal raises some vital questions. Is it a step towards energy security or developing a strategic relationship with the US? Does the deal in any manner constrain our strategic autonomy or the pursuit of an independent foreign policy?

On the demand side, India consumed about 470 MTOE (million tonnes of oil equivalent) of energy in 2003-04. On the supply side,

---

Tehelka.com-the People's Paper, 01 September, 2007

India generates 135 thousand megawatts of power annually. It would have to ramp up its generating capacity to 500-600 thousand megawatts annually. Thus, over the next few decades, India would have to pursue each and every possible energy option.

India is actively exploring a wide array of energy options ranging from bio-diesel, wind energy, hydrocarbons from tar sands, ore emulsion and carbon sequestration, and gas pipelines through turbulent areas of West and Central Asia. Some of these are still at an experimental stage while the gas pipelines are high risk ventures with issues of financial and physical viability. There are reasons for opposing nuclear energy per-se, which somehow have not found a place in the mainstream debate on the issue. They extend from the safety and security of nuclear reactors and cost per unit of electricity to environmental impact and radioactive waste. However, if we do not have an issue with the above, then it makes no sense to oppose the nuclear deal, which clearly provides access to a prudent energy option even though it may constitute only 8 per cent of India's energy mix in the short run, as the scalability potential is exponential.

It would be churlish to contemplate that the nuclear deal has not been influenced by the prevailing global environment and marks the resumption of a larger strategic engagement between India and the US While it would be simplistic to view the evolving strategic relationship between India and the US or defence cooperation with Japan or Australia through the prism of a containment policy qua China, there are certain national security imperatives that just cannot be swept under the table.

The fact remains that China is spending anywhere between USD 85–125 billion annually on defence. The Sino-Pakistani alliance, the Chinese relationship with the military regime in Myanmar and its forays into Sri Lanka to access the Indian Ocean are obvious concerns that should not be glossed over. From a purely national security perspective it makes eminent sense to have a strategic relationship with the US. The only questions that remain are the implications of this deal on India's pursuit of an independent foreign policy and whether the deal constrains, caps or rolls back India's strategic nuclear programme. If India at any stage feels that it needs to carry out a nuclear test, no bilateral or multilateral agreement can constrain it. If a test is vital and would have implications on our economy then we would have to factor in the cost and weigh it on the touchstone of our sovereignty.

If the US were to call off the deal because of domestic imperatives despite the redundancies and safeguards built into Article 14, Clauses 2-6 of the 123 agreement, then we would live with it as we lived with sanctions post-Pokharan I and II. In the worst case scenario, it would only bring us back to the situation we are in today.

It is for the opponents of the deal to answer as to why they stand on the same side as China and Pakistan in opposing the deal, for India, quite clearly, needs this deal.

Nuclear Mess

A CORE ISSUE that escaped analytical attention in the first hundred days is the rather disquieting formulation in the Bharatiya Janata Party's manifesto on India's strategic programme. The construct reads as follows: "BJP believes that the strategic gains acquired by India during the Atal Behari Vajpayee regime on the nuclear programme have been frittered away by the Congress. Our emphasis was, and remains on, beginning of a new thrust on framing policies that would serve India's national interest in the 21st century. We will follow a two-pronged independent nuclear programme, unencumbered by foreign pressure and influence, for civilian and military purposes, especially as nuclear power is a major contributor to India's energy sector. BJP will study in detail India's nuclear doctrine, revise it and update it, to make it relevant to challenges of current times, maintain a credible minimum deterrent in tune with changing geostatic realities and invest in India's indigenous Thorium security programme".

Before coming to the more profound issues, note the characterisation of the Vajpayee government as a "regime". The Oxford English Dictionary defines regime as "a government, especially an authoritarian one". A search for the meaning of the word "geostatic" did not produce any strategic or tactical definition. Perhaps, they

---

The Asian Age, 20 September, 2014

meant geostrategic. Rather sloppy when you are dealing with the "N" word in a nuclearised neighbourhood.

The portentous implications of this rather cavalier phraseology set alarm bells ringing across the world. *The New York Times* in an incisive editorial on April 9, 2014, contrasted the approach of the two political dispensations. Articulating the distinction, it stated, "The lack of clarity about the party's (read BJP) intentions on this issue introduces more uncertainty in an already unstable region", and went on to add that, "in fact last week, Prime Minister Manmohan Singh proposed a global framework to promote a 'no first use' doctrine among nuclear weapon states, a laudable goal." There was naturally consternation not only among the Ayatollahs of non-proliferation, but also in responsible policy-making circles. That must have compelled the BJP's prime ministerial candidate to clarify that "no first use was a great initiative of Atal Behari Vajpayee—there is no compromise on that. We are very clear. No first use is a reflection of our cultural inheritance." Quixotic that a strategic doctrine can be a cultural inheritance and that too in a nation that lacks a strategic culture.

Notwithstanding the clarification, the fact remains that the formulation stays as it is in the BJP manifesto without any amendment. Does the clarification of a prime ministerial candidate override the manifesto commitment of his party? The jury is out on that. It, therefore, becomes imperative that the phraseology is deconstructed, sentence by sentence, to understand its true import. What were those strategic gains acquired during the Vajpayee regime which were frittered away in the UPA era? The facts, unfortunately, are contrary to this rather hackneyed assertion. Despite the nuclear tests of May 1998 that Pakistan soon followed up with its own set of explosions, the Kargil intrusion did take place in May 1999.

During the next few years, Pakistan not only intensified its proxy war against India, but its instrumentalities attacked the Indian Parliament. This resulted in the largest ever mobilisation of the Indian armed forces in recent times—Operation Parakram in January 2001 that ended 10 months later in a whimper. It blunted the most useful instrument of coercive diplomacy almost permanently. The nuclear tests actually froze the power balance in South Asia into perpetuity, thereby providing Pakistan the nuclear shield to carry on with its policies. Were there really any strategic gains that accrued to India in that torrid summer of 1998?

In fact, the opposite is true. It was the adroit diplomacy of the UPA government which, through the Indo-US civil nuclear agreement, was able to demolish the sanction and denial regimes—colloquially referred to as "nuclear apartheid"—institutionalised by the Nuclear Suppliers Group, also called the Club de Londres. This gave India access to much needed sensitive dual-use technologies among other things, and is perhaps the most vital strategic gain made by India in recent times.

Coming to the second sentence of the formulation, we are yet to hear or know what "new thrust" the BJP intends on giving to framing policies in the strategic arena that would serve India's national interest in the 21st century. The third sentence invokes the omniscient though invisible foreign hand guiding our nuclear theology—a conspiracy theory that has no empirical basis to back it. But hilariously, after opposing the Indian civil nuclear agreement, even to the extent of bringing a no-confidence motion on the matter in July 2008, the BJP has suddenly woken up to the virtues of nuclear power. Is the BJP suggesting that India's strategic force posture is not relevant to contemporary challenges? Rather perilous an admission given the parts that we live in. The last, but not the least sentence maintains a credible deterrent in tune with changing "geostatic" realities. Is it an allusion or an implicit admission that our deterrent is not credible?

Ironically, the then NDA government in August 1999 had conceptualised the draft nuclear doctrine after the second round of nuclear tests. It was eventually approved by the Cabinet Committee on Security and officially promulgated in January 2003. It is profane that an issue of such import was not even brought to a meeting of the full Cabinet for discussion much less a decision or at the least a ratification. The doctrine held the field throughout the UPA years, from 2004 to 2014, ostensibly without any change or amendment that was enunciated in the public domain. While strategic ambivalence, if properly leveraged, may be an asset, strategic ambiguity is a lethal liability as it broadcasts portentous and diverging pointers about the very foundations of your nuclear theology that ostensibly bolsters your strategic posture. Given the equivocality, opacity and ineptly worded postulation that the BJP has adopted to deal with India's most sensitive governance paradigm, coupled with the fact that the manifesto commitment remains inviolable, one can only wonder whether the government is up to something that "India does not know".

The Yanks are coming

THE SECOND term of any US President is a good time for intrepid and inspiring foreign policy enterprises. Free of electoral pressures, the President can make his own historical bed to lie in. With less than two years for President Barack Obama's term to wind down and a hostile Congress, will there be any legacy of the Indo-US relationship during the Obama years?

Mr Obama inherited a country in its severest economic crisis since the Great Depression of the 1930s. It was mired in two wars. In the librettos of the US President, the good war was in Afghanistan and the bad war in Iraq. Its reputation was in shreds due to the illegal renditions programme and prisoner abuse at Guantanamo Bay and other offsite locations. How much of that damage has been repaired only time would tell. One of the inadvertent casualties of these preoccupations has been an absence of mind space for the Indo-US relationship. Nothing evidences it more than two superb accounts of the priorities and primacies within the rarefied echelons of the US administration authored by two former US defence secretaries—Robert Gates who served both the Bush and the Obama administrations and Leon Panetta, who first served as Mr Obama's Central Intelligence Agency director and then as secretary of defence. India hardly finds even a passing reference in both these narratives.

The Asian Age, 10 January, 2015

At this point, it perhaps would be worth to step back into time. In the closing years of the Vajpayee administration, the then National Democratic Alliance government initiated the "Next Steps in the Strategic Partnership (NSSP)" with the US. The NSSP was the outcome of a rather capacious dialogue between Jaswant Singh and Strobe Talbott. However, the moment the Bharatiya Janata Party was out of government, it started opposing every aspect of the Indo-US engagement with a vengeance. The intransigence culminated in the confidence motion of 2008 on the Indo-US nuclear engagement that the NDA lost. What the BJP/NDA opposed was perhaps the most "daring initiative" ever envisioned—reform of the international nuclear order to India's advantage. However, after this watershed achievement there has been a hiatus.

What should be the next "big idea" in this relationship? For that, one needs to scan the strategic landscape to discern the significant US initiatives in the Asia-Pacific region. The most obvious one that comes to the mind is the "Asia pivot" or the rebalance of the US force posture towards this region. This entails drawing down from Europe and the Greater Middle East and deploying those military forces in the ratio of 60-40 in this area. Broadly quantified, it translates into 60 per cent of all oversees US military assets in the Asia-Pacific and 40 per cent in the rest of the world. Though there is an economic component to this rebalance but given the sluggish nature of the global economy it is at best fuzzy.

Does India fit into this strategic calculus? Unlikely, given the fact that India should maintain strategic ambivalence and not get tied down to any arrangement that would in any manner constrain its autonomy—the grandiloquent rhetoric about the quadrilateral between Japan, Australia, the US and India notwithstanding. The next big item on the US calendar is the drawdown leading to the eventual wrap up of its involvement in Afghanistan. Were the security situation to deteriorate and the new power structure in Afghanistan is unable to hold the country together, what then would the US do? Would it recommit troops to Afghanistan? Again, this is exceedingly incongruous.

Would it then look around at Afghanistan's immediate neighbours—Pakistan, Iran, Russia, China and the Stans-

Turkmenistan, Kazakhstan, Kyrgyzstan and Uzbekistan to fill that vacuum? Not by a stretch, as some do not have the capacity, while others are players in the Afghan tragedy since the Eighties. And others would be mortified of venturing back. Would then the US look towards India for fulfilling that role given that India has a strategic partnership with Afghanistan? This is unlikely, since it would put Pakistan's tail up and more so as India has been chary, for all the right reasons ,to having an expeditionary presence abroad.

An idea that has been flagged earlier too is perhaps worth cogitating. The Nuclear Non-Proliferation Treaty (NPT) comes up for review this year. India has, perhaps, the most impeccable track record in terms of non-proliferation of nuclear technology, perhaps much more than even the signatories to the treaty. Would it be in India's interest to join the nuclear non-proliferation architecture as a nuclear weapon state? Should India not graduate into the role of a rule maker rather than a rule taker? Is there any downside for India for aspiring to once again change the international order? Prima facie there seems to be none.

However, why would the US or anyone else for that matter do the heavy lifting for India? The US, in any case, feels shortchanged by the supplier's liability provision in the nuclear liability act. The collective belief among the Beltway policy community in Washington DC is that the US got literally nothing in return for all the muscle and torque it invested into getting India the waiver from its own legislature and the International Atomic Energy Agency (IAEA) and the Nuclear Suppliers Group (NSG). The conundrum then is whether India can offer the US something in return? There are going to be no takers for the enhanced foreign direct investment (FDI) limit to 49 per cent in defence howsoever much the Indian government may want to spin it. Maybe the government may not need to do a quid pro quo but pitch it dexterously. Approximating the United Nations Security Council, the NPT is also a vestige of power balance of the Cold War era. If the institutions of global governance have to reflect the contemporary global dynamic they need to reform too.

However, first and foremost, the government needs to start a conversation within its own strategic and policy community to flesh out the pros and cons of this thought. Concurrently, it must explore the US administration's attitude and that of other key nations. Mr Obama's upcoming visit to India at the end of January is the opportune moment. Does the BJP government have the strategic bandwidth to at least think large if not finesse this realpolitik? Indubitably, it is more creative than showing the Yanks some military hardware.

A Faustian bargain

"THE DEAL IS done. We have reached an understanding. We have broken the logjam of the past few years," exulted former foreign secretary Sujatha Singh on the first evening of President Barack Obama's visit to New Delhi to participate in the Republic Day parade. She was referring to the Indo-US Civil Nuclear Deal negotiated by the UPA government. For all her labours, the reward was her removal just two days after Air Force One lifted off from the technical area of the Palam Airport. After moving a no-confidence motion to derail the nuclear deal in July 2008, the BJP had no qualms in attempting to take acclaim for operationalising it in 2015. A day after the 123 Agreement was made public on August 4, 2007, the BJP had termed it as an "assault on the nuclear sovereignty and foreign policy options" of India. So it was from January 25 onwards that the nation was oblivious as to what was the "done deal". Finally, the day after polling in Delhi was over the foreign office come out with an explanation in the form of frequently asked questions on Civil Liability for Nuclear Damage Act 2010 and related issues.

What were the sticking points that Modi and Obama presumably resolved? The first pertained to the interpretation of Section 17(b) of the Nuclear Liability Act. The original clause in the bill read: "The

---

The Asian Age, 21 February, 2015

nuclear incident has resulted from the willful act or gross negligence on the part of the supplier of the material, equipment or services, or of the employee." There was consternation in Parliament about the difficulty of proving intent. Bowing to the will of Parliament, the clause was redrafted to make the liability of the supplier absolute. The amended clause in the Nuclear Liability Act reads: "The nuclear incident has resulted as a consequence of an act of the supplier or his employee, which includes supply of equipment with patent or latent defects or substandard services".

Now let us come to what the government clarification says. "However, the situations identified in Section 17(b) relate to actions and matters such as product liability stipulations/conditions or service contracts. These are ordinarily part of a contract between the operator and the supplier. This situation is not novel but is rather a normal element of a contract. Thus, this provision is to be read along with/in the context of the relevant clause in the contract between the operator and supplier on product liability. It is open for the operator and the supplier to agree on the terms of their contract relying on the applicable law".

Demystified of legalese it essentially means that the supplier-operator contract would have overriding precedence over a statutory provision. If this interpretation was correct then what was the need for this section? The previous provision section 17 (a) states inter alia "the operator of the nuclear installation after paying compensation for nuclear damage in accordance with Section 6, shall have a right to recourse where such right is expressly provided for in a contract in writing." In fact, the unamended and amended Section17 (b) was specifically for situations where such a right of recourse was not specifically written into a contract between an operator and a supplier. Now who is selling the national interest with such self-serving interpretations?

The next sticking point is Section 46. The provision states, "This act shall be in addition to, and not in derogation of, any other law for the time being in force, and nothing contained herein shall exempt the operator from any proceeding which might, apart from this act, be instituted against such operator." The intent of the provision is clear that if a nuclear accident or incident takes place, the option of tortious liability and criminal proceedings would be open to the victims in both Indian and foreign courts. If the accident or the incident happens because of the supplier's fault then obviously the operator or even the government can take him to task for criminal negligence or punitive damages in Indian or foreign courts respectively.

Now discern how the government in its explanation seeks to water it down. "The CLND Act channels all legal liability for nuclear damage exclusively to the operator and Section 46 does not provide a basis for bringing claims for compensation for nuclear damage under other acts. That this section applies exclusively to the operator and does not extend to the supplier. At the same time it does not create the grounds for victims to move foreign courts. In fact, that would be against the basic intent of the law to provide a domestic legal framework for victims of nuclear damage to seek compensation".

Now juxtapose this explanation against the plain meaning of Section 46 and you can draw your own conclusions as to who is batting for the nuclear behemoths when the UPA was batting for the people. Last but not the least the insurance conundrum. Section 6(2) fixes the liability between Rs 100-1,500 crores for different kind of nuclear reactors and plants. Explaining this provision in the Lok Sabha, the then minister of state in the Prime Minister's office stated that the compensation cap to be paid by the operator at Rs 1,500 crore as provided in the bill was not the "limit" as overall compensation would be the decision of the claims commissioner. "Compensation is unlimited. Whatever compensation will be decided by the Claims Commissioner and he (operator) will have to pay it. The limit on compensation was only to enable the operator take insurance cover. How does the ministry of external affairs FAQ interpret this provision? "Section 6(2) of the act lays down that the operator's maximum liability shall be Rs 1,500 crore. In case the total liability exceeds Rs 1,500 crore as per Section 7(1) a of the CLND Act, this gap of Rs 1,100 crore would be bridged by the Central government".

Moreover, the FAQ says that Rs 1,500 crore would also be made up of an insurance pool made up of GIC Re and four other PSUs, which would together contribute Rs 750 crore and the balance would be contributed by the government. The suppliers can also access this insurance pool. In other words, Indian money would pay for a nuclear accident in India and a foreign supplier can virtually take a free ride at the expense of the Indian savers and taxpayers. Does that sound like protecting national interest or selling the sovereign short?

In essence, as long as Section 17 and 46 remain on the statute book, no amount of sophistry or chicanery would allow the government to escape the rigours of the law. These provisions were inserted by the UPA government to protect people from a Fukushima, Chernobyl or a Three Mile Island-type of disaster, while retaining the flexibility to access nuclear power. No formal or informal understanding arrived at by the BJP government can surmount the explicit letter of the law.

V. Oodles of Doodles

The Gulf vacuum awaits the Indian summer

A NEW ERA is dawning in the Middle East. An era that would be characterised by declining US influence and attempts by Saudi Arabia, Iran and Israel to widen their spheres of influence in the region. This would not only aggravate political tensions but also see increasing Shia-Sunni-Judaism violence, consolidation of political Islam and a weakening of nation states in the entire Middle East.

Our quest for equity oil necessitates a seat on the high tables of the Gulf states, if not in the boardrooms. From India's perspective, a holistic approach to sustainable energy security is now an essential pre-requisite for its economy if the target of even 8 per cent growth has to be sustained. As of now, 70 per cent of India's energy needs are imported from the Gulf Cooperation Council Countries (GCC). For the next 50 years, India's energy mix is going to remain hydrocarbon-dependent notwithstanding its emphasis on nuclear and other sources of alternate energy.

The Gulf states have a collective surplus of three trillion USD, most of which is invested in US Treasury bonds, but can be leveraged with an effective strategy for infrastructure development in India. Millions of Indians workers in the Gulf send back remittances that contribute to local economies in a variety of ways. The security and

---

Tehelka.com-the People's Paper, 28 April, 2007

stability of the Persian Gulf states is in turn embryonically linked to developments in the greater Middle East. The Gulf states (GCC countries) are looking towards India, China and Japan—their major energy consumers to fill the void that would be created as a result of decreasing US engagement in the region. It would be worth underscoring that both Japan and China view energy security as directly affecting their defence and security interests. Thus, the Middle East is of critical importance to them too.

So, does India have a role different from the one it was performing earlier? The answer to this question lies in our assessment of the situation in the region and the confidence India has in its ability to be able to respond to it. The developments in Middle East over the past four years have instilled a siege mentality among nations and people of the region. They have served to validate the theories of civilisational/religious conflict between the Occident and the Orient on the one hand and Christianity versus Islam on the other. The Israeli aggression on Lebanon only seeks to reinforce these mythological spectres.

The greatest danger in the Middle East is not a nuclear Iran or the threat of conventional invasion, but internal socio-economic and political changes that might be increasingly hard for leaders to direct or control. The threat emanates from the spreading Iraqi civil war and growing radicalism via violent forms of politicized Islam. Israel's pursuit of nuclear technology and the non-resolution of the Palestinian question also adds to the disquiet in the region.

The sense of triumph among the fundamentalists that they succeeded in vanquishing the atheist Soviet state in the 90s, and have now been able to withstand the collective might of the Western Alliance in the 2000's, has created and consolidated a pan-nationalistic identity that does not bode well for multi -ethnic and pluralistic states.

In the coming two or three years, a regional security organisation would be mid-wifed in the Middle East by the US and other Western powers. While it may be politically difficult to station Indian troops in the region immediately, the possibility of India patrolling the sea lanes from the Straits of Hormuz to the Straits of Malacca should be seriously explored as most of these sea lanes either touch Indian waters or fall within our exclusive economic zone. The Coast Guard could even take on greater responsibility for escorting oil and gas tankers through these waters, as they are potential terror targets.

In the absence of India refusing to do so, Japan, with its blue water capability would be more than willing to take on this role. This would extend the arc of Japanese influence from the East all the way up to the West of Asia. However ,given our vital interests and the emerging power vacuum in the region, India must take a call. The choices are: allowing other Asian powers, including China, a greater presence or pro-actively seeking to be a part of the framework of extra regional powers that is bound to be playing a role in the Middle East in the decades to come.

A new language for energy

THE FIRST World War ended a century of relative peace in Europe brokered by the Congress of Vienna in 1815. Since then energy has been an essential component in the foreign and security dogmas of the great powers. Is the inevitability of these postulates continuing in the 21st century a given? Perhaps the time has come to step back and seriously deliberate as to whether energy needs to be de-linked from foreign and security policies.

There is a great moral hazard in not questioning these strategic tenets of yesteryear that have perpetuated themselves into this century. It is imperative to first delineate the embedded nature of this convergence. Successive presidents of the US have enunciated security doctrines for guaranteed supplies of abundant and cheap sources of energy. In 1980, President Carter declared that access to Persian Gulf oil was a vital national interest and that the US would be prepared to use military force to protect it. President Carter's Rapid Deployment Joint Task force has evolved into the US Central Command, with an area of operations that is contiguous with the energy-rich west/central Asian and Caspian Sea regions.

At the turn of the millennium, the project for 'The New American Century' recommended massive power projection capability globally,

---

The Indian Express, 20 March, 2008

both to intensify pressure on nations labelled as rogue states and for taking action for acquisition of new and existing oil and gas fields. In May 2001, President George W Bush's New Energy Policy recommended that ties with oil-rich countries should be deepened and US presence broadened. The 2001 Quadrennial Defence Review spoke of the need for the US to enhance its ability to send forces to critical points around the globe. It identified overseas oil-producing regions as these critical points.

The net result of these policies and action is that an opinion got created in large parts of the world that Iraq was never about WMDs, Al Qaeda or even democracy. It was all about oil. There are similar perceptions about Afghanistan too, as it lies at the geographical crossroads of strategic pipeline routes. Erroneous as it may be, opinion is more often than not shaped by perception rather than reality. Integrating energy into foreign policy and security also introduces a political element into an essentially economic calculus. There is a school of thought that canvasses that supplies from the Caspian region must not go through either Russia to Europe or through Iran to the Persian Gulf which is the cheapest and the fastest route. Oil should instead flow from Kazakhstan and Azerbaijan through the turbulent Caucasus and end up at Ceyhan on the Mediterranean coast of Turkey, a process that is both expensive and a route that is long. Similarly, gas from Turkmenistan should flow through Afghanistan to Pakistan, and piped through the hostile and volatile regions of Afghanistan and Balochistan, a nightmare for those who have huge investments at stake.

In the past eight years, President Putin has leveraged Russia's energy resources as both strategic and tactical assets towards regaining Russia's erstwhile position in the world. As a vital supplier of gas and oil to Europe and Japan, Russia first experimented by shutting gas supplies to Ukraine. Though the quarrel was ostensibly over tariffs, experts believe that Russia was really testing the 'gas' weapon for possible future use. Russia's cancelling of production sharing agreements with foreign companies is further evidence of these commodities occupying a central place in its aspirations for a greater global role. Russia may have lost the Cold War but is not prepared to lose the energy sweepstakes as the election of Dimitry Medvedev, chairperson of Gazprom, as president clearly demonstrates.

China has made the acquisition of equity oil the pre-eminent objective of state policy. It has made important gains in Africa where it is likely to be in contention with other powers that have similarly elevated the pursuit of equity oil into a similar goal of statecraft.

An equally significant development is taking place in India's neighbourhood. Pakistan has now begun to claim that Gilgit and Baltistan, illegally occupied by it in 1947, are not part of the erstwhile princely state of J&K ceded to India by the ruler of that state. This claim has become shriller of late. This is ostensibly because the proposed overland pipelines from the port of Gwadar (developed with substantive Chinese investment) to Xinjiang and onwards into mainland China would run through these occupied Indian territories. While these proposed pipelines may enable China to mitigate the risks attendant in traversing the sea-lanes from the Hormuz to Malacca and help it resolve the Malacca dilemma itself, let us not forget that this power play is taking place at the tri-section of three declared nuclear weapon states.

In the post-Cold War era, western strategic thinkers, impelled by visions of unipolarity and aided by the occupation of Kuwait and continuing instability in the larger Middle East, started articulating energy interests in the language of competition and conflict. Their arguments stemmed from the zeal to lock down sources of supply amid concerns relating to depleting global supplies, the ostensibly hostile role that major hydrocarbon producers were playing in global politics, and burgeoning demand for energy by the Asian economies.

While their concerns may not be entirely incorrect, it leads the rising political and economic powers to start scouring unstable regions for their own spheres of influence, positioning energy as the pivot to re-energise fossilised 19th century mindsets? Would this century have to contend with further aggression and re-politicisation of energy flows between the emerged and emerging players?

Frequently, the refrain 'hunger for resources' sets off alarm bells of attendant conflict. Can we not turn energy into the fuel of peace? Is it not time to start exploring a framework of global cooperative arrangements that can truly delink energy from foreign and security policies?

India must decide its stance on Gaza

PARADOXICALLY AND concomitantly in Fortaleza, Brazil, the Government signed off on the Sixth BRICS summit declaration with the operative portion affirming... "We call upon Israel and Palestine to resume negotiations leading to a two-State solution with a contiguous and economically viable Palestinian State existing side by side in peace with Israel, within mutually agreed and internationally recognised borders based on the 4 June, 1967 lines, with East Jerusalem as its capital. We oppose the continuous construction and expansion of settlements in the Occupied Palestinian Territories by the Israeli Government, which violates international law, gravely undermines peace efforts and threatens the viability of the two-State solution."

Rupture

Tough libretto avowing a position, at the BRICS, that is endeavouring to emerge as an alternative pole in the global balance of power.

When consternation and outrage mounted, the Government did a U-turn and agreed a week later to a discussion in Parliament. It concurrently then also went right ahead and voted in favour of a Palestinian drafted resolution at the United Nations Human Rights Council, terming Israel's military operations ostensibly as international crimes and called for an investigation by an independent global

Mail Today, 29 July, 2014

commission. Is this sequence of events indicative of the Government's left hand not knowing what the right is doing? Does it reflect a rupture between the Prime Minister's office and the Ministry of External Affairs? Is it symptomatic of the green shoots of policy paralysis manifesting themselves? Should it be perceived as an attempt to run with the hare and hunt with the hound in the naive belief that other foreign offices do not read international declarations?

There could be yet another facet. Was the Government surreptitiously attempting to bring about a policy shift in India's historical position on the Israeli-Palestine conflict that backfired under pressure? Is it then demonstrative of its inability to be able to walk the tight rope that such historical and contentious disputes require without diluting either our relationship or position with either entity?

However, on a weightier note, what is worrying is whether the Government at the political level is even remotely cognisant of the strategic implications of the current round of hostilities on India. First and foremost, it needs to be clearly understood that Hamas is undoubtedly a destabilizing force in that region, whose links with other analogous organisations that believe in violence as a means towards an end is too well-documented to require any reiteration. While the Palestinian Liberation Organisation had at least acknowledged the right of Israel to exist, though not as a Jewish state, Hamas and it's equivalents like Islamic Jihad are committed to the physical destruction of the Jewish state.

Imperative

As a victim of terror, it is imperative for India to make a clear distinction between the Palestinian people and Hamas when it condemns the violence in Gaza or takes a position at any international forum. Second, it needs to be kept in mind that the thaw in the relationship between the Six (US, France, Britain, Russia, Germany and China) and Iran on the nuclear question seems to have run into headwinds with hardliners in Iran accusing Israel of attempting to scuttle an agreement. A breakthrough would help India spread its hydrocarbon sourcing from the region on a broader trajectory and therein lies the rub, the conflict in Gaza has the potential to detract from a resolution of this vital issue, though Shiite Iran and the Sunni organisations are at the opposite ends of the Islamic religious spectrum but unfortunately comprehend a common foe in Israel. Since the United States has been unequivocal in its backing of the Jewish state since its inception, Iran may see the war of attrition between Israel and the Hamas as a strategic counter-lever that may further erode the US appetite to keep playing the outside balancer in the region, thereby giving Iran time, leverage and maneuvering space in the Nuclear negotiations. It is therefore in India's energy security interests to see that the resolution of the Iranian Nuclear question remains a priority. That is why India had voted against Iran at the International Atomic Energy Agency. Stability in the Gulf serves India's strategic interests.

Prudence

The third dimension of the Gaza conflict which India needs to be mindful of is the impact it is having on the proliferating antagonisms across the region, especially in Iraq and Syria. India has a large diaspora scattered across the region whose safety and security is also the responsibility of the Indian state. We still have Indian citizens trapped in Iraq.

If the litany of conflicts that had remained frozen in time all start exploding to life, given that the status quo prevalent for decades in the Middle East and the larger Islamic world, post the dismemberment of the Ottoman Empire, has been disturbed by the Second Gulf war, Arab Spring and the internecine infighting across the Arab expanse, it may entail the flight of a large number of Indians from the region—which could then impact on the remittance economy which provides sustenance to a large number of families in myriad Indian states. It, therefore, is very necessary that India treads prudently and calibrates its responses based upon a clear understanding that historical forces of gargantuan proportions are at play in the Middle Eastern region, which could well reshape the dynamics, contours and even its geography permanently. Any misstep could have serious consequences for our interests in the region.

Imperial ambitions

THE MISSILE assault on Malaysian Airlines MH17, that resulted in the fatality of 290 passengers near the village of Hrabove in Donetsk Oblast, eastern Ukraine, has once again focused attention on Russian interventionism in the region that once constituted the erstwhile Union of Soviet Socialist Republics (USSR). Specifically, it has brought into sharp relief the persistent hostilities between Russia and Ukraine.

What do these developments mean for the peace of Europe and do they have any ramifications on India as it aspires to be a global player riding on the back of an enlightened policy architecture crafted during the United Progressive Alliance years. To contextualise both these questions, it is important to step back two-and-a-half decades. Francis Fukuyama, in 1989, had portrayed the American and western European triumph in the Cold War as follows: "What we may be witnessing is not just the end of the Cold War, or the passing of a particular period of post-war history, but the end of history as such: that is, the end point of mankind's ideological evolution and the universalisation of Western liberal democracy as the final form of human government". Valiant words that unfortunately did not stand the test of even contemporary times. The rout in the Cold War brought in its wake disastrous consequences for the former Soviet Union. Not

The Asian Age, 09 August, 2014

only did it lose all its satellite states in eastern Europe, but it also had to shed its own territory. It was consumed by a crippled economy and an anarchic internal political situation where oligarchs, warlords and the mafia, not essentially in that order, ruled the roost. As a consequence, not only did the ideological construct of Marxism-Leninism lie in ruins, but also the majesty of the Russian continuum that pre-dated the October Revolution of 1917 by many a century. Russia seemed destined for oblivion in the emerging global order.

The ascent of Vladimir Putin to the Russian presidency started to change all that. Not only did the state reassert control but riding on generous oil and gas revenues, it increasingly started resembling the Soviet Union of before. Its absolutism was ingeniously packaged as democracy, characterised not only by a crackdown on civil liberties but more essentially by a consuming obsession to regain the lost glory of the heady days of bipolarity. Naturally, the first target of this assertiveness was what Russia considers its near abroad. It, therefore, adopted a non-linear strategy of conflict. In the August of 2008, it occupied/liberated Abkhazia and South Ossetia from Georgia, depending upon the angle from which the bellicosity is examined. In January 2009, it halted gas exports to Europe accusing Ukraine of siphoning gas from the pipelines without paying for it. It is another matter that once Russia turned the tap back on, Ukraine started playing hardball by blocking the transit of gas to European destinations in a glacial winter.

Insofar as the current stand-off with Ukraine is concerned, in the aftermath of the revolution in Ukraine in February 2014, President Viktor Yanukovych fled Kiev and was succeeded by an interim president Oleksandr Turchynov. Russia did not recognise this regime change. It ostensibly termed it as a coup d'état and, therefore, illegal. Towards the end of February 2014, pro-Russian forces began infiltrating into the Crimean Peninsula and after a disputed referendum a treaty of accession was signed on March 18 between the Republic of Crimea and Sevastopol and the Russian Federation to initiate the process of its formal absorption into the Russian state. On March 21, the Russian Parliament approved the accession from the date of the signing of the treaty. Similarly, since early March, pro-Russian elements have been active in the Kharkiv, Luhansk and Donetsk regions of eastern Ukraine, raising tensions between the two countries to just a degree below the boiling point.

Russia's pugnacious approach has foreboding implications for other frozen disagreements on the periphery of the former Soviet Union like Transnistria in Moldova.

For over a decade now the West has been trying to deal with Russia's desire to build what was the erstwhile USSR as its exclusive sphere of influence. So, does the latest flashpoint in the form of the catastrophe of MH17 provide the European Union and Nato with the leverage to integrate the remaining former Soviet states on the periphery of Russia into the European economic and security architecture?

This would entail the rupture of an informal understanding that precludes the stationing of US or Western European military forces in the former Soviet dominated eastern Europe, particularly the three Baltic states of Latvia, Lithuania and Estonia that are a formal part of both the EU and Nato. Would then this aggressive manoeuvring entail a repeat of history in the prophetic words of the late Winston Churchill, who foresaw on March 5, 1946, the beginning of the Cold War and stated: "From Stettin in the Baltic to Trieste in the Adriatic, an iron curtain has descended across the continent. Behind that line lie all the capitals of the ancient states of Central and East Europe". Are we witnessing the green shoots of a new Cold War in Europe?

What does this mean for India given the relationship that India has enjoyed with the former USSR and its successor state of Russia. Not only does India rely heavily on Russia for military hardware, but there is a broad range of international issues on which there is congruity between the Indian and Russian positions as evidenced by the sixth Brics Summit Fortaleza Declaration on July 15, 2014. Trade between India and Russia stood at $6.2 billion between January and August 2013. Simultaneously, India has a very important stake in consolidating its relationship with the European Union. The total trade between India and the EU in 2013 was 72.7 billion euros. Coupled with that are India's bilateral equations with key players in Europe—Britain, France and Germany and, of course, the US—all of whom are naturally alarmed at the Russian spectre. With the EU and the US imposing Phase 3 sanctions on Russia, can India take a principled position on the larger question of Russia's assertive ambitions in its neighbourhood? The jury is out on that.

Dhokla diplomacy

EIGHTY DAYS after the new dispensation came into existence there seems to be nothing to suggest there is a higher political direction, let alone a long-view of India's engagement with the world. Its foreign forays have been characterised more by form than substance. Champions of the government would contend that the government invited the extended neighbourhood to its coronation. The Prime Minister travelled to Bhutan and Nepal. The Foreign Minister visited Bangladesh and Myanmar for the ASEAN confabulations, and therefore the neighbourhood is 'the' priority of this dispensation. If indeed that is the case then what is the government's game plan for the region? With 23.4% of the world's population and only 2.96% of its land area, a toxic history and a serrated geography, South Asia is perhaps the most un-amalgamated region of the world. Given this reality, can SAARC be revitalised to make it more efficacious? What about South Asian Free Trade agreements transiting to a free trade area, pruning of the sensitive list of products, and the fundamental question: does the division of the region into non-least and least developed states require a relook?

There is no evidence to suggest that these issues have even been pondered, forget evolving a Monroe doctrine that outlines a security doctrine that can ensure India's centrality in the region. Prayers cannot

---

Mail Today, 13 August, 2014

substitute for policy. In today's nuanced eco-system, India's influence will really be defined by its capacity to embrace and influence a spectrum of complex colloquies on multilateral matters. How then has the government performed on this parameter? The manner in which, at the eleventh hour, it blocked the trade facilitation agreement at the WTO did not cover it with any glory.

Even if India had legitimate concerns that once the pact on simplifying custom rules is concluded, developed countries would have no interest in finalising a separate deal on food subsidies. Thus, the 2017 migration path agreed to at Bali would be a chimera. It should have then endeavoured to build a coalition that would have supported its position rather than being left isolated in the company of Cuba, Venezuela and Bolivia. India's veto may well signal the rise of a world of fragmented trading blocs which would have their own rubric and processes for settling divergences like the Trans-Pacific partnership. How does this square up with India's position of being a vocal proponent of global trade reform? Turning from multilateral to bilateral contexts—what is that India wants out of its engagement with the US? With the Indo-US Civil Nuclear engagement having served the purpose of breaching the global nuclear apartheid and terminating India's isolation, what is the next big 'idea' that should benchmark the relationship between these two democracies? Similarly with China. Though their Foreign Minister visited India, followed by an Indian delegation's visit to China commemorating the sixtieth anniversary of the Panscheel, were there any concrete takeaways from these interactions except renewed cartographic aggression?

The European Union and its constituents remain important partners of India. With the 10th Asia–Europe meeting or ASEM summit coming up in Milan in October under the overarching theme of "Responsible Partnership for sustainable growth and Security", has this administration applied itself to the question as to how India could possibly take a leadership role in energising this engagement as opposed to pro-forma participation. The total trade between Asia and Europe was to the tune of 1.37 trillion Euros in 2012 .That accounts for a substantial chunk of the global trade.

The BRICS has matured over the years and the fructification of the New Development Bank ostensibly has invested it with a gravitas notwithstanding the intrinsic fault lines that underscore its existence. However, the unresolved argument is, what is the future that India sees in this partnership? Would it serve India better to restrict it to an Economic Union or does India see a larger political role for it, and if so, how does India then reconcile bloc equations with its larger commitment to multilateralism?

This, then, takes us to the vexed question of the reform of both the ossified structures of the United Nations, as well as the Bretton Woods institutions. Are there any new ideas, initiatives or energy that India would like to put on the table or does this government think that India would be better served by investing vigour into partnerships with other regional organisations that have become more cohesive and potent entities over the years?

Moving to the maritime domain—how does India intend consolidating its dominant position, sitting as it does on the head of the Indian Ocean? How would it ensure that the stability of the Indian Ocean region is not endangered by the rebalance of the US force posture towards Asia & China's blue water aspirations, given that India's near abroad extends from the Straits of Hormuz to Malacca and the assertiveness that is increasingly at play east of the Malacca straits?

As India has committed itself to the inviolability of the global commons, what should be its role in ensuring that globally enforceable rules of engagement evolve expeditiously in the cyberspace and an aggressive push is provided to ensure that militarisation of outer space does not become our gravest security quandary in the near term?

This is an illustrative not an exhaustive menu of strategic dilemmas that confront India. This is without even factoring the 'P' word into the calculus. The moot point being that the nation is perplexed if not confounded by the enigma as to whether the political establishment even grasps the complexity of India's imperatives, or is it episodic "Dhokla Diplomacy" at play?

Wars of the 21st century

THE 20TH CENTURY was defined by five tectonic geo-strategic events. The First World War, the Second World War, the Cold War, demise of imperialism and colonialism coupled with the rise of neo-imperialism and neo-colonialism and, lastly, the end of the Cold War and the ghoul of uni-polarity. As the millennium turned, it brought with it the prospect that the 21st century would be tranquil, as humankind would have drawn lessons from the death and destruction that had stained the previous century. However, these expectations were soon belied. After 9/11, the world was acquainted with new terminologies like "war on terror", the "coalition of the willing" and the sardonic "if you are not with us you are against us". It was straight out of the fables of the Wild West—the irony being that the frontier this time around was the Middle East and South Asia. Recently, China's President Xi Jinping injected a fresh dynamic into an already unstable global environment by instructing the People's Liberation Army to "improve their combat readiness and sharpen their ability to win a regional war in the age of information technology."

Is then the 21st century also coasting along the trajectory of the 20th? Would the template for the future be drawn from the Great War of 1914 that heralded eight decades of turbulence, or the Concert of

---

The Asian Age, 04 October, 2014

Vienna two centuries earlier in 1814 which brought a centenary of peace to Europe?

The answer, perhaps, lies in an objective analysis of the opening years of this century itself. Thirteen years after the US and its allies commenced operations against radicalism on a global scale—is the world a more stable, safer, peaceful place to live in? The jury will remain out on that for quite a while. It all commenced on October 7, 2001, with a colossal bombing campaign against Afghanistan by American and British forces. The trigger was the safe havens provided by the Taliban to the Al Qaeda. The focus shifted to regime change in Iraq, followed by Iran, Libya, Syria, and the paroxysms that convulsed other regimes in the Middle East followed.

Today, Osama bin Laden is dead, neutralised as he was in a military cantonment in Pakistan. But the Al Qaeda has mutated and is alive and kicking. The Afghan Taliban, led by Mullah Omar and his cohorts of the Quetta Shura, the Haqqani Network, are all still around, augmented by terrorist organisations patronised by the permanent Pakistani establishment. Afghanistan continues to be volatile with the political transition having miscarried. The presidential elections, mired in allegations of electoral fraud, required an American-brokered Band-Aid arrangement that now sees two centres of power, namely a President and a Chief Executive, that has no basis in Afghan election law. The security transition has also floundered with the Afghan Army failing to step up to the plate. The economic transition has gone belly up with the Afghan state literally broke and requiring a $537 million emergency bailout to pay salaries to half a million government employees this month.

Iraq is in the throes of a civil war with the Islamic State of Iraq and the Levant (ISIS) threat requiring American re-intervention. Syria has been reduced to a shell state primarily because of the patronage extended by the West to forces inimical to the Baathist regime. Libya is in a mess with warring factions continuing to fight for domination and control, prompting the United Nations and 40 nations to issue an appeal to desist from violence that has displaced over 300,000 people since July this year. The nuclear talks with Iran have stalled and the stalemate seems to be becoming pervasive, if not ubiquitous.

If the objective was to reorder the world and promote the values of democracy, liberalism and economic engagement, then the last 13 years have been a botch with radicalism aggravated, extremism enhanced and terrorism exacerbated.

Moving East, there are two important dates in the Chinese calendar that are looming over the horizon. The first is 2020, a year that would mark 100 years of the Chinese Communist Party, and the second is 2049, the centenary of the Chinese state. What do these two years have to do with President Xi's exhortations for a regional war? The answer lies in the internal dynamics of China. As perhaps the only influential communist state to survive the vicissitudes of history, the overriding objective of the Chinese leadership is to maintain single party domination. To achieve this, the Chinese Communist Party has constructed a chronicle founded on certain critical claims, namely political stability, economic betterment and preservation of core interests. Decoded, they mean sovereignty, territoriality and universal veneration.

This narrative is challenged in that country on a daily basis. A class divide has taken root within one generation, exemplified by a rich-poor, urban-rural, coastal-inland fault lines. Added to this hot-mix are a range of issues that intensify social cynicism. All this pent up dander finds a ready outlet on Weibo, the Chinese Twitter, and a million mutinies play out in the virtual space on a daily basis. What holds this shaky edifice together is passionate nationalism that has an overwhelming echo across the Chinese social ethos. This is where the rhetoric of regional war, unfortunately, fits in. It acts as a social adhesive by immortalising the aspirations of supremacy.

However, these domestic imperatives leave a very disquieting ricochet in their wake. Since China has a host of land and maritime disputes with its neighbours, coupled with opaque defence numbers, it compels countries in the region to take recourse to pre-emptive strategies, which include bolstering their defence capabilities. This ends up putting an additional strain on already stretched national budgets. It also puts a very large swathe of Asia on the edge as it shatters another carefully cultivated myth that China's rise would be peaceful and would not create any major dislocation in the existing world order.

This is the quixotic saga of two pre-eminent global powers who considered themselves to be a potential G-2. Tragically, their policies have been an unsettling force rather than a stabilising influence in the last one and a half decades. It, therefore, becomes imperative that truly multi-polar, alternative global security architecture, without the omnipotent veto emerges, one that subsumes the possibility of unilateral action by any nation or nations acting in consort, disrupting the peace of the 21st century.

The new cold war

WHY DID the former president of the erstwhile Soviet Union, Mikhail Gorbachev, on the 25th anniversary of the fall of the Berlin Wall caution that the world is on the brink of a new Cold War? He stated, "Some say it has already begun. Instead of building new mechanisms and institutions of European security and pursuing major demilitarisation of European politics, the West and particularly the United States declared victory in the Cold War. Euphoria and triumphalism went to the heads of the Western leaders. Taking advantage of Russia's weakening and the lack of a counterweight, they claimed monopoly leadership and domination in the world. The enlargement of Nato, Kosovo, missile defence plans and wars in West Asia had led to a collapse of trust. To put it metaphorically, a blister has now turned into a bloody festering wound."

The central concern that former President Gorbachev was flagging is whether there has been a failure of statespersonship in evolving a new world order transcending the frozen hostility of the Cold War era. To explore this trepidation it is imperative to trace the evolution of the institutions of global governance over the century. The League of Nations emerged out of the wreckage of the First World War that killed 25 million people and marooned the prevailing global order. It

---

The Asian Age, 29 November, 2014

was founded on the standard of a "just peace" enunciated by President Woodrow Wilson.

The principal nation-states of those times wanted to ensconce their distaste for war into a new form of international order. The League and a series of mediation accords proposed to supplant conquests for dominance with licit means of dispute resolution. Participation in these new structures was open to all and theoretically comprehensive. Every form of defilement of peace was strictly proscribed, yet no state was alacritous to apply its terms. Timeworn mindsets reigned.

Two superimposing yet conflicting post-war orders came into existence. The sphere of covenants and treaties charted by the Western democracies in their relationship with each other and an unimpeded precinct arrogated by countries that had voluntarily extracted themselves from this edifice of restrictions to attain greater latitude of action. Ultimately, the instability inherent in the architecture of this order failed to keep the peace and the Second World War engulfed the world.

Out of the shambles of this great conflagration emerged the United Nations in 1945. The structure of the United Nations and the balance of power enshrined in the veto system of the Security Council was representative of the power dynamic that existed at that point in time. The vision being that the United Nations would implement collective security via a global concert.

Over the past seven and more decades, the track record of the United Nations has been variegated. A myriad number of wars and violent conflicts have taken place around the world that have killed, maimed and rendered homeless millions of people, but what the United Nations has successfully prevented is a conflagration on a global scale of the kind seen in the First and Second World Wars. However, the end of the Cold War provided the victors a golden opportunity to redesign the institutions of global governance to reflect the transformation in the trans-continental scheme of things between 1945 and 1989.

The obvious low hanging fruit was the restructuring of the United Nations Security Council. By posturing the enigma as to which nation can possibly be kept out rather than which country must be brought into the zone of perpetual membership, the entrenched five have effectively stymied any attempt to contemporise the most important organ of the UN system to reflect the current influence equilibrium. The failure to do so has contributed to the increasing redundancy of the UN. Member states and "coalitions of the willing" have simply ignored the UN with impunity and resorted to unilateral action on more than one occasion.

Similarly, regional groupings, private initiatives and platforms outside the formal United Nations structure have become more fashionable and influential in the economic arena. The World Economic Forum, emergence of the G-20 and other quasi-formal structures outside the UN framework are all manifestations of the resistance to reform.

Another such outmoded legacy is the Non-Proliferation Treaty that comes up for review next year. The NPT entered into force in 1970 and effectively divided the world between nuclear haves and nuclear have nots. Over the years ,various other constructs were put in place to perpetuate this nuclear apartheid, including the Wassenaar Arrangement and the Nuclear Suppliers Group that came into existence as the London Club in response to India's first nuclear test in 1974.

While the pillars of the NPT—non-proliferation, disarmament and the right to peacefully use nuclear technology are extremely relevant even today, what is missing is a reality check on the current situation. Over the years ,certain countries who are not signatories of the NPT have emerged as nuclear weapon states—India, Pakistan and North Korea being the overt ones, while Israel has maintained a strategic ambivalence with regard to the status of its nuclear weapons programme. However, here lies the rub. While Pakistan and even China, which is one of the recognised Nuclear Weapon States, have been involved in proliferation to North Korea, allegedly Iran and some erstwhile regimes in West Asia, India's track record has been impeccable. By way of an example, the Ayatollahs of non-proliferation may consider it worth their while to even belatedly recognise India's imperative to test both in 1974 and then again in 1998. They should take cognisance of its non-proliferation credentials and offer to admit it as a nuclear weapon state into the hallowed portals of the Non-Proliferation Treaty. It would only lend gravitas and further credibility to the NPT regime. In the remaining decades of the 21st century, it would be worthwhile to heed the sage advice of President Gorbachev. It is a worthy endeavour to try and construct a new international order that reinforces the concept of order within regions, reassesses the concept of balance of power, reaffirms sovereignty of nation states, democratises and broad bases institutions of global governance to surmount the impending new variant of the old Cold War.

Can India board the Kabul Express

DISTANT FROM the annual dosage of midsummer cricket sleaze there are extremely sombre developments that are unfolding in India's near abroad. They do not augur well for both our national security or even our strategic priorities. The government claims that it is crafting a regional policy that would bypass Pakistan. It touts the Chabahar port in Iran as an example of its intent to boost trade, commerce and connectivity with Afghanistan after Pakistan refused to sign the Saarc agreement on motor vehicle and rail connectivity in Kathmandu last November. It is an entirely different matter that Chabahar was quietly incubated during the United Progressive Alliance's time despite Western pressure. The present government has precious little to do with it except enter into a generic memorandum of understanding that, in fact, is fuzzily worded if not sloppily drafted. Be that as it may, by the time the Chabahar port becomes operational, if it ever does, there may be nothing left in Afghanistan to trade with as the Talibs are advancing with utmost dispatch. The attack on the Afghan Parliament by six terrorists on June 22 once again underscores the rather perilous security situation in that country, coming as it did on the day that the Afghan legislature was considering the appointment of the unity government's nominee for defence ministership. Ironically,

---

The Asian Age, 27 June, 2015

Mohammed Masoom Stanekzai is considered to be the principal interlocutor of the Kabul dispensation with the Taliban. It is believed that he spent the past three years discreetly negotiating with a host of non-state actors. Veteran observers of the Afghan scene believe that he has been the fundamental proponent of the talks and in bringing the Taliban on board.

However, this does not seem to have impressed the Taliban that claimed after the attack that the specific objective of the Fidayeen assault was to disrupt the hearing that was supposed to confirm the defence minister. Like in the United States of America, under the Afghan Constitution also, every ministerial appointment requires parliamentary approval. A month earlier, on May 14, the Taliban had attacked a guest house in Kabul and butchered 14 people, including nine foreigners.

In less than one year, ever since the Nato troops left the country and the US has virtually ridden off into the sunset with a very thin ground presence—9,800 military personnal—the Taliban has made ominous gains all the way from Afghanistan's borders with Pakistan and Iran to its frontiers with Uzbekistan, Turkmenistan and Tajikistan. From Kunduz and Badakhshan in the north, to Helmand, Musa Qala and Uruzgan in the south ,the Taliban juggernaut is on a complete roll. There has been a quantum jump in the fatalities of Afghan National Army combatants in the first four months of 2015, compared to the same time last year. Even over a short-term horizon this is an unsustainable level of damage for any military force to absorb. The bottomline is that the security situation has gone belly up and the governance crunch is reaching a watershed extremely rapidly. The unity government of Ashraf Ghani and Abdullah Abdullah holds sway over a diminishing amount of territory day after day.

If the current dispensation in New Delhi believes that India has strategic interests in Afghanistan, if it considers that India's 106-km long non-contiguous border with Afghanistan is more than just bellicosity to be trotted out occasionally for airing at some talk shop, it then begs the obvious question—What does it propose to do about the situation?

New Delhi, because of its tactical naiveté, finds itself between a rock and a hard place, as the current government in Afghanistan is not as "friendly" to India as the previous Karzai administration.

Right after assuming office, President Ghani has leaned heavily towards Pakistan and China. In fact, he has invested a lot of political capital in cultivating various players in China and Pakistan, including paying an unprecedented visit to the General Headquarters in Rawalpindi to pay tribute to Army Chief, General Raheel Sharif. Heads of nations do not call on Service Chiefs in democracies, but Pakistan has always danced to a different dynamic and Afghanistan has been a cynical playground for a succession of Inter-Services Intelligence director-generals and other uniformed mavericks right from the days of the Afghan jihad fronted by Pakistan and bankrolled by the US, Saudi Arabia and a host of other fellow travellers. It is another matter that Pakistan has responded with increased levels of violence to this overture of Mr Ghani, clearly underscoring through merciless assaults that its interest lies in an unstable Afghanistan where it can keep playing ducks and drakes with the Taliban and the rest.

Even the non-formal talks between the Afghans led by Mr Stanekzai and the Taliban in Ürümqi were midwifed jointly by the Pakistani and Chinese intelligence services. The Pakistani military establishment and the People's Liberation Army of China (PLA) are so deep in bed together that it should not have come as a surprise to Prime Minister Narendra Modi that China has put a hold on the Lakhvi resolution at the United Nations.

There are three realistic options that the National Democratic Alliance/Bharatiya Janata Party government has qua Afghanistan. The first is it could stop parroting the spiel that India has strategic interests in Afghanistan when it actually has none, and allow the situation to reach its natural equilibrium. After all, Afghanistan has been for myriad reasons correctly characterised as the graveyard of empires over the millennia. In the past 35 years alone, both the superpowers of the 20th century, the Union of Soviet Socialist Republics and the US have had to quit the rugged Afghan territory—the former after the ignominy of the Amu Darya moment and the latter out of a honed sense of self-preservation. India should allow the Pakistanis, the Chinese and whosoever else has big power delusions to stew in their own juice and finally meet their nemesis. It should continue to extend humanitarian assistance when asked and even exit its infrastructure commitments in Afghanistan. Rather than bleating about the $2 billion that we have pored into Afghanistan over the past one and half decades, we must acknowledge that it is really chickenfeed compared to the approximate $2 billion a day spend of the US and Nato war machine over the same span of time.

The second option is to engage with the new Afghan leadership aggressively and drill into their heads that their salvation does not lie with Pakistan or China, but in balancing them out by engaging with nations on their outer periphery like India, Turkey and even Russia that do not have a common border with Afghanistan but have a stake, if not a strategic interest, in a stable Afghanistan. If India feels that the advance of the Taliban and the infiltration of the Islamic State of Iraq and Syria into Afghanistan could expand the terror footprint in India, then it should go beyond the strategic partnership agreement of 2011 and offer boots on the ground to the government in Afghanistan. After all, strategic interests are not secured by platitudes, they are safeguarded by investing blood and treasure.

The third option is that if India has been completely cut out by the current Afghan government because of its excessive reliance on the Sino-Pakistani nexus, then India should consider opening dialogue with the Taliban. An upside of this engagement would be that, god forbid, if there is an IC-814 like situation ever again, we would not be left scrambling for even a rudimentary contact with the new power brokers—the Taliban of Afghanistan. And the NDA/BJP would be spared the alleged, contrived or real "suitcase stories" that have still not found a resting place even 15 years after the hijack at the turn of the 21st century.

Fortress Europe

EUROPE IS besieged. Millions are on the march. They are fleeing to its shores escaping the bestiality of the nine odd civil wars that are raging across the arc of instability in Afghanistan, Iraq, Syria, southeast Turkey, Yemen, Libya, Somalia, Sudan and northeast Nigeria. Syria and Libya have almost ceased to exist as Westphalian entities that cartography comprehends them as. Half of the twenty three million Syrians have been rendered homeless and are on the move searching for refuge. The ISIS has rendered another three million odd Iraqi's as refugees. Another million and a half have been displaced in Southern Sudan. The waves of humanity are just roiling into Europe causing both social and political turmoil. The stampede that left hundreds injured on the Serbian-Croatian border is but the latest manifestation of frontiers getting overwhelmed by the multitudes.

The response is also conflicted. Initially, European nations welcomed the refugees with the German Chancellor Angela Merkel even clicking self-serving selfies with the evacuees. However, soon the sheer numbers swamped even the efficient German response system as the trains continued rolling into Munich and other cities. Under pressure from the politicians of Bavaria and other states, the Federal government was compelled to set up controls along its borders with

---

The Asian Age, 18 September, 2015

Austria to regulate the incoming human traffic. Austria, in turn, has pretty much done the same on its Hungarian border and Hungary has fenced its border with Serbia and now Serbia has put its army on high alert on the Croatian border.

Greece and Italy, the first port of call for refugees fleeing across the Mediterranean Sea, may just be compelled to opt for more coercive measures in the near future as they too are swamped. Overnight, the open borders policy of the European mainland has regressed to the old days of ingress and egress checkpoints at national borders. Xenophobia, racism and anti-immigrant violence may be the logical corollary of the influx as the loony fringe on the right of European politics may find a renewed raison d'être.

As the Interior Ministers of the European Union nations got together in Brussels to wrap their arms around the conundrum, a poignant full page open letter in the Newspapers by a Non-Governmental Organization "Medecins Sans Frontieres" underscored the enormity of the worst displacement crisis the world faces since the second world war.

Urging the EU Ministers to dismantle the fences and provide safe passage to the migrants, the first and the last paragraph of the letter are worth reproducing. "We send you this letter today, together with a life jacket belonging to one of the 15,000 people rescued at sea by the Medecins Sans Frontieres (MSF) since May. The poor quality life vest was the only security a man, woman or child had while trying to cross the sea to Europe. These jackets sometimes feature handwritten prayers for a safe passage or phone numbers of relatives and friends to be contacted in case the person wearing it does not make it. This is a reminder that people embarking on these journeys are fully aware of the risks they are undertaking, and of the sheer desperation motivating to put themselves and their families in so much danger".

The letter ends with a heart-wrenching plea. "Europe is faced with an increasing number of people seeking assistance and protection. These people are only a small portion of the millions who are fleeing intolerable suffering. No matter the obstacles, they will continue to come. They have no other choice. The current policies are untenable in the face of the situation. The only way that Europe can prevent a worsening crisis on its territory is to the smugglers with a safe, legal and free alternative. We ask you to provide safe passage. Legal crossing of sea and land borders must be authorized for asylum seekers into and inside EU. All forms of legal avenues allowing refugees to reach Europe must be put in place urgently. Efficient solutions to relocate asylum seekers from one member EU state to another must be found. Effective access to coherent asylum procedures and assistance should be provided at entry points, throughout Europe and along migratory routes. Swift registration and access to temporary protection should be provided upon arrival. Legal migration pathways must be created. Dignified reception conditions must be offered to all. Make this life vest redundant. Provide humane, dignified and safe alternatives." The underlying message of the missive is all but clear. It instructs the leaders of the European powers to take responsibility for the immense human suffering their actions over the past decade have caused in the greater Middle East.

For the responsibility for the current mass migration can be squarely laid at the doorstep of these eminences. The continuing tragedy in Afghanistan is the result of the cold war rivalry between the erstwhile Soviet Union and United States dating back to the early eighties. It was renewed afresh by Operation Enduring Freedom in 2001. It is not that removing the Taliban- Al-Qaida nexus was wrong but then after their previous joust in Afghanistan, the US should have had the stomach for the long haul once it decided to go in again.

The situation in Iraq, Libya and Syria is again the result of a disastrous attempt by the US and it's allies to reopen the settlement of the Middle East, frozen in time post the dismemberment of the Ottoman Empire after the First World War. If Saddam Hussein, Muammar Gaddafi and Assad were or are fiends then those who have replaced them are not paragons of virtue. They are, in fact, even bigger ogres. The current situation in Yemen is again the consequence of the assault by Saudi Arabia, UAE and other frontline allies of the US in the Gulf region. The perennial problem in the Middle East—the Israeli-Palestinian conflict that has spawned the largest number of refugees in the world, the unfortunate Palestinians, again has an eternal Western and European dimension to it. For the neo-conservatives of the twenty-first century, high on the success of the "end of history" with the disappearance of the iron curtain in Europe, the chickens have unfortunately come home to roost rather early in the day. That is not to say that 9/11 and whatever else followed in its aftermath should be condoned. The question that the "coalition of the willing", ISAF and thousand other acronyms should ask themselves in retrospect—was there a smarter way of handling the situation? For the world is carrying the can for their Ramboism and the American electoral cycle may TRUMP up another-"Bush" version 3.0. However, there is no institutional introspection much less a critique in mainstream western media about the trigger of the current crisis.

For India the nightmare may have just about begun. If the fences in Europe keep becoming impenetrable by the day the multitudes would inevitably be compelled to turn east. The events in the Spanish Enclaves of Ceuta and Melilla in Morocco, in 2005, are a menacing reminder. Imagine if a million people were to land up at the Wagah border demanding protection and asylum and this may happen without even Pakistan unravelling?

The spectaclisation of diplomacy

IN THE PAST 16 months, the Prime Minister of India has travelled abroad 29 times. It roughly translates into two overseas visits a month. In the next four months another eight trips are on the anvil. Are there any substantive upsides of these outings for India?

In the initial flush of victory, the Prime Minister invited all the Saarc and regional leaders to his coronation and triumphantly proclaimed a neighbourhood-first policy. In pursuance of that, Narendra Modi visited Bhutan, Nepal, Sri Lanka and Myanmar. The relationship with Nepal today is stretched to almost breaking point, with the Nepalese Constituent Assembly cocking a snook at India's purported concerns. The grapevine has it that the main reason for New Delhi's dander is not as much the denial of equity to the plains people and the indigenous inhabitants as it is the refusal of the Nepalese leadership to formally declare Nepal a Hindu Rashtra, which the Rashtriya Swayamsevak Sangh ostensibly wanted. They rubbed it in by enshrining secularism in their Constitution, notwithstanding the creative spin that they may have imparted to the concept to mollify the forces of right reaction in New Delhi.

The drift of both Sri Lanka and Maldives into the Chinese orbit has only quickened with the advent of this government. The Maldivian

The Asian Age, 03 October, 2015

President has virtually told New Delhi to take a walk by continuing the persecution of former President Mohamed Nasheed who had sought refuge in the Indian embassy. Sri Lanka is continuing with the policy of allowing docking facilities to Chinese naval assets. China has replaced Japan as the numero uno donor to Sri Lanka.

In Afghanistan, India is not even a player in the game after the withdrawal of the Nato-led International Security Assistance Force in December 2014 and the American plan to hitch their saddles and ride off into the sunset. Not only is the government of President Mohammad Ashraf Ghani and Chief Executive Abdullah Abdullah leaning towards Pakistan, but even negotiations between the Afghan government and the Taliban are midwifed by the Inter-Services Intelligence-Chinese Intelligence combine, with the Americans playing chaperone, both in Urumqi in China and later in Murree, Pakistan. Serving and former senior US officials bluntly and publicly articulate that they see India as a part of the problem, and not the solution, in Afghanistan.

The relationship with China is also going nowhere if not heading south. The buzz in strategic circles is that during his visit to Xi'an, Beijing and Shanghai in May when Mr Modi expressed his unhappiness at the slow pace of border negotiations to President Xi Jinping and Prime Minister Li Keqiang, he was coldly rebuffed and the gist of the Chinese brush-off even found its way onto the Chinese Sina Weibo and other social media platforms. Pakistan is a case of the Prime Minister's left hand not knowing what even its fingers are doing. In a span of one year the Prime Minister invited Nawaz Sharif to his coronation in May 2014, then three months later cancelled the foreign secretary-level talks because the Pakistani high commissioner met the Hurriyat. He then sent his foreign secretary on a tour of South Asia to find a fig leaf of an excuse to land up in Islamabad to resume the dialogue. It was followed by the ecstasy of Ufa, on the sidelines of the Brics summit, with an agreement to hold a dialogue at the level of the national security advisers.

However, even before the ink had dried on the joint statement read out by the two foreign secretaries, the world witnessed the riotous exhibition of the Indian foreign minister and the NSA of Pakistan paying verbal, if not virtual, kabaddi over the airwaves. The latest bout is playing itself out in the United Nations. All these shenanigans have once again ensured the hyphenation of a relationship that took the United Progressive Alliance 10 long years to de-hyphenate. From the sublime to the ridiculous is the only expression to describe Mr Modi's handling of the Pakistani interface.

Similarly, with the United States there is no "big idea" to take the relationship to the next level. In the five interactions that Mr Modi has had with US President Barack Obama, he has not been able to walk away with even a single big takeaway. Despite the histrionics in the Indian media space, the cold reality is that on both his visits to the US Mr Modi was given short shrift by Mr Obama. In fact, on the most recent visit, the snub could not have been more obvious with Mr Obama hosting a state banquet for Mr Xi and fobbing off Mr Modi with a working meal.

This is despite the National Democratic Alliance government completely subscribing to the American vision of regional security on the Asian continent, thus virtually becoming a junior partner if not a client state of the United States. This is evidenced by the imminent joint meetings between the foreign ministers of the US, Japan and India, the proposed ocean dialogue, cooperation between India and the US in developing an aircraft carrier, and the inclusion of Japan, and possibly Australia, in the India-US naval exercises—the notorious quad. All this and much more is playing itself out under the auspices of the India-US Joint Strategic Vision for the Asia-Pacific and Indian Ocean, a policy document that India was practically coerced into signing as the quid pro quo for Mr Obama agreeing to be the chief guest at the Republic Day parade earlier this year. This will have serious implications on the independence of our foreign policy and our ability and flexibility to navigate between the various emerging poles of the global power dynamic in the 21st century.

If it wasn't humiliating it could have been termed hilarious—while Mark Zuckerberg of Facebook fame flew to Washington DC to pay his respects to the Chinese President by marking his presence at Mr Obama's state dinner, the Indian Prime Minister flew to the West Coast to pay obeisance to the founder of the new media enterprise.

Incidentally, Facebook, Twitter and all the other Western new media platforms are not allowed to operate in China. They are all blocked.

One wonders why Narayana Murthy was never accorded this courtesy with the Prime Minister making a dedicated visit to the Infosys headquarters in Bengaluru or, for that matter, what is happening to the ambitious proposal cleared by the UPA Cabinet to build foundries for chip manufacturing which would put India at the heart of the new economy rather than merely remaining a body-shopping paradise. Has that also been given an ignominious burial to kowtow to the old masters of the new information order?

Even on the entire business of a permanent seat on the United Nations Security Council, the reality is that there is no text for negotiations before the United Nations General Assembly. What is there before it is a compilation of the opinions of various countries. Three members of the Security Council with veto powers—the US, Russia and China—have not given their views. In side letters to the compilation, the US and Russia have all but reneged on the lip service they have been paying to India's claim to a permanent seat with veto power. China's attitude towards India leaves nothing to the imagination and will only harden as India wittingly drifts into the US orbit. In any case, the conundrum with the expansion of the UNSC has been—who do you keep out rather than whom do you take in. The G-4 gang-up may not be the smartest way for India to press its claim. With Europe also, except for the promise to buy arms from some countries, there is no fresh impetus or traction to the relationship. The negotiation on the free trade agreement with the European Union remain deadlocked. It stands where the UPA had left it in the May of 2014.

What then has been achieved except for collecting the diaspora in stadia around the world and pontificating on all and sundry? The simple answer is: zilch. There is an inherent danger in whipping up diasporic xenophobia about India's great-power ambitions, exploiting their nostalgia and search for a sense of identity in societies where they are materially well-off but have not been able to root themselves.

You set the Indian overseas community up as a vulnerable object and a soft target. It even impedes the process of their natural assimilation in the adoptive countries of their choice. With the immigrant crisis in Europe at a flash point and an inevitable backlash a reality, the Prime Minister needs to be very careful about his histrionics. Furthermore, it irks the host countries which may be indulgent the first time around but may not be that magnanimous if such gigs are perceived as the routine and not the exception. It belittles India to witness the Prime Minister working as a cheerleader for some of the most decadent sheikhs in the Gulf by getting the Indian community to raise slogans in their support. That is the inherent hazard in the spectaclisation of diplomacy. Not only will it pay no dividends to India, but questions are also now being asked—Who, pray, is writing the cheque for these one-man and half-an-act theatrics?

Make 'Indo-Pacific' meaningful

THE BHARATIYA Janata Party-led National Democratic Alliance government has been on an overdrive in international relations, with the Prime Minister travelling abroad every other fortnight. However, a conceptual clarity about India's global vision over the medium term is absent, as the current administration marches beyond the 18-month mark. India's foreign policy, and the strategic choices it makes, would be determined by its ability to manage relationships that are simultaneously complimentary and adversarial. These interactions are symbiotically intertwined with overlapping priorities, interests and conflicts concomitantly at play.

The issues on the table include both bilateral and multilateral conversations on the disconnect between the neo-liberal economic order and the urgent need to provide better quality of life to millions of people in the developing world, a consensual architecture to mitigate the toxic effects of climate change, restructuring of the institutions of global governance, balancing the fight against terror while preserving civil liberties and persevering towards the emergence of agreed rules of engagement in the virtual civilisation—the Internet.

Some of the basic premises that would need to be revisited include the traditional Westphalian template itself: What is India today and

---

The Asian Age, 28 November, 2015

what part of India does foreign and strategic policy seek to serve? Should territorial limits alone define India or would it include its hydrocarbon interests in Africa, Latin America, Russia and West Asia? Does it also include the defence of the Indian diaspora—its wealth and resources included? Should it include the transnational corporate empires of Indian oligarchs? Will and should India be prepared to leverage its hard power to protect and preserve these interests?

Who does India engage with in the world as nations alone do not affect India's interests—non-state actors, rouge nations and private interests impact India too. Is it time to keep both the formal and the back channels open to them?

An example would be the Afghan Taliban or the Somali tribes that have elevated piracy to statecraft. Not in the same basket by any stretch but more central is the question of full diplomatic relations with Taiwan, either within or outside the "One China policy" and, finally, does India have both the institutional structures and the intellectual capacity to be able to absorb, assimilate and synthesise these different strains and weave them into a long view of the world from Delhi's perch?

On the state side, till yesterday, the US and its allies wanted India to proscribe Iran and even arm-twisted India to bring its oil import from Iran below the 10 per cent threshold but today, after the nuclear deal between Iran and the West, they may want a greater Indian engagement with Iran—which would also be in India's interest, to offset the Chinese from gaining an upper hand. China has demonstrated its capacity to influence both totalitarian regimes and democratic states by virtually colonising large parts of Africa over the past two decades. Similarly, would the India-China and, by extension, the emerging economies' bonhomie be evident at the climate change conference in Paris, despite the continuing territorial disputes and the resultant chill in Sino-Indian interaction? These are realpolitik realities that would need to be surmounted by India if it wants to evolve from a big player in the little league to, conceivably, a budding player in the big league.

On a related note, are there any medium-term strategic opportunities that India can leverage? Just two grand sweeps, one towards the East and the other towards the West would suffice. As India looks towards the East, it does so from its roost at the head of the Indian Ocean, straddling the sea lanes of commerce as they traverse from the choke points of the Strait of Hormuz right up to the Malacca Strait. In years to come, this station at the head of the Indian Ocean is going to become all the more germane as the $46 billion China-Pakistan Economic Corridor comes into play. This corridor of highways, railways and pipelines, primarily to transport oil and gas from the port of Gwadar in Baluchistan to the city of Kashgar in Xinjiang province in northwestern China, would enable China to surmount it's "Malacca dilemma". This could, in turn, lead to increased assertiveness by China in the South China Sea, as it would seek to act on its historical claims. It would make the littoral states of the South China Sea—Indonesia, Malaysia, Vietnam, Philippines and Taiwan—justifiably more jittery than they are today. There lies an opportunity to draw all these states into a loose coalition, notwithstanding their individual economic linkages with China or India. For, whatever the one belt one road (OBOR) may be worth, all the minerals and other resources extracted by the Chinese through sweetheart deals in Africa and other parts of the world cannot go right up from Gwadar to Kashgar. Most of them would still have to traverse the Indian Ocean, Andaman Sea and the Bay of Bengal. India's airbase in Campbell Bay is just 240 km from the mouth of the Malacca Strait. It can come into play to counterbalance Chinese intentions in the South China Sea.

The net upside for India would be transforming the concept "Indo-Pacific" from an abstract Indian fantasy into a strategic and economic reality. Coupled with American presence in the western Pacific and it's hub and spoke security relationships all the way from Japan down to Australia, this coalition would be germane to keep the global commons open and stable across the Indian and Pacific Oceans, whose conjunction is the South China Sea. Thus, if leveraged properly, Pakistan's economic big ticket opportunity can also be India's windfall.

This would be the perfect power dynamic to "act East" rather than just keep looking East.

From the East, as India turns it's gaze towards the West, it discerns tectonic forces of religious bigotry and chilling cruelty galloping across the region, erasing territorial boundaries. The inane attempt to reorder the Middle East order that emerged from the ashes of the Ottoman Empire has miscarried miserably. However, in this fiasco lies another opportunity for India. As the Al Qaeda, Islamic State of Iraq and Syria, Taliban and numerous other militant Islamists prepare for the final push from Turkey to Pakistan, it should automatically draw the democracies of Europe and India into a closer embrace.

Not only would closer security cooperation become an imperative, as the Paris massacre has once again demonstrated, but at a syncretic level too India is perhaps the only country where, for over a thousand years now, Islamic influence has been absorbed into its culture without fundamentally allowing it to alter the social ethos. The unique experience that India brings to the table is the interface between an aggressive Islam and Indian ethos of multiculturalism that has held the field down the ages. The former, despite the sword, was not allowed by the latter to substantially alter either the demographics or even the cultural moorings of the subcontinent. It created, through assimilation as opposed to a clash of civilisations, an enlightened version of Indian Islam that has existed cheek by jowl with other religious narratives for hundreds of years now. This knowledge was one of the things that India offered to the United States after 9/11, i.e. to how to find an honorable accommodation with Islam over the long run, but the binary mindset of George Bush's advisers failed to grasp it. This is the unique experiment that the Christian civilisation on the western frontiers of the Islamic spread would have to factor into its sociological strategy, as a supplement to tryouts with multiculturalism.

Otherwise, the challenge of reining in religious revivalism and terrorism emanating from it may continue to bedevil liberal democracies for quite a few centuries to come. Since the US is the global outside balancer of power in every continent and the state of Israel has an existential stake reining in militant Islamism, they are both natural allies in this struggle. India, therefore, would have to evolve its own version of exceptionalism to engage with the world as it consolidates itself internally. Therein lies the classical dilemma for policy wonks—while strategic opportunities are not open indefinitely juxtaposed to them are the realities of the Indian state, the most conspicuous being lack of institutional capacity to deal with the world and itself simultaneously.

NSG Bid: Wrong long view from Delhi

ON A DAY that Britain decided to divorce the European Union, another important development was playing itself out in faraway Seoul, South Korea, where the Nuclear Suppliers Group (NSG) was meeting to decide on India's admittance to this exclusive club as its member. Before coming to the outcome of the Seoul meeting it would be worthwhile to recount what exactly this club is all about. On its website this 48-nation assembly describes itself as follows: "The NSG is a group of nuclear supplier countries that seeks to contribute to the non-proliferation of nuclear weapons through the implementation of two sets of guidelines for nuclear exports and nuclear-related exports.

"The NSG guidelines also contain the so-called 'Non-Proliferation Principle', adopted in 1994, whereby a supplier, notwithstanding other provisions in the NSG guidelines, authorises a transfer only when satisfied that the transfer would not contribute to the proliferation of nuclear weapons. The 'Non-Proliferation Principle' seeks to cover the rare but important cases where adherence to the Non-Proliferation Treaty (NPT) or to a nuclear-weapon-free zone treaty may not by itself be a guarantee that a state will consistently share the objectives of the treaty or that it will remain in compliance with its treaty obligations."

The Asian Age, 26 June, 2016

Founded in response to the Indian nuclear test in May 1974, the NSG first met in November 1975. Nations already signatories to the NPT saw the need to further limit the export of nuclear equipments, materials or technology. Colloquially referred to as the "London Club" due to a series of meetings in London from 1975 to 1978, the confabulations resulted in agreements on the guidelines for export. These were published as the Zangger List and the Trigger List by the International Atomic Energy Agency (IAEA). Listed items could only be exported to non-nuclear states if certain IAEA safeguards were agreed to or if exceptional circumstances relating to safety existed.

The Trigger List remained unchanged until 1991, although the Zangger List was regularly updated. The non-revelations about the Iraqi weapons programme following the first Gulf War led to a tightening of the export of so-called dual-use equipment. At the first meeting since 1978, held at The Hague in March 1991, the participating governments agreed to changes, which were published as the Dual-use List in 1992. Since then, a regular series of plenary meetings take place and the lists are periodically updated. In the wake of the Indo-US Civil Nuclear Agreement, the NSG gave a clean waiver to India on September 6, 2008, that allowed the US and other NSG countries to export nuclear materials to India essentially for civilian and peaceful purposes. That effectively paved the way for operationalising the agreement. The waiver came about primarily because India has an impeccable record of non-proliferation. It was considered to be a responsible emerging power. At that point in time, too, there were naysayers and recalcitrants, but the then US President, George Bush, did the heavy lifting, including calling up the Chinese President to ensure that no one stood in the way of consensus.

What has changed between then and now is that a number of NSG members have expressed reservations about giving India membership. China, of course, has been most vocal and vociferous in leading the pack. The argument being put forth is that there is a distinction between a waiver and membership and therefore a criterion needs to be formulated. How to deal with non-signatories to the NPT may be a cogent reason, but, as is the case with international politics, most such rationalisation is filtered through the prism of national self-interest of the member states.

It is here that India's failure becomes starker. After creating all that hype and hoopla over the past one month, including visits to Switzerland and Mexico by the Prime Minister and personal entreaties to Chinese President Xi Jingping, the entire effort has all but come to zilch. Contrast this with 2008, when Prime Minister Manmohan Singh did not stir out of New Delhi to lobby for the waiver but used his acute understanding of international affairs to dismantle the entire architecture of nuclear apartheid that had been put in place after "Smiling Buddha", as the 1974 peaceful nuclear explosion (PNE) by India was codenamed. A system created three decades ago as an angry reaction to India's assertion of strategic autonomy was skillfully demolished by taking on both belligerents outside and inside, including the ruling Bharatiya Janata Party which had moved a no-confidence motion in Parliament accusing the then United Progressive Alliance government of selling out India's national interest.

All that the current Prime Minister and his foreign policy team had to do was to take that process forward, but they faltered. The reason is not very difficult to discern—the National Democratic Alliance government has failed to finesse the delicate trapeze act that is required to manage the relationship between the big powers, particularly United States qua China and independently with Russia. China has been going through a strange metamorphosis because of its declining economic numbers. The legitimacy of the Communist Party from 1980 onwards rested on a very simple premise: We will be able to make the quality of your life better than that of the preceding generation. With growth declining, assertive nationalism has become a way of managing internal discontent. Given that India is also an emerging power, it suits China, both domestically and internationally, to ring-fence India into South Asia.

The NDA government also neglected to gauge the larger ramifications of the proposed $46 billion investment by China in the China Pakistan Economic Corridor (CPEC). Not only does it broaden the strategic and military relationship between the two countries but also creates an automatic Chinese buy-in into Pakistani foreign policy objectives in South Asia. The manner in which the NSG discourse has been structured with regard to the evolution of principles to deal with non-NPT countries has once again hyphenated India with Pakistan, a paradigm that the Indo-US Civil Nuclear Agreement and the clean waiver had surmounted.

Moreover, even the response of Russia has been ambiguous—while they have been historically supportive they do not seem to be willing to walk that extra mile any longer. Even President Barack Obama did not go that extra stretch that his predecessor did despite America's public pronouncements of support for India's inclusion in the NSG. Given that there was a domestic consensus on the NSG issue, unlike in 2008 when there were raucous allegations of a sell-out, it may just be worth Prime Minister Narendra Modi's while to seriously reflect upon how they have got their long view of foreign relations from New Delhi all wrong.

